ADVANCE PRAISE

"Equity, like any layered or compelling concept—freedom, say, or democracy—cannot be neatly or easily defined, and yet its critical dimensions are straightforward: equity demands a recognition that every human being is of infinite and incalculable value, and that all human beings are entitled to decent standards of conduct concerning justice from all earthly powers and institutions. With this valuable book, Manya Whitaker illuminates the often deliberate and sometimes inadvertent violations of those standards, and provides a handbook for creative and courageous resistance. *Public School Equity* summons us to dive into the contradictions and swim as hard as we can in the direction of our dreams—more than a moment, it's an invitation to a Movement."

—**William Ayers**, author of *To Teach* and *About Becoming a Teacher*

"When school leaders ask, 'How do I begin, continue, sustain, and drive equity within my school, system, or staff?' recommend *Public School Equity: Educational Leadership for Justice*. Dr. Whitaker provides a road map that meets educational leaders, their teams, and staff where they are on their individual and collective journeys. This is a step-by-step guide that centers teachers as the focus for achieving systemic educational equity and transformation."

—**Aaron J. Griffen**, Vice President of Diversity, Equity and Inclusion, DSST Public Schools

"Equity is at the heart of the radical hope that systems of oppression can be eradicated. Whitaker's powerful and inspirational book pushes readers to move away from the racist trappings of equality and toward the full light of equity in moving but totally pragmatic ways. This book is necessary for school-based practitioners and those who prepare practitioners to inspire change."

—**Kenneth Varner**, Professor of Education, University of Nevada, Las Vegas

"Whitaker has constructed a powerhouse book that every leader in prekindergarten–12 schools should read. During a time when school leaders across different sociopolitical contexts are struggling to address, respond to, and solve unprecedented problems inside and outside of school, this book reminds us that equity must be at the center of all we do! Drawing from robust and deep stories of educators, this book helps educators think about and plan for the important work ahead that must include communities, families, parents, policymakers, educators, and especially young people. A resource about the intersectional nature of cognition and behavior, this book is transformative for the individual and the collective."

—**H. Richard Milner IV**, Cornelius Vanderbilt
Distinguished Professor of Education, author of
Start Where You Are but Don't Stay There

PUBLIC SCHOOL EQUITY

Educational Leadership

for Justice

Equity and Social Justice in Education Series

Cheryl E. Matias and Paul C. Gorski, Series Editors

Routledge's Equity and Social Justice in Education series is a publishing home for books that apply critical and transformative equity and social justice theories to the work of on-the-ground educators. Books in the series describe meaningful solutions to the racism, white supremacy, economic injustice, sexism, heterosexism, transphobia, ableism, neoliberalism, and other oppressive conditions that pervade schools and school districts.

Equity-Centered Trauma-Informed Education
Alex Shevrin Venet

Social Studies for a Better World: An Anti-Oppressive Approach for Elementary Educators
Noreen Naseem Rodríguez and Katy Swalwell

Learning and Teaching While White: Antiracist Strategies for School Communities
Jenna Chandler-Ward and Elizabeth Denevi

Public School Equity: Educational Leadership for Justice
Manya C. Whitaker

Ableism in Education: Rethinking School Practices and Policies
Gillian Parekh

PUBLIC SCHOOL EQUITY

Educational Leadership

for Justice

Manya C. Whitaker, Ph.D.

Routledge
Taylor & Francis Group

NEW YORK AND LONDON

Designed cover: Lauren Graessle
Cover Image: ©Klaus Vedfelt/Getty Images

First published in 2022 by W. W. Norton

Published in 2024 by Routledge
605 Third Avenue, New York, NY 10158
4 Park Square, Milton Park, Abingdon, Oxon, OX14 4RN

Routledge is an imprint of the Taylor & Francis Group, an informa business

Library of Congress Cataloging-in-Publication Data
A catalog record for this title has been requested

ISBN: 9781032596778 (pbk)
ISBN: 9781032677958 (ebk)

DOI: 10.4324/9781032677958

This book is for my students, who give me lessons in leadership every day. I am a better educator and human because of them.

Contents

Part I
Envisioning Equity   1

Part II
Staffing for Equity   83

Part III
Sustaining Equity 137

Acknowledgments

I'd like to thank the many teachers, principals, and district administrators whose insights motivated this book. Despite your overwhelming workloads, you always find time to advocate for justice.

I also want to acknowledge Bridgette Hylton, Esq. for her brainstorming energy as I conceptualized this book; my graduate research assistant Pesha Mabrie for her willingness to read drafts of less-than-stellar writing; Carol, Jamie, and Marne for their guidance and suggestions during the publishing process; and Dr. Paul Gorski for creating a literary space where I could put my passion into words.

I'd especially like to thank Ms. Harburger, Ms. Berry, Mr. Pillsbury, Mr. Gray, and Ms. Perkins for enabling me to experience the joy in learning, no matter how disruptive I was in class. You all will be happy to know that in college I learned the value of listening instead of speaking from Dr. Abigail Baird, who shocked me into silence by modeling what it looks like to embrace and celebrate students' multiple identities. I credit my eventual recognition of her practices as equity-oriented to Dr. Rich Milner, who remains the largest influence on my scholarly path. But it is my parents, Rocky and Linda, to whom I am most grateful for always encouraging me to dance if I want to dance, because in doing so, they taught me how it feels to liberate myself.

Finally, I want to extend love and gratitude to my partner, Dr. Michael Sawyer, for his unwavering belief that what I have to say is valid and important. When I didn't believe in myself, I kept writing because you believed I should. Thank you for making me feel how I hope students feel in school.

Introduction

The COVID-19 pandemic exposed the reality that America's public education system is perilously close to collapse. This is especially true for minoritized and marginalized youth who do not live in communities that can fill the access and opportunity gaps that schools do not. The haste to reconfigure schooling made it clear that educational inequities exist beyond school discipline policies, a Eurocentric curriculum, and even beyond school funding. And despite the hyper-focus on resolving the "newly" discovered digital divide, justice won't be had by providing up-to-date technology and internet access. The pandemic crises forced us to accept that a focus on individual schooling factors will not produce educational equity if we do not also attend to how those factors operate together, across and within schools.

Framing the Problem

More than 65 years after *Brown v. Board of Education*, 58% of Black students and 60% of Hispanic* students attend schools where students of color compose more than 75% of enrollment (U.S. Department of Education, 2019a). Overlay that with economic segregation by which 45% of Black and Hispanic students attend schools where more than 75% of the students qualify for free or reduced lunch (U.S. Department of Education, 2019b). Within these segregated schools are classrooms

* I utilize *Hispanic* and *Latinx* according to the demographic label used by the author(s) of the cited source.

led by a majority white teacher workforce, even in urban areas where Black, Indigenous, and teachers of color (BITOC) constitute just 30% of the faculty (U.S. Department of Education, 2017a).

We decided long ago that separate schools are inherently unequal, not because of the segregation of people but because of the segregation of resources people bring with them to schools. While school budgets are largely determined by state per-pupil revenue, wealthy schools with active Parent–Teacher Associations (PTAs) and Parent–Teacher Organizations (PTOs) can raise and contribute additional funds that many low-income schools cannot. These additional monies are in part responsible for extracurricular and cocurricular opportunities to which many students in low-income schools do not have access. Especially in urban areas where charter schools reign supreme, Black and Latinx students attend schools where the curriculum is focused on standardized tests at the expense of non-tested subjects such as science and history (Whitaker, 2018).

These students are also learning in environments with harsh zero tolerance discipline policies that result in disproportionate suspensions and expulsions (Milner et al., 2018). Perhaps most important is the lack of teacher experience in racially isolated schools. Racially minoritized students, students from low-income communities, and students with disabilities are more likely to be taught by teachers with fewer than 5 years' experience (Goldhaber et al., 2017; Grier, 2019; Lai et al., 2020; Rogers & Doan, 2019), which matters because there is a positive relationship between teachers' years of experience and students' test scores (Ladd & Sorenson, 2017).

A lack of economic, social, and cultural resources has created a schooling system in which racially minoritized students, multilingual students, undocumented students, students with disabilities, and students who are a part of the LGBTQIA (lesbian, gay, bisexual, transgender, queer, intersex, and asexual) community often feel excluded, unwelcome, and misunderstood. They do not see themselves nor their histories represented in their textbooks. They do not feel comfortable in a space that denies their existence. They do not automatically know the rules by which their wealthier, white, able-bodied friends play the game of life. It is no surprise then that minoritized students have test scores that are one-third to a full standard deviation below national averages (National Assessment of Educational Progress, 2019a, 2019b).

Solutions Thus Far

Myriad solutions have been implemented and oftentimes lauded to address these inequities, yet many education policies exacerbated them. Mandates that schools desegregate in 1955 led to the closure of Black schools and the eradication of a Black teacher workforce, the consequences of which we feel today with just 7% of public school teachers identifying as Black (U.S. Department of Education, 2019c). As part of a war on poverty, Title I of the Elementary and Secondary Education Act (ESEA) of 1965 established a capitalist framing of equity that utilizes income as the criterion for deciding student eligibility for academic supports. This narrative was influenced by culture of poverty theories (Lewis, 1959) that persist in educational discourse where children from low-income communities are perceived as deficient and middle- and upper-income children are thought to never need help.

While the Education for All Handicapped Children Act (now the Individuals with Disabilities Education Act [IDEA]) of 1975 required us to also consider students' cognitive, social, and behavioral needs, it is those whose parents have cultural capital that actually receive supports. This was exemplified in 1983 when after "A Nation at Risk" demonstrated racial gaps in literacy, science, and math, instead of strengthening Black, Indigenous, and students of color's (BISOC) learning interventions, they were tracked into remedial courses with lowered expectations. Black, Brown, and neurodivergent students remain overrepresented in special education courses (U.S. Department of Education, 2018).

It is not only students who suffer from poorly designed and executed policies, as was evident shortly after the implementation of No Child Left Behind (NCLB) in 2001. The creation of high-stakes testing also meant that teachers of historically underserved students were penalized for low test scores, increasing teacher attrition in Title I schools. We hoped that a Black president would reverse punitive policies that disproportionately affect schools with racially minoritized students, so it was disappointing when President Obama implemented Race to the Top (2009) that asked those same schools to compete for grants to "turn around" test scores by firing staff or restructuring as charter schools.

States were more likely to receive a grant if they adopted the newly designed Common Core State Standards (2010) and committed to using some of the funds to create curriculum and assessments aligned with the new standards. The only winners were publishers who made millions producing textbooks that did not represent diverse students' histories or experiences.

Nearing the end of his second term in 2015, President Obama admitted that perhaps educational equity would not be achieved with heavy federal oversight, so he authorized the Every Student Succeeds Act (ESSA) that gave decision-making power back to states. Though this gesture was well-received by a public with long-standing beliefs in local control, ESSA added fuel to the school choice flames, making it the reform du jour. School choice advocates argue that achievement gaps are caused by poor student–school fit that is resolved if parents can choose the best school for their child. What they fail to mention is that those with the most choice are those with the most informational, social, and economic capital. In a country founded on ideals of meritocracy and individualism, it is unsurprising that capitalist-based reforms have exacerbated educational inequities that are only partially mitigated by a few promising initiatives.

For example, there are programs to recruit BITOC who could potentially be more effective than the 79% of teachers who are white and may not understand their culturally and linguistically diverse (CLD) students' sociocultural needs. Yet, despite less expensive alternative licensure programs, an increase in Grow Your Own (GYO) programs, and organizations such as Teach for America that fast track teacher preparation, the number of BITOC continues to rise slowly, increasing by just three percentage points between 2011–2012 and 2017–2018 (U.S. Department of Education, 2019d). Such growth is undermined by the fact that the few BITOC we do have exit the profession at a higher rate than white teachers (Albert Shanker Institute,

2015), decreasing the likelihood that BISOC will ever experience the advantages of a teacher who looks like them.

Advocates of teacher–student ethnic matching highlight the emotional benefits of role models, asset-based perceptions of students, and cultural constructions of knowledge when teachers and students have similar social positionalities (Acosta, 2015; Flores et al., 2018; Gershenson et al., 2016; Gist, 2014). But the reality is that there simply aren't enough BITOC to ensure that at some point, every racially minoritized child will have a teacher who shares their heritage. What's more is that white students need diverse teachers just as much, if not more, than BISOC if we have any hope of disrupting the culturally reproductive nature of U.S. public schools.

It is not that by virtue of being racially minoritized you are endowed with better pedagogical skills or more content knowledge. It is that BITOC are likely to have experienced firsthand the necessity and the value of teaching through a multicultural lens. They bring with them the dedication to bear witness to the needs of students who are often rendered invisible by traditional educational processes that ignore how identity shapes learning (Easton-Brooks, 2019).

Teaching to and through students' frames of reference (Gay, 2013) is extremely promising. We know that if teachers embrace diverse linguistic codes, interpret behavior within students' sociocultural context, expand what counts as knowledge, and utilize curriculum reflective of students' lived experiences, academic outcomes will certainly rise. We know that students feel valued in a classroom that bridges home and school and truly keeps their interests and needs at the core of instruction. Multicultural education *should* be an answer to educational inequity.

But too often teachers are expected to engage in culturally responsive teaching without a schoolwide commitment to inclusion and opportunity. No teacher can be a change agent if their pedagogical practices are undermined by exclusionary discipline policies, expectations to teach to a test, or mandates against having parents in the classroom. Further, teachers need ongoing professional development, mentoring, and feedback related to multicultural teaching to ensure they can consistently and effectively respond to students' needs. Eradicating educational inequities that fuel opportunity and achievement gaps requires a comprehensive schoolwide approach to social justice.

Theoretical Framing

Most education practitioner books are largely focused on *practices*. We talk about what teachers and administrators should do to support students' learning. Are they using culturally responsive instructional practices and tracking students' academic needs via Response to Intervention (RTI) protocols? Are teachers and staff responding to students' behavior according to the tenets of positive behavioral intervention and supports (PBIS)? The appeal of a "what" and "how" perspective is obvious—it is quick and easy to assess someone's behaviors. However, behaviors are performative, short-lived, and are not always reflective of the beliefs that motivate them. Such a narrow measuring of social justice facilitates trending and quickly discarded instructional reforms, while also ignoring structural inequities.

This book takes a different approach to issues of educational equity by using what we know from social cognitive psychology about how people develop, enact, and sustain specific belief systems that in turn, shape their decision-making. Each part of the book is guided by a different theory:

Part I: Envisioning Equity. This part utilizes organizational role theory (ORT) (R. L. Kahn et al., 1964) as the guiding framework for creating a school climate focused on equity. From social psychology, ORT examines how well people assume preplanned roles in hierarchical structures by revealing the determinants of peoples' workplace behaviors. I use this theory to help school leaders backward design their school culture by considering the roles necessary to achieve school goals, and by thinking through how those roles will interact to affect organizational objectives. I urge school leaders to strategize around three principles of ORT: role confusion, role strain, and role conflict.

Part II: Staffing for Equity. The second portion of the book relies on social identity theory (SIT) (Tajfel & Turner, 1979) as a way of understanding how people develop social identities, how they group themselves together, and how they collectively develop and maintain behavioral expectations. In applying this theory to schooling, I walk readers through typical school-based social groups (e.g., administrators, veteran teachers, novice teachers, support staff), the norms and behaviors endemic to those groups, how leaders emerge in each group, and how the groups interact to acquire and maintain dominance. The purpose of using this theory is to make clear how social grouping can be detrimental to school functioning, but also how it can be leveraged to meet organizational goals.

Part III: Sustaining Equity. The final part of the book explores how school and district leaders can support, assess, and promote teachers in an equitable fashion. I return to role theory, but this time using cognitive role theory (CRT) (Biddle, 1979) as a framework for examining the factors that influence teachers' abilities to meet professional expectations. I highlight issues such as role taking, role conformity, and role consensus as explanatory variables when schools fail to truly create an equitable work environment.

Book Organization

The purpose of this book is to offer educators guidance for leading a school or district grounded in social justice by centering *teachers*—not just teaching practices. It details a three-phase process of envisioning, implementing, and sustaining a school culture that recognizes the multidimensionality of social justice education. I walk readers through what it takes to establish a balanced organizational structure and an empowering school climate, before moving to the nuts and bolts of identifying, recruiting, hiring, and onboarding teachers with positive multicultural dispositions. Part III of the book describes equity-oriented professional development, evaluation, and promotion practices aimed at retaining effective teachers of diverse students. The final chapter acknowledges the value of formative and summative feedback in education and thus offers readers guidance on conducting schoolwide equity assessments. The book concludes by imagining what schools could be if we centered equity in service of justice.

Along the way, you will meet a principal of a struggling middle school in a newly gentrified neighborhood. We follow along as turnaround principal Shelby Patterson works to rebuild a school with equity at the core. She models what it looks like to lead for justice by engaging in a long-term process of imagining what the school could be, creating a plan to achieve the vision, and of making the sometimes hard, but critical changes necessary to do what it is best for students and families. Principal Patterson serves as a gentle reminder that change takes time and not everything will happen as you hope.

Chapters are organized to move readers chronologically through the process of developing, leading, and contributing to an equity-oriented school, but each chapter can stand alone. Anyone with professional responsibilities at the classroom, school, or district level will find this text useful because it offers concrete how-tos for enhancing equity through processes, policies, people, and practices. It is a valuable text for anyone interested in teaching in urban environments and for teacher educators working with those preparing to do so. Much of the content of this book is drawn from over 40 interviews with teachers, principals, and district leaders across 5 years. Here, I highlight the seven educators (with pseudonyms) whose wisdom and advice appears throughout the book.

Educator Profiles

Mr. Clayton Barry
Manager of District-Wide Supports and Related Services
Rhode Island
Former Special Education Specialist

> "Equity to me is removing barriers to access and providing the ability for students to succeed if they so choose. We can't make the students succeed, but I feel like we have an obligation as the educational body to provide resources and access, knowledge of the system itself, of education, access to education, be it technology or special services or whatever they need."

Dr. Marcus Carmichael
District Vice President of Diversity, Equity, and Inclusion
Colorado
Former High School Principal, Assistant Principal, and Middle School Teacher

"Educational equity to me means restructuring education not to fit the needs of everyone, but to fit the needs of the most vulnerable, the most marginalized first. We want to fit everybody's needs, but we're going to restructure this to make sure that we're going to give those who have been systemically and historically oppressed the leg up they need in order to close the 'gaps' and to meet the same expectations as everyone else."

Ms. Taylor Fisher
Assistant Professor of Educational Leadership
California
Former Vice Principal and Department Chair

"Equity looks like addressing the needs the students have in ways that help them get to the places where they want, and should be able, to go."

Dr. William Houser
Assistant Professor of Educational Leadership
Texas
Former Principal, Assistant Principal, Guidance Counselor, and Middle School Teacher

"Equity means making sure that each student gets what they need to succeed, whether it's resources, whether it's TLC. That's not just instructionally, but also the affective domain. We're talking about their needs are being met inside and outside of the school as well."

Mr. Samuel Lewis
Elementary School Principal
Colorado
Former Elementary Teacher

"I've always related to the kids. Of course, I care about my staff. I care about my parents. I care about my community. But at the end of it, my start for everything is thinking about kids and equity for kids and making sure that as school leaders, we are aligning all the resources in order to support kids. Educational equity to me means that students are first."

Ms. Linda Nash
District Director of Special Education
Washington
Former Special Education Teacher, Student Services Specialist, Director of Outreach and Organizational Learning, and Director of School Improvement

> "My definition of educational equity is actually intersectional. To me, it's really about any kind of a protected class . . . and instruction to all those [identities]. That's who we should be thinking about. If it's gender identity, if it's disability or ability, if it is language, it's much more expansive [than race]. When I think practically what that looks like in a school setting, I think you have to think about the complexity of how the various different intersectionalities of people and identities show up and how we school for them."

Ms. Emily Richardson
Health and Wellness School Program Coordinator
Colorado
Former Elementary and Middle School Teacher

> "I don't think it has a look. I think it has a feel. It is when you walk into a building or a classroom and not only are students engaged, but family and community are present in the building, and students are celebrated for who they are, not who they are thought to be able to become. Equity to me is where they literally highlight every culture, every cultural celebration, they lean into it and embrace it. We are a crew and we're together."

What You Can Expect

The fight for educational equity occurs in courtrooms, communities, and certainly in classrooms. Across these spaces we conflate equity with equality, tolerance with inclusion, and access with opportunity. In the coming pages I use these terms often, so I want to operationalize them in the context of K–12 schools:

- *Equity* is providing teachers, students, and families with resources and supports aligned with their individual needs.
- *Equality* occurs when teachers, students, and families are given the exact same resources and supports whether they are aligned with their individual needs or not.
- *Tolerance* is reluctant recognition of differences with little commitment to leveraging them toward positive outcomes.
- *Inclusion* requires acknowledging, respecting, valuing, and celebrating differences.
- *Access* is the presence of educational and professional resources.
- *Opportunity* is the ability to take advantage of those resources.

While I would like to have written a book with *the* solution to what I consider to be one of the nation's most pressing problem, I have not. What I have written is something I think is missing from educational discourse about the failure of our education system: a realistic process for long-term improvement. There are dozens, if not hundreds, of education reform books but to be frank, I find the solutions too broad, too vague, too expensive, too disconnected from the realities of schooling. Especially with respect to educational equity, solutions are too narrow in scope. It is not enough to diversify the teacher workforce or to implement restorative justice practices. It is not enough to take students on college tours and enroll them in art classes. These are Band-Aids for a gaping wound.

I am suggesting an intentional and strategic process for affecting and effecting educational equity across multiple aspects of school functioning simultaneously. I admit that focusing on one school at a time will not quickly change a failing system. But I also recognize that top-down approaches have failed to do that very thing for decades. Here, I build upon the commitment of frontline educators doing what is best and what is right for students by offering them concrete steps to do so.

Part I

Envisioning Equity

MEET SHELBY

It is late June and Shelby Patterson has just moved into her new apartment four blocks from Roger Gates Middle School, where she will begin as the principal in just six weeks. Shelby has 15 years of experience as a school administrator but knows her new position will not be easy. The state department of education has labeled Roger Gates a Priority Improvement school for the last two years and has now placed the school in "turn around" status. That is Shelby's job: to turn Roger Gates around. Shelby has successfully transformed two other schools, but in addition to low achievement, a lack of resources, and dilapidated facilities, Roger Gates' problems are exacerbated by gentrification and an increasing divide between new and old neighborhood residents.

Roger Gates has historically served Latinx and Black students from blue collar families, but because the neighborhood is part of the city's revitalization program, there are many more higher income white families moving in. On the surface this is a good thing because higher incomes bring home ownership, which yields higher property taxes and, ultimately, increased school funding. But Shelby knows that the new families will expect much more out of Roger Gates than it currently delivers. What's more worrisome is that the arrival of new students has revealed racial and income-based achievement gaps that are fueled by massive inequities within and beyond the school.

Change takes time, but the state has given Shelby just three years to achieve what seems to be impossible. She makes a list of her year 1 priorities:

1. **Lack of resources**. *Roger Gates' budget allots $6,700 per student, which is 28% lower than in neighboring districts. Shelby cannot wait on property tax revenue to increase the budget, so she must be creative when thinking through how to expand school resources.*

2. **Family and community morale**. *Recent gentrification efforts have resulted in skyrocketing rents, raises in grocery store prices, and a crippled public transportation system on which Roger Gates' families heavily rely. With so much going on in their lives, families do not have the capacity to dedicate time and resources to their children's schooling. Many parents attended Roger Gates themselves and hope that their positive experience will carry over to their children. But still, parents know that things are different now, and they can't help but feel pushed out of their neighborhood and their school.*

3. **Closing achievement gaps.** *Shelby knows that achievement gaps are the outcomes of opportunity and access gaps. Roger Gates has a limited range of academic offerings and very few extracurricular activities. It seems as if the prior principal was focused more on school policies than school practices. This has led to a lot of bureaucracy and very little action. Given families' life contexts, Shelby acknowledges that if she is going to raise achievement, she will need to surround students with in-school supports.*

Experience has taught Shelby that such large goals are better accomplished in collaboration with others. She revisits staff files, student profiles, and explores the neighborhood as she searches for people who can help her envision equity at Roger Gates.

It is not uncommon to hear people talk about wanting to open a school. These proclamations are usually the result of someone learning the depth and breadth of inequities and inefficiencies in education. While their intention is admirable, the reality that anyone who has enough money and proper social networks can open a school is terrifying.

That people think they are equipped with the knowledge and skills to run a school speaks to how little respect we have for educators in the United States. School leadership requires a mixture of interpersonal and organizational skills; financial literacy; and deep knowledge of local, state, and federal education policies and practices. It requires humility, compassion, and selflessness, and a willingness to put the needs of our most vulnerable first. When enumerated in such a way, leading a school is a daunting endeavor, but it does not have to be. This first part of the book uses organizational role theory (ORT) to help school leaders backward design their school culture by considering the professional roles necessary to achieve school goals, and by thinking through how those roles will interact to affect organizational objectives framed around equity.

Organizational Role Theory

Drawn from social cognitive psychology, ORT focuses on how people understand their job expectations *given their relationship* to others in the organization (i.e., school). This emphasis is important because it highlights the fact that people do not just read a job description and immediately know what to do. They compare their job to others' jobs to ascertain differences and similarities in professional expectations. Organizational role theorists assume three things:

1. Jobs are designed based upon organizational needs.

2. Job expectations are learned through experience.

3. People are aware of the expectations they have of their own and others' professional behaviors.

These tenets hold true in schools where positions are often created retroactively after realizing a gap in school functioning. Take for example the dramatic increase in resource officers and counselors after school shootings in Colorado, Kentucky, Florida, and Texas. Or the chronic need for special education teachers as technological advances, sociocultural trauma, and an increasingly diverse student population coalesce to reveal the breadth of students' needs. Of course, it is ideal if schools are fully staffed prior to opening, but there is no way to know exactly which positions will be most critical. ORT encourages us to anticipate needs when creating the organizational structure by engaging in a strategic planning process that aligns needs with capacities.

The second tenet of ORT is supported by data reiterating the positive correlation between years of teaching experience and students' academic achievement. The art and science of teaching are realized through professional practice with various pedagogies in different settings with diverse students. Staff responsibilities are also constantly evolving in response to emerging school needs. ORT therefore suggests that job descriptions should be written with flexibility and space for interpretation.

Finally, and most importantly for school leaders wanting to educate for equity, is a reminder that people are aware of their work environment and are continually assessing their fit within that environment. Constant comparison of one's own job expectations and performance with others' can result in negative outcomes that affect the overall school climate. For instance, many novice teachers are often assigned to classrooms where students have lower prior achievement and more diverse learning needs (Kologrides et al., 2012), which, for new teachers who've yet to fill their pedagogical tool kit, can engender feelings of role strain: being overwhelmed by professional expectations.

Educators are often asked to simultaneously serve as social workers, psychologists, and parents, which can cause role conflict: tension between competing job expectations. Blurred boundaries are inevitable in a complex field like education, but a clear organizational structure can help people prioritize their professional responsibilities. This would minimize possible role confusion that emerges when people are uncertain about their unique contributions to the organization, especially if other people appear to have similar job descriptions.

When schools have clear organizational structures and when people fully understand and are equipped to perform their duties, everyone can focus their attention on optimizing student outcomes. Part I of the book unpacks the complex considerations of establishing a school grounded in, and working toward, equity and justice. After reviewing the 15 steps of school planning, we turn our attention to choosing an organizational structure and accompanying leadership style, developing equitable policies and practices, and cultivating family and community partnerships that supplement potential gaps in the school organization.

1 School Planning for Equity

When you hear the phrase *educational equity*, what do you immediately think of? Like the experts you met in the Introduction, most educators think holistically about students' diverse needs and how best to meet them in an effort to ultimately erase opportunity and achievement gaps. They emphasize the affective nature of learning through the importance of teacher–student relationships, a welcoming school climate, and a culture of positivity. They talk excitedly about high expectations, tough love, and shared accountability. Principals discuss hiring and retaining high-quality teachers who love the students, love the school, and love the community.

If only schools came predesigned with each of these elements in place. Equitable schools, or any schools for that matter, do not just appear. They are thoughtfully designed, planned, executed, and constantly evaluated and adjusted. This does not mean that designing a school culture grounded in equity can only happen before a school opens. On the contrary, because it is an iterative process, designing an equitable school can and should happen in stages. Depending upon a variety of constraints (district support, time, resources), each of the three phases of the 15-step process will take at minimum 3–4 months, totaling approximately 1 to 1.5 years from envisioning to assessment.

While this seems like a long time to enact change, it is important not to rush the process or think of this as a checklist for equity. Decades of hasty school reforms have yielded quick-fix solutions that did little to eradicate educational inequities. We need to approach school reform dialectically, considering top-down structures and policies in conjunction with bottom-up practices. We then need to consider the third space (Bhabha, 1994) by intentionally connecting schools to communities. Strategic planning will ensure coherence and consistency across all elements of schooling for teachers, students, families, and school leaders.

Planning

The first and most critical phase in designing equitable educational experiences is the planning phase. This is the time when everything must be carefully thought out from multiple perspectives. Most initiatives that fail do so because they lacked strategic planning.

THOUGHTS FROM THE FIELD

I always do things in one year, three years, five years, and beyond increments. I have a medium- and a long-term plan. I think part of the thing that administrators think is "I have to do it. I have to solve the world in one year." But as a new administrator, you probably have at least 15 to 20 years left in your career, so pace yourself.

Director Nash

Step 1: Create an Advisory Board

Not only wasn't Rome built in a day, it wasn't built by one or two people. While most school districts have a school board, very few public schools have their own advisory boards. An advisory board is a collective that provides advice and guidance to school leaders, which sometimes means challenging a principal's idea or decision. The board is not an evaluative body; it is a brainstorming body meant to provide feedback, generate ideas, and anticipate outcomes.

Think proactively and construct the board at least 2 months before you hope to conduct a needs-assessment (Step 2). Board recruitment should be thoughtful and intentional. In the corporate world, the board president picks the other members based upon their resume, but this approach is exclusive and antithetical to equity because we tend to prefer people who think as we do. This leads to groupthink that minimizes the creativity necessary to reimagine schooling. Instead, host a town hall where you share your goals for the school, the anticipated timeline, and the role of the board. Invite interested parties to meet with you individually about how they hope to contribute to educational equity.

If this sounds like an interview it's because it is. Too often, school leaders rely upon others' goodwill to do what is best for students. But when the rubber hits the road and people get busy, volunteer work is not prioritized. It is therefore important that the advisory board be branded as a professional commitment as well as a personal one. Strive to develop a board with members who represent different investments in the school and thus, interact with and in the school differently. These stakeholders should include students (as age appropriate), alumni of the school, families, teachers, staff, and community members—each with equal voting power such that there are no roles or positions (e.g., chair/director, secretary, treasurer) on the board. They should also represent different social identities and positionalities so that the board includes people with diverse life experiences, particularly as they relate to schooling.

Finally, each member should commit to being on the board for the duration of the process. The board should meet at least once a month, but during the planning phase, twice a month would not be a bad idea. These meetings should take place on a day and at a time when everyone can attend, so it is best to schedule them at the same day and time each month (e.g., second Thursday of the month at 6 p.m.). Meeting at the school is the logical choice, but it is okay to rotate meeting locations as long as everyone agrees in advance and has transportation. School leaders are responsible for scheduling and for creating and disseminating detailed agendas prior to meetings.

Before moving to Step 2, make sure you've completed the following:

- scheduled a town hall
- advertised the event to the school and neighborhood communities

- met with interested parties
- assessed potential board members' investment in educational equity
- identified how each potential board member will uniquely contribute to the board
- secured board members' commitment to remain involved throughout the process

Step 2: Conduct a Needs Assessment

As education scholar Gary Howard (2016) noted, we can't teach what we don't know. In other words, you can't design an equitable school culture without first recognizing existing and potential inequities through a needs assessment. This can be tricky if you are new to educational equity because inequities are rarely blatant. Factors limiting students' achievement can be relational in nature (e.g., teacher bias), operate outside of the classroom or school (e.g., students who work after school may not be able to complete daily homework), or be driven by students' cognitive, social, or emotional needs (e.g., a learning disability). Unmasking inequities requires deep inquiry into surface-level observations focused on fairness (e.g., Black students get in trouble more than white students) that reveal underlying causal factors motivating unequal outcomes (e.g., Black students get in trouble more than white students because Black children are perceived as threatening and older than they are). Such critical analysis is best facilitated by a properly designed needs assessment.

Assessment is different than an evaluation that is done to measure if goals were met at the end of a process (product-oriented). Assessment occurs throughout a process to ascertain current capacities and performance levels. A needs assessment offers an opportunity to identify possible strategies for increasing equity across multiple school factors including student enrollment, staffing, curriculum, policies, organizational structure, resources, evaluation, compensation, and even the school's physical spaces (process-oriented). But an equity based needs assessment goes even further to clarify: (a) who has what needs, (b) existing programs or practices that can be leveraged or expanded to meet those needs, and (c) available resources.

There are five steps to conducting a needs assessment:

1. Determine what needs to be assessed.
2. Determine who will participate in the assessment process.
3. Determine how information will be collected.
4. Determine how findings will be used.
5. Determine how findings will be communicated to the school community.

Step 1 is most critical as it is easy to forget to assess important but invisible aspects of schools such as the school climate for diversity and inclusion. How do students, teachers, and families *feel* in the school? What elements of school functioning affect someone's sense of belonging? When do students most often experience success and when are they experiencing failure? What messages about involvement do families perceive receiving from the school? While it is easy and faster to assess the dress code for inclusivity, it is much harder—but equally necessary—to assess lived experiences that offer a thorough view of the overall school culture.

Keeping that bird's-eye view in mind, the answer to Step 2 is simple: Everyone. Well, not every single person in the school, but a representative sample of each demographic, much like the advisory board. You will certainly need the core perspectives from students, teachers, staff, and families, but you should also invite participation from community organizations and community members, especially parents or caregivers of prospective students. Gathering opinions beyond the school can provide insight into the school's reputation and engender strategies for marketing, as well as for teacher and student recruitment.

Collecting data from such a wide pool of people will require not only time, but also careful consideration about how best to get useful answers from specific groups. For example, students give far more detail in conversations than they do on written questionnaires. Young people also talk more when they can build upon others' comments, so focus groups facilitated by a trusted adult are an excellent way to gather intel. Families with minimal time and scheduling constraints will appreciate a survey that asks them to quickly rate or rank explicitly stated school factors. Interviews might be most useful with community members who may have questions as well as opinions.

Once you've decided *how* to collect information, you also need to determine *who* will collect information from whom. If you are a new principal, teachers may not yet know you well enough to share their honest opinion about hiring practices, school policies, or the organizational structure. Students may not feel comfortable sharing their thoughts about instructional practices or the curriculum with teachers with whom they don't have positive relationships. Situations such as these may necessitate confidential or anonymous approaches to data collection. There are a multitude of free and low-cost online platforms that can gather, organize, and store survey and recorded interview data so that people do not feel like their answers can be traced back to them. Online databases have the added benefit of being digital so there is no need to keep track of hundreds of pieces of paper. Table 1.1 is an example of how you might organize the many elements of a needs assessment.

Table 1.1 Example Needs Assessment Organizer			
	Needs Assessment		
	Dress Code	**Curriculum**	**School Climate**
Respondents	Students; families	Teachers; students	Students; families; all staff
Data Collector	Counselor; administrator		
Data Collection Method	Focus groups; online survey		
Data Collection Timeline	End of first semester		

An online database will also be useful as you make sense of the data. You may want to categorize data by the visible and invisible factors you identified prior to conducting the assessment. This will provide clear feedback on each element of schooling. Within each factor, further organize information by demographic to make certain all voices and perspectives are represented. What did students say about the school? Teachers? Finally, locate points of overlap between key constituencies to determine priorities. Present these findings to the advisory board, at a staff meeting, and to the community.

Once you've completed the following, you are ready for Step 3:

- identified specific instances of educational inequity in your school
- determined which groups are most affected by inequities
- identified underlying patterns of inequities across findings
- shared findings with the school community

Step 3: Identify Core Values

How did the outcomes of the needs assessment make you feel? What were you proud of and what were you motivated to change? Your answers to these questions likely reflect your core values: the beliefs that guide behavior. If you felt happy that families reported feeling welcomed and respected by the school, you likely value collaboration. If you were upset that students said the dress code was "unfair," you may value self-expression. It is important to remember, though, that your personal values are not on the table; the focus is the values the school should uphold. Put another way, core values are the shared beliefs among school members.

While there is no must-have list of core values for equity, keep in mind that school values should translate into equitable policies and practices. For instance, many Waldorf schools promote positive self-esteem; consequently, they do not have punitive discipline policies that might make children label themselves as "bad." Or take diversity as an example of a core value. In a truly equitable school this value suggests the presence of a pronoun policy, an inclusive curriculum, academic schedules that honor religious holidays, and least of all, a demographically diverse staff. Yet, many schools that claim to value diversity operate in ways that ignore, minimize, or penalize cultural differences. Alignment between values and practices is an easy way to see if purported equitable schools are walking the walk and not just talking the talk, so make sure you:

- translate core values to actionable behaviors
- share a draft of the new core values with the school community
- revise core values based upon community feedback

Step 4: Write a Vision Statement

A vision statement is a description of why you have certain core values. What will operating according to your core values help you achieve in the long term? What do you want to be known for? This one-sentence statement should clearly articulate the impact you want the school to have on its students, teachers, and community, so it should be developed in consultation with the advisory board. The vision statement serves as a guide to ensure the school stays on track toward its ultimate goal. School districts often have well thought-out vision statements:

- Every child succeeds *(Denver Public Schools)*
- Each student will graduate ready for college, career, and life *(Seattle Public Schools)*
- To be a premier urban school district *(Dallas Independent School District)*

Step 5: Write a Mission Statement

The mission statement explains how you will achieve long-term goals. A mission statement is a short summary of the school's core purpose by describing day-to-day practices. This single sentence should be motivating, proactive, and jargon free. Here are the mission statements that accompany the aforementioned vision statements:

- providing all students the opportunity to achieve the knowledge and skills necessary to become contributing citizens in our diverse society
- ensuring equitable access, closing the opportunity gaps, and excellence in education for every student
- educating all students for success

Because vision and mission statements guide school functioning, be sure the entire staff understands how their daily responsibilities contribute to both. It is wise to:

- explain the distinctions between new and old statements to the school community
- ask staff to recommit to the school's vision and share at least two ways their professional practices will change given the new statements

Step 6: Set Goals

The easiest way to begin drafting goals is to write one goal for each aspect of the needs assessment (even for the factors for which there was positive feedback) using the popular SMART approach: **S**pecific, **M**easurable, **A**greeable, **R**ealistic, **T**ime-framed. Establishing SMART goals ensures a detailed and well thought-out process for creating an equitable school.

Specific goals (the "S" in SMART) answer the six "W"s: Who is involved? What do we want to accomplish? Where will it happen? When will it be done? Which constraints are most prominent? and Why do we need to accomplish this? Without such specificity, it is easy to overlook an important component of the process. For example,

General goal: *Implement restorative justice practices.*

SMART goal: *All teachers will implement restorative justice in their classroom by the end of first semester.*

In the former, it is unclear who will be using restorative justice in what instances for what purposes. This formulation creates role confusion and allows people to transfer responsibility because they were not specifically named. The SMART goal explicitly states the responsible party, the behavior, and the time frame for execution.

Such clarity makes the goal easily measurable (the "M" in SMART) but it could be further improved by including the "why" behind the goal. This allows you to create logical measures of success that indicate not only know if a goal was completed, but also how well it was completed. A 10% reduction in suspensions and expulsions is good but a

45% reduction is much better. You should therefore create cumulative SMART goals:

SMART goal (1a): *All teachers will implement restorative justice in their classroom by the end of first semester.*

SMART goal (1b): *All teachers will reduce disciplinary referrals by 25% by the end of the academic year.*

Cumulative smart goals underscore the reality that equity will not be achieved in one step, so tracking progress is necessary for continued motivation. Keeping spirits up is incredibly important because not everyone will have the same ideas about what needs to be done to create an equitable school. Therefore, the third element of a SMART goal is that it needs to be agreeable, such that even though everyone may not think a particular goal should be a priority, they at least recognize its contribution to the school's mission.

Collective feedback might also help you detect unrealistic goals (the "R" in SMART). If people don't agree on the goal, they won't be motivated to achieve it, but that doesn't mean that it won't eventually get done. But if a goal is unrealistic, it can't be accomplished regardless of who is doing the work. Budgeting constraints and know-how are common barriers to goal achievement in education. It sounds great to have a goal of limiting class sizes to 20, but if your funds are earmarked for specific purposes, you may not be able to reallocate money toward hiring more teachers or securing additional buildings to accommodate more classes. Schools that are hoping to be more equitable often have inclusive classrooms where students with moderate to severe learning disabilities are mainstreamed into general education classrooms with teachers who may or may not have the skills to properly differentiate. This is a common mistake in which providing an equal education (everyone in the same classroom) actually undermines equitable learning opportunities (everyone getting what they need to optimize their learning) because someone did not assess the school's capacity to equitably achieve this goal.

Given enough resources, it is reasonable for a school to want to have small class sizes and inclusive classrooms. The problem then is not the goal itself; it is the time frame in which the goal is accomplished (the "T" in SMART). Goals must have clear beginnings and endings, particularly in the context of schools where everyone is already overwhelmed with professional duties. Without a clear deadline, people will understandably push new initiatives off in favor of more immediate tasks. Time-framed goals not only allow people to integrate new projects into their workload, but they also convey a sense of urgency that helps people understand its importance.

List your goals on a single document and review the following *before* Step 7:

- Are they each clear and specific?
- Is each goal explicitly written to increase equity?
- Do they collectively address multiple areas of school functioning?
- Will they promote long-term change?
- Are they spaced out to prevent role strain?

Step 7: Draft an Action Plan

With the framework for building an equitable school laid out, it is now time to translate the big picture into concrete actionable steps. An action plan is a guiding document that details how you will achieve the goals determined in Step 6.

An action plan must contain the following:

- Objectives for each goal that delineate the necessary steps to achieve the goal. Returning to our example of reducing suspensions and expulsions, an objective toward achieving that goal might be to train teachers how to use restorative justice practices.
- Actionable steps for each objective that detail what it will take to make that objective come to life. For example, I must first assess teachers' understanding of the data indicating a need for restorative justice. Next, I should evaluate teachers' existing knowledge and skills about restorative justice to determine if professional development (PD) is warranted.

- Methods for evaluating objective outcomes. How will you know when an objective has a successful outcome? Objectives need to have measurable outcomes that detail progress toward the larger goal. How will you assess the efficacy of the PD (i.e., if teachers truly learned restorative justice practices and feel prepared to implement them)?
- Contingency plans if an objective is not fully met or if a step toward meeting an objective falls through. Some goals will have enough supporting objectives that if one isn't successful, the ultimate goal can still be achieved. Other goals will be heavily reliant upon one or two objectives so it is critical to have a backup plan. If I cannot find someone to facilitate an in-person PD on restorative justice, I should have already located online learning opportunities. If not enough teachers feel competent after the training, I should have a structure for one-on-one mentoring among teachers. Utilizing an alternative plan will of course necessitate changes to the overall timeline but having a safety plan will also ensure that the larger action plan is adhered to.

Writing objectives for each goal will result in a substantive document with a lot of details, but despite the effort that went into creating the action plan, you must remember that it is a living document subject to revision at all times. Be mindful of revisions because changing a single objective or goal could potentially reshape the entire process of becoming an equitable school. Each minor revision requires a review of the entire action plan to maintain comprehensive coverage of equity issues and alignment in approach.

Resource Assessment

It is easy to have a vision, but it is much more difficult to realize that vision. Most education reforms or initiatives never come to fruition or are short-lived because schools lack district support and the accompanying resources to sustain them. As exciting as it is to have a clear action plan, you must pause and assess your ability to implement it. The second phase of school planning requires a careful and honest review of information, human, and economic capital.

Step 8: Conduct a Knowledge Assessment

There is undoubtedly a lot of wisdom among the advisory board and among the teachers and staff in the school. However, it is very unlikely that for every goal there is a person with the relevant knowledge and skills to lead in that area. Guided by your action plan, do a staffing inventory and indicate where you are best situated to lead and where others have more pertinent knowledge and skills (whether or not they are willing to lead is discussed next). Work with the advisory board and consult with school leaders to determine how to fill knowledge gaps in the action plan. We've already discussed hiring an expert to facilitate restorative justice trainings. In what other areas might teachers need deeper understandings? This is a point at which you, as a school leader, need to be critical in your assessment. Do teachers know how to diversify their curriculum? Facilitate difficult dialogues? Create a trauma-sensitive classroom? Do you and other leaders know where to recruit diverse teachers? How to assess their cultural consciousness? How to conduct equitable teaching evaluations?

Don't be nervous about reflecting on these questions. If the answer to some of these questions is "no," there is no need to panic and no need to reinvent the wheel. Many schools have been successful moving toward equity in one or some of the areas specified in your action plan. Research schools with similar demographics in similar geographic areas and see what they've done to be more equitable. Are there opportunities to collaborate with other schools in or near your district?

If there are no schools that model exactly what you're looking for, look toward community partners. While the context may differ, the processes are similar. Nonprofit organizations are especially conscious of employing equitable practices because they are often funded by government-backed grants that require adherence to equal opportunity laws according to the Office of Civil Rights. Their primary constituents are also community members who are often engaged with them because of issues of inequity. Affinity-based organizations such as the National Association for the Advancement of Colored People (NAACP), United

We Dream, and GLSEN (Gay, Lesbian & Straight Education Network) are excellent resources for support developing equitable policies and procedures. If district funds are available, education-based nonprofits like the National Equity Project and Learning for Justice provide professional development and coaching to school leaders, teachers, and staff to build capacity for equitable educational practices. Finally, it is worth contacting local colleges and universities that have a community engagement office. They may be able to fill some of the gaps in your knowledge assessment or refer you to others who can.

In Step 9 you will determine staffing needs based upon this knowledge assessment, so it is important that you've accurately captured knowledge gaps. If not, you will likely waste time searching for external support or end up asking people to do things they cannot do. Make sure you've:

- shared the action plan with staff and invited them to identify their own knowledge gaps
- documented the objectives and goals that few people feel prepared to achieve
- verified that staff do have the knowledge and skills to achieve remaining goals

Step 9: Conduct a Staffing Assessment

The knowledge assessment will reveal where the school needs content support, but a thorough staffing assessment identifies where the school lacks capacity. That is, you may not have enough people, or the right combination of people, to fully implement the plan. Role theory urges us to remember the importance of role consensus—people understanding and agreeing to their job expectations—for the well-being of the organization. When people don't know how or don't want to do what is asked of them, it is highly unlikely that their efforts will yield desired results. All action plan job duties should therefore be distributed in consultation with teachers and staff rather than assigned to them. Their ability to effectively lead in relevant areas is dependent upon their expertise, time, interest, and leadership skills, as well as their commitment to the core values and their motivation to achieve the new vision. Not everyone will be asked to take responsibility for an objective, but everyone should be aware of how they can contribute to successful objective outcomes.

In developing the action plan implementation team you may need to temporarily revise some employees' job descriptions. If a teacher is going to lead the equitable school discipline initiative, they may need to relinquish some teaching duties to make time for this new professional role. This will avoid role strain which is among the leading causes of attrition in education. You may need to hire aides, paraprofessionals, substitute teachers, and others who can step in when teachers may be otherwise occupied. You will likely also need to add new staff such as counselors, social workers, nurses, and translators. Resist the urge to hire a dean of diversity because such a position sends the message that diversity, equity, and inclusion are someone else's responsibility. It is important that all members of the school community are held accountable for creating an equitable school culture.

The final staffing consideration is timing and time. When should existing employees begin their new roles and when should new employees start work? Because some of the objectives in the action plan are cumulative, the implementation team does not need to be fully staffed at the onset, nor do people need to be in these new roles forever. Work with the advisory board to decide who needs to be hired when and for how long. You should also consider if these roles are volunteer or paid positions, and if they are full-time or part-time. You will determine how to pay for these new positions in the next step of the process.

Step 10: Conduct a Financial Assessment

In an ideal world where money is not a limitation, what would you need to fully implement the action plan in the desired time frame? Review your existing budget and look for places where you can reallocate funds. Was every budget line fully spent last year? How does each budgeted item contribute to an equitable education? It is not uncommon for schools to invest a lot of resources into things that have tremendous benefit for few students. For example, some schools that have been forced to cut music, art, and technology courses have opted to fill this gap by transporting interested students to community organizations or other schools with those course offerings. Many schools with dual enrollment programs spend a lot of money on students' community college tuition, fees, and transportation. These are excellent enrichment opportunities but only if enough students participate in them. Could music, art and technology classes be offered after school by a preservice teacher who needs practicum hours? Can students take online college courses rather than be transported to the community college? Think outside of the box for opportunities to enhance equity and save money.

Second, ask the district for support. Most school districts reserve funds in a discretionary budget line that are utilized as situations arise. Draft a proposal for a grant (preferably a multiyear grant) that explains the rationale for your revised mission and vision statement, and that overviews your action plan and any cost-saving efforts you've already made. Include an itemized budget proposal with strong rationales for how each item will increase equity, and ultimately, student achievement. This last point is important because while you may care about equitable opportunities, the school district is concerned with outcomes. Be sure to link the overall initiative to test scores, teacher retention, and other common metrics of school effectiveness.

Third, take the template of that proposal and adapt it to apply for federal, state, and nonprofit grants. If there is not grant writing expertise among the advisory board members, check with the state department of education, the school district, local nonprofits, and students' families. Writing grant proposals is best done in collaboration with an experienced other because grant applications can be incredibly tedious and time consuming.

Fourth, partner with a college or university. Education departments are always looking to collaborate with local public schools. They need sites for preservice teachers to complete their teaching practicum and participants and data for their research. If you can create a true partnership (see Chapter 4), you may meet people who can support your action plan by helping write grant proposals, offering professional development, and filling staffing gaps while teachers work on their action plan objectives. The best case scenario is that a faculty member has an existing grant and needs a school site to conduct the research. This may give you access to grant funds for which you didn't even need to apply!

Finally, fundraise. Work with your school district to create an online donation page that describes the school's vision, mission, and timeline. Redo the school's website with this updated information and a link to the donation page. Use your (and the teachers' and staff's) professional and personal networks to advertise the page on social media. Host a town hall and invite community members to hear about the new initiative and suggest ways they can support the action plan.

After all of this, if you find that your staffing needs are unreasonable given resource constraints, go back to your goals and reprioritize them. Based upon existing information and human capital, what *can* you accomplish? Remember that you are working *toward* equity so each step is valuable even if you can't walk as fast as you'd like.

**ADVICE FROM THE FIELD:
HOW TO ACHIEVE YOUR GOALS WITH LIMITED RESOURCES**

We owned everything. We owned our own PD. We would see what it was that we needed and we would find experts in the building who could lead that PD, and then also go observe them in the classroom actually doing it. Like Kagan structures. I'm not very strong with Kagan structures, but I had several teachers who were, so they would do Kagan strategy sessions and then have staff come observe them, and we would get them our coverage. Or I would cover. I like doing that.

Another way to cut corners is to rely on the experts in your community and on the kids. You'd be surprised what kids can teach other kids and adults. So, you rely on the staff that you have, rely on the community you have, rely on the kids you have, and start to build relationships with organizations. There are people who love to fund grants for high poverty schools that are doing innovative things.

You've got to think outside of the curriculum, you've got to think outside of the scope and sequence, you've got to think outside the school district, because if you don't think outside of it, then you don't qualify for those grants. When we talk about saving money, we would literally interview people and look at their resumes and see if people wrote grants. Like, "Ooh, we have a person who can write grants." "Ooh, we have a person who can DJ." "Ooh, we have a person who's an English teacher, but also was a theater teacher. Can this person support our theater teacher so we don't have to pay that consultant?"

It's all about leveraging the people and hiring the people with skill sets that you need, in addition to communicating with the community. "Hey, is there anybody in this community who can come help us teach math? Who can come do a math program at our school?" We partner with the YMCA, which is how we were able to do all of our ACT and AP testing. One of the churches sent us to the state capital for the HBCU college fair. I was just asking for $5. They said, "How much is the trip?" They came and gave us $1,500.

So those are the types of things. You have to open up and ask. But you also need to show people, because everybody wants to invest in a winner. Show people what you're doing and where you're going, and that's how you get so many people to start to jump on. Tell your story.

Dr. Carmichael

Praxis

The third phase of the school planning process is praxis: reflection and action. You've spent the previous 10 steps reflecting on your goals and your capacity to achieve them. Now it is time for action. The final steps comprise a cyclical process of implement, assess, and revise before you eventually expand your action plan.

Step 11: Implement the Plan

Now is the time to exchange your school leader hat for that of a project manager who oversees the rollout of the action plan at a micro and a macro level. You will need to be alongside teachers and staff to provide ongoing support as they work on their first objective(s). You don't need to micromanage; you need to be in constant dialogue with your team about what is working, what is not working, and what additional resources may be needed. Teachers and staff should feel comfortable suggesting improvements that deviate from the initial plan but may be more effective at achieving the larger goal.

It is important however, not to get bogged down in the minutia of each objective; that is why you have an implementation team. While you are supporting and problem solving, you also need to attend to the big picture. Are things happening according to the timeline? Is everyone doing what they need to do? Are we getting the outcomes we'd hoped? Keeping an eye on the overall project will help you see if the objectives truly contribute to their respective goals and if they create a coherent path toward equity. Don't be afraid to make adjustments on the fly. The beginning of the implementation will be messy so clean up small spills now to avoid large floods later.

Step 12: Gather Progress Reports
Remember the time you put into creating measurable goals and objectives? Now is when that pays off. It may not be time to evaluate the outcome of an objective, but you should be measuring progress toward the outcome at regular intervals based upon the timeline indicated in the action plan. If the objective was to reduce suspensions and expulsions by the end of year, quarterly data reviews are necessary to determine how close you are to the ultimate goal of a 25% reduction. You then want to share those data points with teachers in the context of their developing capacity to utilize restorative justice strategies. Consistent accountability checks can identify areas of concern and areas of success within the action plan before it is too late to pivot.

Step 13: Revise the Action Plan
Based upon the findings in Step 12, you will almost certainly need to work with the advisory board to revise the action plan. Unexpected obstacles may have arisen that necessitate a leadership change, reallocation of resources, and the reprioritization of objectives or goals. It is easy to feel discouraged at this stage if you are not as far along as you'd

like. It can also be demoralizing to alter a document that so much hard work went into, so celebrate the small victories. Bolster your energy by returning to your vision and mission statements. Focus on the process and don't worry so much about the product at this point. As long as everyone is doing their best to ensure students get a high-quality and equitable educational experience, you should be proud.

Step 14: Monitor

After the first few months of implementation, things should begin to run more smoothly. The implementation team will have figured out how to balance their job responsibilities and with consistent communication, everyone should know what needs to be done. Empower your team to conduct their own mini-assessments and share progress reports at staff meetings. Remain in contact with the advisory board, especially when revisions need to be made. Maintain that bird's-eye view and focus your efforts on summative evaluations at the end of each semester.

Step 15: Expand the Action Plan

After successful implementation of the first 50% of the plan, brainstorm with the advisory board and the implementation team about how you can expand the plan to include more foci. This is important because it captures your momentum and helps maintain progress, especially if some objectives or goals were deprioritized. Now is the time to build up, build out, and build in.

Building up occurs when you leverage successes for "more." After identifying which objectives and goals were accomplished, determine how you can increase those outcomes. For example, if positive family contacts (i.e., communicating positive things about a student to their family) outpaced negative family contacts, how can you ensure twice the number of positive contacts than negative for next semester? Building up repeats what worked in the past.

Building out takes what has worked and applies that process to a related area. Diversifying the teaching staff likely required new recruitment and hiring methods. Those same methods may be equally as effective in diversifying school staff or even the student body. Some other positive outcomes may have been unintentional but can still be informative. This year's applicant pool could have been abnormally diverse, but if you do some digging, those applicants may have come from the same teacher preparation program. Moving forward, you should partner with that particular program and create a teacher pipeline. Building out is how you expand equity initiatives.

Building in is about enhancing capacity to do equity work by accumulating more resources. It should be clear at this point where the pressure points are in the plan. Engage in strategic planning with the advisory board to determine how you can improve your ability to achieve outcomes. This is a good time to revisit the objectives and goals that were deprioritized. Do you have new staff that could contribute? Were you awarded a grant recently? Are there new partnerships that can be leveraged? Create a marketing campaign that advertises recent accomplishments because nothing begets success like success.

Exemplars in the Field

Fifteen steps can feel overwhelming and impossible, but rest assured it is doable. Many states have developed educational equity plans that contain most of the elements described in this chapter. For example, the Maryland State Department of Education (2020) released a 21-page "Guide to Educational Equity in Maryland." In it they explain why they are focusing on equity and then identify four foci that form the core of their action plan. Their plan is data driven, and it contains clear rationales and explicit SMART goals.

If you want a shorter term, smaller example of an educational equity action plan, Cedar Rapids Community School District (CRCSD) in Iowa successfully completed Phase 1 of their three-part action plan. In summer 2020, they hosted six townhalls about anti-racism, diversifying the curriculum, district diversity, and school climate. These conversations yielded five areas in which they have developed SMART goals to increase equity, inclusion, and anti-racism. While CRCSD has not completed the full 15-step plan detailed in this chapter, they were able to successfully enact Phase 1 by conducting a needs assessment, setting goals, and drafting an action plan, demonstrating that school planning for equity need not be an all-or-nothing proposition. It need only be strategic and intentional.

Reflection Questions

1. What are the most pressing issues in K–12 public schools? What are the most pressing issues for minoritized and marginalized students?
2. What in-school factor is most important for educational equity?
3. What education reforms would you like to see implemented at your school and how would they address inequities?
4. What do you need to know more about to better support culturally and linguistically diverse students?
5. How can you leverage your personal and professional networks to contribute to an equity action plan?
6. What can you change in your daily practices to mitigate inequities for students and families?
7. Why might potential equity initiatives be unsuccessful? How can you help the school avoid these pitfalls?

2 Choosing an Organizational Structure Aligned With Your Leadership Style

One aspect of the building-in process discussed at the end of Chapter 1 is making sure the organizational structure of the school facilitates the implementation of the action plan, and more globally, educational equity. I distinguish between organizational structure and organizational practices (Chapter 3) because, although they are related, each deserves special attention when planning for equity. The former is about how positions relate to one another with respect to supervision, authority, and decision-making. The latter refers to what people within an organization do (i.e., how they perform role expectations) as determined by the organizational structure.

This chapter digs deeply into organizational structures by first reviewing traditional and alternative ways of organizing *positions* before describing the leadership styles that determine how *people* within those positions interact. Organizational role theory (ORT) affirms the need to consider positions and people as distinct factors within an organizational structure. Positions are static titles with a list of professional expectations. People within positions perform professional duties according to their interpretation of those expectations. How they interpret expectations is largely influenced by how leadership constructs the relationship between positions and people.

Many education reformers describe shared governance, teacher agency, and schoolwide collaboration as prerequisites for educational equity. Each of these variables speaks to how people within positions are empowered to perform. In other words, they speak to leadership. I argue that leadership decisions are more important than, but dependent upon, structural decisions. When designing a school, the question is not which structure is most equitable (position-focused). The question is which structure best provides people the necessary support and resources to educate for equity. Which structure is most people- and performance-focused?

THOUGHTS FROM THE FIELD

I don't think it matters what floor people are on or other superficial stuff. Equity is about the conversations you're having about the students. You can all be on the same floor, but never be talking to one another. It's richer than that. When I think of equity, it's in terms of relationships. Equity would look like the faculty who have students in common talking with one another and planning, and the conversations would be around student learning, student needs and faculty learning, and faculty needs so that they could improve student learning.

Ms. Fisher

Traditional Structures

Hierarchical

The most popular organizational structure is reflected in a hierarchy of positions, connected by lines that indicate the flow of supervision (Figure 2.1). Positions are organized such that similar jobs are grouped under a supervisory position that oversees those beneath it. Midlevel positions have a similar direct line to a more senior position that reports to the top position.

Such clarity in reporting lines and distinct positions minimizes role

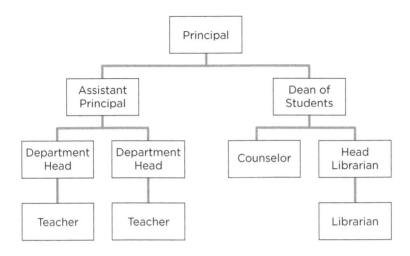

Figure 2.1 Hierarchical School Organization

confusion and role conflict. Everyone knows what is expected of them and who will evaluate them. The benefits of a hierarchical structure is its efficiency and emphasis on productivity. But the trade-off occurs in processes wherein there is no overlap between positions and certainly not between positions grouped under different reporting lines. This could lead to a very siloed school with no shared mission or vision. A hierarchical organization requires strong leadership to communicate equality of positions in what could be a very competitive structure.

Matrix

An offshoot of a hierarchical structure is the matrix structure, which differs in one way. Rather than a position reporting to one supervisory position, they can have lines to two higher positions. This occurs when a classroom teacher is supervised by a team lead or mentor teacher and then also by their department head (Figure 2.2). Solid lines represent the formal reporting line (i.e., the evaluative line) whereas dotted lines can reflect a more casual relationship between the two positions. A drawback here is the possibility of role conflict if two supervisors have different expectations for their shared supervisee.

Both of these more traditional approaches to school organization can assist staff to educate for equity. Among their strengths are distinct

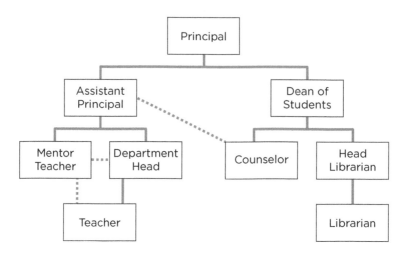

Figure 2.2 Matrix School Organization

divisions of labor, clearly articulated job expectations, and explicit accountability mechanisms. When you think about implementing the action plan, these structures make it easy to assign objectives and measure outcomes in a timely fashion. It is also easy for a school leader to keep track of everything because work is so clearly delineated. The biggest hurdle when wanting to ensure equity given these structures are the multiple levels of bureaucracy. Teachers and other staff at the lower levels do not have built-in role flexibility to respond to students' needs in the moment. These structures may be too rigid and consequently, lean heavily toward an ethos of "best practices" rather than a more equitable ethos of responsiveness.

Flat/Horizontal

Another option for an organizational structure is most often found in cooperative schools. Flat or horizontal structures do not have midlevel positions; there is administration and the staff (Figure 2.3). This model is attractive because it facilitates direct communication between leadership and staff, which can increase the speed of organizational functioning. However, without assistant principals or department heads, positions may not be well defined for people who are used to more

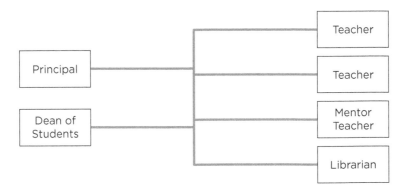

Figure 2.3 Flat School Organization

hierarchical structures, resulting in role confusion. This is likely to lead to role strain if too many responsibilities are ascribed to a single position. Role failure then becomes a possibility because people do not have complete or accurate understandings of their job expectations, or in the worst case, the ability to meet them.

When considered through a lens of equity, a flat structure is the most responsive among the traditional organizational options. Without a direct supervisor with whom to check, teachers can immediately do what they think is best for students without getting approval. The concern, though, is that flat structures allow for a lot of generalists but no specialists. If everyone is a classroom teacher or an administrator, where are the special education teachers, nurses and counselors, and the curriculum specialists? Flat structures prioritize people over performance, which could make it difficult to ensure students are getting what they individually need to be successful.

An Alternative Structure

Team Based
The final organizational structure that rarely appears in schools is team based, which is drawn from sociocracy or more commonly, dynamic governance. This model is very different from traditional structures

because it eschews positions in favor of people *and* performance. There are job titles and associated responsibilities but there is very little hierarchy among the positions. Positions are grouped together in working circles not by title or job function but by people's expertise.

Each circle is composed of a team of people working on a specific task or project. Group members are self-selected based upon interest, skill, knowledge, and time. While there may be roles within each circle (e.g., circle leader, note taker, facilitator), no single person has more authority than any other. Decisions are made through consensus, not voting. Communication between working circles is maintained through delegates who report their team's progress to an adjoining circle of which they are also a member. Thus, overlap in circles represents an overlap of people, not tasks (Figure 2.4).

The organization of circles is fluid, but bigger circles represent projects that affect school functioning more broadly, whereas smaller circles are narrow in scope. This model could easily lead to role strain if people are present in too many circles, but it does a good job minimizing role confusion because each circle has a very specific task on which to work. And because circles operate with autonomy, it can be a very efficient way to accomplish multiple goals simultaneously. It facilitates educational equity because it aligns people's competencies with their

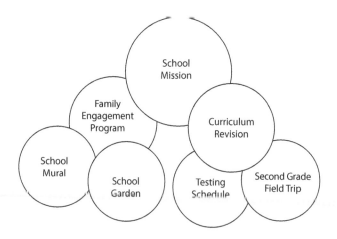

Figure 2.4 Team-Based School Organization

job expectations so that the best people are addressing issues as they arise. No one person's biases can influence final results because there are checks and balances within each circle. A team-based organization does require a lot of trust between people and constant communication, or, like a hierarchical structure, work may become too siloed and unrelated to larger school goals.

Additional Considerations

While it is tempting to choose a structure that is familiar or conversely, innovative, the overarching organizational structure has implications for the school's academic model. The curriculum (what we teach), instructional practices (how we teach), and learning objectives (why we teach) are shaped by how teacher and staff positions interact with one another. For example, the most common academic model is *departmental* where each subject is placed in a division or department with similar subjects (e.g., biology, physics, and chemistry comprise the science department). A departmental academic model is best aligned with either a hierarchy or matrix organizational structure because they support clear delineations between positions with different job functions (e.g., science teacher versus Spanish teacher).

Similarly, an *academies* model, where subjects are grouped together based upon a theme, is best realized through a matrix structure. An "Outdoor Exploration" academy would have a different grouping of positions than a "Global Cultures" academy. The former would likely be led by science teachers and the latter by a mix of geography, language, and art teachers. The academies model necessitates independent functioning of each thematic grouping; yet, teachers within an academy would need to report to both a grade-level team lead and a content-area lead to ensure multidisciplinary coherence within a grade and content coherence across grades.

Another form of multiple academic options within a single school is the *school within a school* design. The most common iteration of this occurs through academic tracking when students are housed in an isolated track (oftentimes physically located in their own building or their own hallway) within a larger school. For instance, the International

Baccalaureate (IB) program is an advanced track with its own curriculum and specially certified teachers. High school students in the IB program take core classes, languages, and some elective courses (e.g., culinary arts, photography, art) within their "school" but could take an additional elective (e.g., health, physical education, band) within the larger school with non-IB students.

Because these schools function largely autonomously from, but operate within, a larger school (with their own teaching staff, schedule, students, etc.), a flat structure is ideal. As a mini school, it is too small for the creation of working circles in a team-based structure, but ideally sized for someone at the top to monitor day-to-day issues, have relationships with all staff working within the school, and ultimately make informed decisions quickly. The rigid curricular expectations in an IB program or, similarly, a language immersion program, minimize the likelihood of role confusion that sometimes emerges in flat organizations. The direct communication between leadership and staff is optimal for adapting polices and practices of the larger school for the self-contained school.

A spin off of the school within a school model is the creation of *small learning communities* designed to provide personalized instruction through deep peer-to-peer and teacher–student relationships. Many schools attempt to do this through homerooms or advisories but a true *communities model* is structured such that students take all of their classes together (like in elementary school) and have a dedicated group of teachers who also serve as their academic advisors. Students are assigned to communities based upon their academic needs, personal interests, or other metrics aligned with the school's vision and mission. Teachers within each community loop with their students in an effort to maintain personal bonds and academic consistency across grades.

Learning communities are best suited for a team-based organizational structure because each community operates largely independently of the others and should therefore have the authority to make their own decisions. While staff may serve as delegates across multiple community circles, the teachers within each circle have personal investment in their community's well-being and considerable knowledge of academic and social expectations. As teachers work collaboratively in multiple roles within a community, there is no need for midlevel positions or

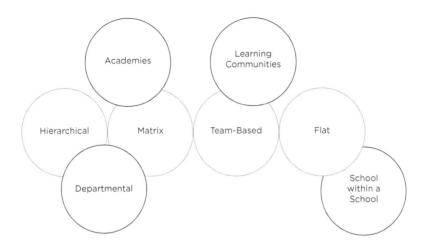

Figure 2.5 Organization Structures and Academic Models

hierarchy across positions. Students' unique needs would be appropriately met by those who know them best.

Alternatively, small learning communities might also fit well within a flat organizational structure, or possibly a matrix structure. In fact, each of these academic models could be executed within any organizational framework, but we want to make certain that all elements of the school's structure are compatible with one another and with a goal of educational equity. When expectations for how a job is performed (i.e., the academic model) are misaligned with the context in which it is performed (i.e., the organizational structure), role failure is inevitable. Equity is about giving everyone—not just students—what they need to be successful, and it begins with a working environment that maximizes the performance potential of each position (Figure 2.5).

School Leadership

The third element of school organization is focused on another "P": people. An organizational structure amounts to a drawing on a page and is only brought to life by how a principal engages the elements of the structure through their interactions with staff. The "how" of actualizing a structure is what determines the school culture: expectations for decision making and actions. Put simply, culture is about permission. Many principals purport to want a collaborative school culture but utilize authoritarian leadership strategizes wherein they make all decisions. On the other side of the coin are principals who describe their school as "traditional" and "structured," yet there is no shared understanding of who is responsible for what. These contradictions are a direct result of leadership styles that are not aligned with the school structure and that ultimately fail at creating a cohesive culture.

Some leadership styles are better suited than others to facilitate educational equity when we consider not only if the leadership style itself fosters equity but also how leadership decisions interact with the organizational structure to enable the implementation of the equity action plan. While there is no best leadership style just as there is no best organizational structure, there are combinations of the two that establish the necessary conditions for equity: schoolwide coherence, collaboration, accountability, trust, agency, and capacity building.

Transactional Leadership

A leadership style that is becoming less common is transactional leadership. This is a behavioristic approach that utilizes rewards and punishments to motivate staff. Leaders emphasize the successful completion of individual tasks that will collectively engender large-scale achievement. For example, a transactional principal might ask teachers to submit weekly lesson plans according to a specific template. The logic is that a high-quality lesson plan promotes high-quality instruction, which yields student learning. Transactional leadership prioritizes the "what" and "how" of teaching, with less attention paid to the "who" and "why." These principals spend their time monitoring and evaluating staff, creating accountability systems, and looking to improve workplace processes. Principals who prefer this leadership style are outcome-oriented, direct, objective, prefer structure and clear expectations, and often work independently. As the school manager, they expect compliance and efficiency.

Potential for Equity

Transactional leaders are problem solvers who act quickly to resolve issues but who may not always be forward thinking. Their attention to current outcomes overshadows possible outcomes, creating a cycle in which they work to improve practices rather than change them. There is little room for innovation for these leaders who are hesitant to think outside of existing systems and structures. This means that the more concrete aspects of the action plan, such as discipline policies, may receive more attention than more-abstract elements like developing community partnerships.

Similar to a hierarchical organizational structure for which transactional leadership is a good fit, there is concern about the school culture being cold and meritocratic rather than collaborative. Staff may not feel like a community working toward shared goals when there is not collective responsibility for task completion. Transactional leadership can be too procedural, stressing the science of teaching over the art of teaching, which ignores the affective side of education that draws many into the profession.

But if done humanely, transactional leadership has the power to produce impressive results quickly. These are principals whom districts ask to turn around failing schools in short time frames. The clarity of work expectations and timelines leaves little room for role confusion and could result in a staff that is competent, self-aware, and invested in improving their practice. The principal can therefore focus on supporting staff as they work toward individual SMART goals, while keeping an eye on schoolwide progress.

Instructional Leadership

In the 1990s, along with the emergence of magnet schools, the first charter schools, and an interest in "progressive" pedagogies (e.g., Montessori), came a new leadership style focused on teaching and learning: instructional leadership. Principals who embrace instructional leadership focus most of their attention on what happens in the classroom. These leaders place teaching at the core of school functioning and believe that if instruction is effective, other school operations will run smoothly. "Good" teaching is evidenced by high student engagement and high achievement. Teachers are rewarded for effective teaching by leadership opportunities that are often accompanied by stipends or course reductions.

Instructional leaders are highly visible and spend their time observing classrooms, examining curriculum, locating and providing instructional supports, and reviewing student outcomes. These principals allocate a large portion of the budget to paraprofessionals, specialists, and professional development, often at the expense of administrative positions. This leadership style is usually adopted by principals who have considerable classroom teaching experience and know the importance of both content and pedagogical knowledge. These principals have good interpersonal skills, are organized, have a positive attitude, and believe strongly in continuing education. Instructional leaders are always teachers first.

Potential for Equity

Instructional leadership has been criticized for being too unidirectional, for positioning the principal as the authority, and for leaving teachers without agency to act in the best interest of their students. Unless implemented within a flat organizational structure, these leaders may devalue department heads and other midlevel staff in their desire to work directly with teachers. By spending the majority of their time in classrooms, instructional leaders can lose sight of other school issues needing their attention as well as of contextual factors that support effective instruction such as family and community engagement.

But instructional leaders' commitment to improving teaching and learning will address many educational equity concerns *if* they are culturally responsive instructional leaders who expect teachers to utilize culturally sustaining pedagogy. This would eliminate many of the difficulties minoritized students experience in the classroom related to the culture of power (Delpit, 1988) and Eurocentric curriculum. The provision of professional development and structured leadership opportunities means that teachers are supported and motivated to perform well and are less likely to become apathetic, burn out, and leave the school. Because instructional leaders are accomplished teachers themselves, they can anticipate obstacles to effective instruction (e.g., classroom management, attendance) and proactively prepare teachers to meet challenges, negating the need for punitive actions toward students. A trickle-out approach to educational equity may not be fast but it will be comprehensive.

Servant Leadership

Also aligned with a flat organizational structure is servant leadership. Borrowing from Maslow's hierarchy of needs (1943, 1954), servant leaders promote self-actualization: realizing your full potential. Rather than utilizing extrinsic motivators, servant leaders foster trust and buy-in through interpersonal relationships. Principals who consider themselves servant leaders prioritize people over processes and products, believing that emotional fulfillment yields high performance.

Servant leaders determine their daily work by asking, "What can I do to help?" They spend time in one-on-one meetings providing mentorship and designing personalized professional development plans for staff. They believe in formative, rather than summative assessment, and in using observation scores and student achievement data informatively, not evaluatively. Servant leaders are asset-oriented role models who practice what they preach through active listening, compassion, collaboration, and a spirit of altruism. This leadership style is for feelers, who are invested in the whole person—not just the professional person.

Potential for Equity

The most obvious drawback of a servant leadership style is the possibility of viewing people too positively. In an effort to maintain social bonds, servant leaders may avoid conflict and not hold people accountable for professional expectations. While capacity building is critical for educational equity, people ultimately need to be able to carry out their duties effectively. It is not always possible to prioritize growth over performance, especially when children's futures are at stake.

Yet, there is something to be said for leaders who create a culture of hope within the school. A positive environment in which staff see the value of their work can generate intrinsic motivation to accomplish school goals. Providing tailored opportunities and support is the definition of equity. Modeling equitable practices will help teachers and staff realize the power of doing the same for students. A leader who aims to serve others has the right attitude for social justice work.

Transformational Leadership

Transformational leadership couples a justice orientation with a visionary mindset. These leaders seek to inspire employees by encouraging them to take ownership of their professional practice and ownership of the school. Transformational leaders cultivate intrinsic motivation by giving staff the agency to innovate and create change. Because the principal is not the sole authority or decision-maker, this leadership style is well suited for a team-based organizational structure where staff work in tandem to solve problems.

If servant leaders look to help, transformational leaders look to improve. Their daily tasks revolve around assessment (not evaluation) of people, practices, and products, always looking for faster, more effective, less expensive ways to reach goals. These principals seem to be everywhere at once, doing more than one task at a time. Transformational leaders are strategically working toward the school's vision on multiple fronts simultaneously. Such complicated work is ideal for high-energy people who are charismatic, open to change, and creative. Transformational leaders are doers, willing to get their hands dirty and take risks that others may not agree with.

Potential for Equity

The biggest critique of transformational leaders is that they are spread too thin so are likely to experience role strain and become overwhelmed. Their trust in staff capabilities can be misplaced if they are too busy to truly understand individual people's strengths and weaknesses. If personal relationships are not nurtured, staff may feel as if their individuality comes second to their professional identity. Transformational leaders can be overly enthusiastic in executing their vision, which may be interpreted as a desire for compliance instead of collaboration.

But if they can reign in their excitement, transformational leaders can cultivate a school culture that embraces praxis. The combination of a unified vision and shared responsibility means that people are empowered to integrate elements of the action plan into their daily routines. So instead of a series of objectives and goals to achieve in addition to their existing duties, the action plan becomes their duty. Progress toward equity should be fast and widespread in a school where everyone shares a commitment to improving education for all students.

Distributed Leadership

Principals who prefer to take a step back but still operate on a fast timeline might take a distributed leadership approach to school functioning. This model uncouples positions and responsibilities in favor of capitalizing on relevant expertise wherever it exists. Aligned with a team-based structure, distributed leadership is about the effective execution of tasks. Unlike transformational leaders who welcome innovation and experimentation, distributed leaders prefer to stick with what works and make it work better. Staff are motivated by the successful completion of tasks of which they had full responsibility.

Less affective and interpersonal than transformational leaders, distributed leaders spend their days monitoring task progress, fostering communication between staff, and disseminating information. These principals may not always be visible around the school as they are focused on the big picture of school functioning, making sure that everything is working together smoothly, and intervening with supports when they are not. Their daily work is therefore guided by where they are needed most at the moment, operating as backup. Principals who successfully utilize distributed leadership strategies are very organized, detail-oriented, trusting, and trustworthy. These leaders are thinkers, constantly gathering, synthesizing, and evaluating information to make data-driven decisions.

Potential for Equity

Distributed leadership can be a bit too hands-off and a little too reliant on staff to ask for help when they need it. Because these leaders are not involved in everything, they may be unaware of some projects and ultimately be unable to ensure coherence across school operations. There is also concern that a distributed leadership model focuses too heavily on existing capacities and not enough on potential capacities, resulting in too few professional development opportunities. Staff may feel stagnant if they are not given proper mentorship and those who are not frequently asked to lead projects may feel unappreciated and disrespected, eventually reducing their motivation to perform at a high level.

For staff whose abilities are well matched to school needs, a distributed leadership model promotes agency and can increase motivation. Staff might find it rewarding to work on projects outside of their job description, allowing them to engage in hands-on professional development. Elements of the action plan become exciting challenges with high emotional and professional payout. A distributed approach to educational equity means that no single person is burdened with ensuring success but that everyone has the opportunity to affect positive change.

Leading for Equity

No single leadership style will perfectly address school needs all the time, so equitable leadership requires flexibility. Principals must consider the context, the people, and the issue when deciding how best to proceed (i.e., contingent/situational leadership). There are times when achievement data makes it clear that instructional leadership is necessary, when a crisis requires transactional leadership, and when a long-term project is best accomplished through distributed leadership. The same principal who is a servant leader when interacting with staff can be a transformational leader when recruiting new students/families. Khalifa (2019) suggests that educators build their leadership practices around the eight characteristics of culturally responsive leadership:

1. connectedness to the school and surrounding communities
2. courage to make unpopular decisions
3. decolonization of policies, practices, curriculum, and structures that promote oppression

4. deference to community knowledge, language, and customs
5. distribution of power, especially when decisions affect multiple entities
6. humanization of bureaucratic curriculum, policies, and pedagogies that render culture invisible
7. humility through praxis
8. intolerance of discrimination, marginalization, and oppression

This list reflects the complexities of leading for educational equity. It is not solely what you do as a leader that begets equity, but how you do it, with whom you do it, and why you do it. It can feel daunting to embody all of these characteristics all of the time—and you won't. What matters more is establishing an organizational framework that facilitates the consistent realization of these attributes through careful attention to structural, academic, and leadership models. No matter which combination of the three you choose, remember that effective leadership is dynamic, requiring constant evaluation of how positions, people, and performances align to serve students.

**ADVICE FROM THE FIELD:
FIRST STEPS IN LEADING FOR EQUITY**

I would say, if you want to lead for equity, make sure that you understand equity yourself. Make sure that you understand other experiences. Maybe not deeply understand or know, because you're not that person of color or you don't know what it feels like to be a woman, or you don't know what it feels like to have Down syndrome. But at least have done your research to understand the experience of different cultures and backgrounds.

Know first, in yourself, that you have exposed yourself to those experiences. You've taken the steps to learn, to be open to new understandings, and to recognize that you have a lack of information on some topics. Are you going to lead for equity in those areas? Probably not, because you don't know enough.

Because when you get in front of folks and start trying to

lead for equity and don't personally commit to equity first, you will not be successful. When equity begins to fall, it's because folks know that who's standing in front of them is not leading for equity themselves.

If I didn't believe in it and do it myself, then I couldn't preach it.

Principal Lewis

Reflection Questions

1. If you rank-ordered the potential of each organizational structure to facilitate equity in your school, which would be first and which would be last and why?
2. How might a hierarchical or matrix structure contribute to educational inequities for students? What potential do they have to mitigate student inequities?
3. How do you imagine including students and families in a team-based organizational structure?
4. Based upon the staffing assessment you conducted in Chapter 1, which organizational structure best facilitates successful implementation of the action plan?
5. Based upon the knowledge assessment you conducted in Chapter 1, which leadership style best supports your staff?
6. How are the eight characteristics of culturally responsive leadership reflected in your action plan goals or objectives?
7. How are the eight characteristics of culturally responsive leadership embedded within other leadership styles?

3 Embedding Equity Within Organizational Practices

W hen most people dream of designing a school, they think about what it would look like, what classes would be offered, and all the things they'd do to ensure student success. They skip over the mundane elements described in Chapters 1 and 2 in favor of more-visible organizational practices. *Organizational practices* refer to the day-to-day routines in which students, teachers, and staff engage. These routines are performed within the context of the school climate and are guided by school policies. Organizational role theory (ORT) borrows from dramaturgy (Goffman, 1959) and likens one's behavior in a particular setting to playing a character (or role) in a play. For example, students understand that when they are a student (as opposed to a child, athlete, or sibling) they are expected to attend school with proper props (e.g., notebook, pencils, paper, textbooks) and to perform certain behaviors, both prompted (standing in the lunch line) and unprompted (raise your hand if you have a question). Similarly, the staff roles decided upon in Chapter 2 have associated props and behavioral expectations that fit within your chosen organizational structure. In this chapter, we move forward and discuss how to best set the scene (school climate) and develop scripts (role expectations) that ensure successful role performance.

School Climate

School climate is the overall feeling of a school. It can be welcoming and energetic or cold and daunting. Climate is a difficult variable to measure because it is not only defined by a building's physical features but also by affective elements resulting from a combination of invisible factors like interpersonal relationships, school rules, and the curriculum. It is also heavily influenced by the school's history, its relationship with the surrounding community, and most of all, by the students.

But just as students (and teachers and staff) contribute to the school climate, schools are spaces that shape students. Organizational practices ranging from the dress code to extracurricular options can either invite or reject students' identities, implicitly communicating what and who is acceptable. Inclusion is not about different types of people occupying the same physical space at the same time. Inclusion is about everyone feeling welcome, respected, valued, and affirmed. This is distinct from diversity rhetoric that advocates for tolerance and acceptance. Educational equity requires more than a reluctant acknowledgement of difference; it requires a celebration of difference.

Many schools choose to celebrate difference in superficial and performative ways that do not meaningfully affect organizational practices. For instance, Black history month (and women's history month, Latinx history month, Indigenous People's Day, etc.) are when schools host culture days and ask students to complete special projects that are unrelated to the curriculum and learning objectives. Such "feasts and fiestas" allow non-minoritized people to be entertained by others' cultural practices and traditions with little understanding of their importance.

Schools also use language that subconsciously affects students' developing identities. For example, many schools still label BISOC, students from low-income communities, and students who live in urban and rural areas as "at risk." These students are likely to attend schools that proudly boast about improving students' "character" by teaching them "grit," "self-control," and "gratitude." And when students do not demonstrate these traits as determined by hegemonic standards, they are further labeled "slow" and may be demoted or held back. The underlying assumption in these linguistic practices are that students are lacking fundamental human characteristics by virtue of their racial, economic, and/or geographic location. Over time, students may internalize these beliefs and view themselves as deficient and incapable of success.

THOUGHTS FROM THE FIELD

I feel like the language that people use is really a dead giveaway. I was on a post about the removal of the SRO officers in a school and a woman hopped on, and she's a teacher, and her response was, "Well, I've worked with high-risk populations for years, and those kids are going to escalate when police walk in the building, regardless." She was like, "We don't need the officers." I said, "Well, thank you so much for realizing that we don't need the officers, but what about the language we're using when you say, high-risk population? That sounds to me like diseased animals quarantined in a facility somewhere, not these beautiful, bright students whose future we're supposed to be shaping."

Ms. Richardson

Implicit messages are complemented by explicit branding in the physical environment that reflects the school's core values, vision, and mission. For example, many college preparatory charter schools name classrooms and hallways after universities. Doors have pennants representing teachers' colleges. On Fridays, staff wear clothing advertising their alma mater. As soon as you walk in the school, there is a display case of college acceptance letters and pictures of graduating seniors. The physical environment leaves little confusion about the school's educational goals.

Even more important, especially when working with students who have experienced neglect, marginalization, and erasure throughout their educational experiences, is the emotional environment. How do students feel when they are at school? Are they proud of their school? Do they look forward to seeing teachers and friends at school? The answers to these questions reflect students' sense of belonging. Researchers continue to reiterate the influence of students feeling seen and supported on their academic achievement, attendance, engagement, and mental health (for a review, see St-Amand et al., 2017). A strong sense of belonging helps prevent delinquency, social rejection from peers, school dropout, as well as psychological and health problems (Anderman, 2002).

The single variable that best predicts students' sense of belonging is their relationship with teachers. This is more important than their race, socioeconomic status, academic achievement, and their relationships with peers (Chiu et al., 2016). Strong teacher–student relationships can mitigate the cumulative effects of misbehavior, apathy, and failure due to poor teacher–student relationships (Martin & Collie, 2019). By improving students' motivation, engagement, academic self-regulation, and overall achievement (Allen et al., 2013; J. A. Baker, 1999; Roorda et al., 2011; van Uden et al., 2014), teacher–student relationships offer schools continual opportunities to support students' learning.

Such support is both interpersonal and instructional. Qualitative interviews (Emdin, 2016; Farrington, 2014; Michie, 2019) reveal students' preferences for teachers who respect them (i.e., don't yell, pronounce their names properly), trust them, and don't police minor behaviors (e.g., head on desk, sitting sideways in a chair). They like it when teachers initiate help so that they don't have to ask questions and risk embarrassment in front of peers. When they perform well, they expect positive feedback. When they are not doing well, they appreciate teachers who communicate about their progress and offer opportunities to improve.

Teachers who fail to connect with students interpersonally or instructionally may be disengaged from their teacher role. While teachers report leaving schools because of a lack of administrative leadership (Carver-Thomas & Darling-Hammond, 2019), they also report job dissatisfaction because of students. Student tardiness, student absenteeism, class cutting, student dropouts, poor student health, and student apathy contribute to teachers' lack of professional enthusiasm. These factors are compounded by teachers' complaints about high poverty and low family involvement (Moore, 2012). Because of the correlation between race and income in the United States, these variables are present in most schools serving minoritized youth where cultural mismatch between teachers and students further complicates the development of strong teacher–student bonds (discussed in Chapter 5). This is not to say that students from underserved communities will never experience a strong sense of belonging. On the contrary, students whose schools are committed to inclusion will naturally feel welcomed and appreciated.

Framing Equity

Cultivating a school climate for equity requires careful attention to the creation of emotional, cognitive, and behavioral spaces throughout the school. It is useful to think of the climate through three lenses (Shulman, 2005):

- Habits of heart—core values; why do you teach?
- Habits of head—ways of thinking and knowing; what do you believe?
- Habits of hand—what you do; how do you practice your values and beliefs?

These habits will be enacted differently through interactions with students versus staff, but for each, the goal is to foster their motivation to perform to the best of their abilities by creating an environment where they want to be, where they see the purpose in being, and where they experience success. An expectancy-value theory of motivation (Eccles et al., 1983) offers four suggestions for increasing intrinsic motivation:

1. Create a space where people enjoy themselves and can do things that interest them. For students, this means a variety of course options, multiple extracurricular activities, and innovative, hands-on learning experiences. For teachers this may mean variety in teaching assignments, autonomous decision-making, and opportunities to develop new classes.

2. Keep your revised equity-focused vision and mission at the core of school functioning. Clearly and consistently communicate your vision and explain how every decision contributes to the realization of the vision. The key here is transparency and honesty when explaining the utility of a particular assignment or class to students, and a new policy to staff.

3. Affirm everyone's contribution to the school community. This could be asking students to facilitate lessons or be peer mentors. You might invite staff to lead an initiative or promote them into a new position.

4. Minimize emotional costs by making sure that role expectations are reasonable (i.e., that the outcome will be worth the effort), that they leave time for other enjoyable tasks, and that they do not engender negative emotions. Students and staff should not be given busywork, be overworked, or be asked to do things of which they are not capable.

Each of these contributes to a positive school climate because it recognizes and leverages individuality, acknowledges accomplishments, and encourages continual engagement in the school community. School leaders can mistakenly put the climate on autopilot thinking that it will run on its own once people understand their role and are given their scripts. But a school climate is dynamic, open to influence from a variety of sources so it must be consistently monitored and adjusted. Most importantly, because it is largely people who both shape and are shaped by the school climate, they too must be nurtured.

THOUGHTS FROM THE FIELD

I saw someone post online that their school had "The Well." It was a lounge with nice couches and teachers couldn't bring phones or laptops or work. Every Friday they had free lunch and there were always snacks. There was calming music and spa smells. Once a month they got massages and they would bring in inspirational speakers. The next step was "Teacher Timeout." This was for teachers who had a conflict with a student. They would send someone to cover the class while the teacher went to The Well to recover. She said that she felt like the principal really cared about the teachers so they could care about the students.

Mr. Barry

School Policies

Conversations about educational equity begin with policies because they determine what is and what is not allowed in schools. Many educators, students, and families interpret policies as if they are laws when in fact, they are not. Policies are guidelines used to achieve specific goals. They are locally determined and implemented at the discretion of relevant decision-makers. In the United States, education is overseen by individual states that pass most decision-making to local educational agencies (LEAs) or, school districts. Most education policies originate from school districts overseen by a school board composed of 4–10 elected or appointed volunteers. School leaders have flexibility about when and how to implement district policies.

The problem with policies is that they are written as one-size-fits-all guidelines, which, while equal, is not equitable. Inequities are exacerbated by school staff's inconsistent application of policies such that implicit biases and explicit prejudices mean some students are disproportionately subject to school policies whereas others are not. The most frequently cited policy that is inequitably enforced are zero tolerance school discipline policies. Though initially proposed at the national level in response to school shootings, since its inception in 1994, zero tolerance has expanded beyond weapons to minor infractions such as dress-code violations and subjective offenses like disrupting class, offensive language, and disrespectful behavior. In schools designed according to white sociocultural norms, it is BISOC who experience disproportionate rates of detention, suspension, and expulsion (National Center for Education Statistics, 2018a).

Consequently, racially minoritized students, especially Black and

Latinx students, miss critical learning opportunities. The Civil Rights Project (2020) found that in one academic year, U.S. students lost 11 million days of instruction due to suspensions. When suspension data is disaggregated by race and gender, Black boys lost 132 days per 100 students enrolled and Black girls lost 77 days per 100 students, 7 times higher than white girls.

It is important to emphasize that discipline policies themselves are not automatically inequitable. The biased implementation of them is what creates discipline gaps that sustain opportunity gaps. This is true of most education policies, especially academic ones. For instance, tracking and sorting dictate students' opportunities to learn (OTLs) by placing them on an educational path that restricts the courses in which they can enroll in the future. The existence of academic courses with varying levels of rigor is not in itself problematic. The issue lies in how students are placed into certain courses.

It is common for individual teachers to use their discretion to decide which students can succeed in which tracks and make recommendations for placements. Teachers' perceptions are informed by their observations and interpretations of students' behavior, and their assessment of their academic work compared to other students. Academic sorting methods are exceedingly subjective and worrisome. As with discipline policies, teachers' biases against BISOC, students with disabilities, and boys means that white and Asian girls are those most often enrolled in gifted programs (National Center of Education Statistics, 2018b). Even when school policies require academic testing for course placement, students can be incorrectly sorted because standardized tests are culturally biased, lack predictive validity, and do not account for children's cognitive variability (Dixon-Román, 2017).

This is especially true for English language learners (ELLs) who, after being assessed in English, are frequently sorted into academic tracks that do not reflect their true capabilities. Some multilingual students are mainstreamed into courses with English-speaking students and are pulled out for intensive English instruction. Others experience full English immersion and receive no English instruction. In both cases, students are given far fewer OTLs because they are not receiving instruction in their heritage language *and* in the case of pull-out programs, are missing content area instruction while receiving English language instruction.

Academic policies should enhance educational opportunities, not limit them. Whether students experience reduced OTLs because their school simply does not offer certain courses, they are prevented from enrolling in courses, or because they are absent from class, has long-term implications for their educational achievement. For example, certain courses (e.g., Algebra 1, Biology, Chemistry 1) function as prerequisites for future courses, so without the opportunity to enroll in early courses, students will never be able to advance in that subject area. Even for the same course, content variation can greatly differ across academic tracks resulting in unequal preparation for future learning (for reviews see Oakes, 2005 and Schmidt & McKnight, 2012).

The cumulative nature of learning means that students' early school experiences can and do predict future OTLs, but they do not predict students' future abilities. It is never too late to disrupt the cycle of educational inequity by expanding students' OTLs through equitable school policies.

Policing Success

THOUGHTS FROM THE FIELD

A lot of times, when we create policies, we tend to do so from a reductionist and a deficit point of view. We create policies with the expectation of failure. We expect people to fail, so we're going to put this policy in place to try to keep them from failing versus putting a policy in place that ensures people succeed. So why would I create a student handbook that focuses on suspensions? Because I think kids are going to be suspended. But if I create a handbook that minimizes suspensions because I'm going to put systems in place to make sure kids don't get suspended, that's a whole other thing.

Dr. Carmichael

As Dr. Carmichael points out, school policies should be designed to facilitate success, not in anticipation of failure. Organizational role theory suggests that when people know what's expected of them, they behave accordingly. Psychological research affirms the idea of self-fulling prophecies, imposter syndrome, stereotype threat, and other mechanisms through which explicit and implicit expectations guide behavior. School policies, as guidelines for goal achievement, should provide the framework for realizing the school vision. If the school's vision is that students will graduate career, college, and life ready, then each policy must in some way prepare students for the next phase of life. Discipline policies shouldn't target students for misbehavior but instead, help them acquire and practice context-appropriate behaviors.

There are multiple strategies for engaging in culturally responsive discipline that are trauma-informed, grounded in care, and that emphasizes social and emotional learning (see Milner et al., 2018 for an overview of equitable classroom management). Restorative justice practices teach students that their actions can cause communal harm. De-escalation and inquiry-based dialogue help teachers understand students' emotional and cognitive states. Consensus building and noncontingent reinforcement are proactive methods of reducing student misbehavior. Mindfulness practices help students self-regulate their emotions. Positive behavioral intervention supports (PBIS) can reinforce behavioral expectations and school norms. Teachers should use each approach as necessary, remembering that educating for equity means providing for students, not policing them.

When we punish students for what they don't know or aren't able to do, we are essentially blaming them for their lack of cultural knowledge (referred to as cultural capital). Students from low-income families are particularly likely to be unaware of school norms as their parents' knowledge is often limited to their own and family members' schooling experiences (Lareau, 2011). We cannot assume that all students understand the rationale behind dress codes or utilizing formal English, nor that all families understand the differences between academic tracks.

The most obvious way to resolve knowledge gaps is to create academic policies that mitigate relative (dis)advantage. One example gaining in popularity is a movement to detrack academic courses so that all students experience the same level of rigor. This is usually complemented by a dual enrollment program that allows high school students (particularly those who might have otherwise been in advanced courses) to simultaneously enroll in college courses for academic credit. An alternative detracking complement is *linked learning* where all courses are college and vocation preparatory with equal emphasis on content and skills.

These academic options need to be implemented in conjunction with an English language program that allows English learners to take advantage of increased OTLs. Educational equity for ELLs can be achieved through an academic model that has three goals: learning English, learning academic content, and improving heritage language literacy. A maintenance approach to language (as opposed to a subtractive approach) requires gradually transitioning students' academic instruction from their heritage language to English as their English fluency and their comfort dictates within each subject area. A student might receive science and language arts instruction in their heritage language but receive math and history in English. In all courses, students should have access to learning materials in multiple languages as well as to translation technology.

If and when a student struggles, remediation should be available while they are still enrolled in the course. They should be allowed to revise and resubmit previously failed coursework for full credit and to submit missing work without a late penalty. Students in need of more intensive remediation can attend before or after school tutoring or, if they can't be at school outside of regular hours, exchange an elective for a study hall period. In worst case scenarios, students may need the option of academic recovery if they fail a course. Because academic failure is typically the result of missing or inadequate work and not a lack of competency, students should be allowed to recover credit as soon as possible. Credit recovery can occur through evening classes, Saturday school, through one-on-one tutoring, or during winter and spring breaks. Students who almost passed a class should progress to the next course with the stipulation that they simultaneously complete prior coursework.

Equitable academic policies acknowledge that students will sometimes make poor, but developmentally appropriate decisions that warrant multiple opportunities to reengage in their learning. Educators can proactively address negative outcomes by strategically monitoring students' academic progress. Each school should have care teams comprised of teachers and staff who are assigned a group of students to monitor. Teachers can reach out to the care team when students begin to struggle and provide them with necessary background information to intervene with supports. The care team is responsible for initiating interventions such as RTIs, 504s, IEPs, and BIPs. They then work closely with classroom teachers to ensure effective implementation. Care teams reduce teachers' workload so they are only monitoring students whose care team they are on, while also giving students multiple advocates across the school who can collectively meet their needs.

Teaching and Learning

What happens in the classroom is almost exclusively up to the teacher. There is no checklist of equitable pedagogical approaches as each of the major four learning theories are suited for different types of learners (for a review see Whitaker, 2016). Some educators prefer social constructivism because of its emphasis their on critical thinking and hands-on learning. Others like humanistic approaches that recognize students' social and emotional needs. Many teachers value socioculturalism's prioritization of community-based learning. However, behavioristic teaching styles receive critique, especially in conversations about educational equity.

Behavioristic learning is about teaching and reinforcing positive learning behaviors. This pedagogical style is most prominent in "no excuse" charter schools that require students to do things like keep their desks organized, raise their hands when they have questions, and keep their eyes on the teacher or their task (termed *tracking*). Teachers pace activities quickly, utilize call and response, and are constantly asking questions. None of these expectations or practices are inequitable or unfair. In fact, they are effective at improving students' on-task behavior, which is why they are present in most classrooms regardless of a teacher's pedagogical approach. Behavioristic learning is ideal for students who prefer structure, routine, and independent work.

The problems many perceive with a behavioristic teaching style is not with the theory itself but with teachers' implementation of it. Teachers often conflate classroom management with instruction under this model. Instead of focusing on students' behaviors as a means to enhance organization, engagement, and attention—which ultimately improve learning—teachers police irrelevant behaviors (e.g., oral language use, type of pencil or pen students use) and spend too much time punishing negative behaviors and not enough time reinforcing good ones. Thus, the inequity of behaviorism, like school policies, lies in teachers' employment.

Students experience inequities when teachers' practices are misaligned with students' needs and/or abilities. Misalignment happens on a micro level when teachers can't differentiate instruction, and on a macro level when they fail to consider students' life contexts when making pedagogical decisions. Many students are unable to spend hours on homework every day because they work or have family responsibilities after school. Assignments that require additional expenses or trips to special locales are unfeasible for low-income families and those with time constraints. Assumptions about access to technology, familial support, and other resources place students in the uncomfortable position of having to disclose personal information or risk failure. In Chapter 6, we discuss proactively hiring teachers with equity mindsets who are likely to avoid these missteps, but here we focus on how school leaders can create an educational structure that reduces the likelihood of academic inequities.

Equitable Teaching

While the "how" of instruction is best left to teachers, the "what" and "when" should be intentionally designed by school leaders. This includes the curriculum and accompanying assessment, as well as the academic schedule that determines the extent to which educational equity can be realized.

Curriculum

Teachers are expected to teach toward state-determined standards using state-determined curriculum, but there are no restrictions against supplementing the curriculum or reorganizing it. The core curriculum is outdated in most states and does not reflect the experiences of non-white, non-Christian, nonheterosexual people. English classes favor texts written by white men, history courses act as though time began in 1620 with the arrival of the *Mayflower*, and women are absent in science and math curricula despite well-documented contributions to both disciplines.

Teachers must create an inclusive curriculum in which students can see their current and future selves. This cannot be accomplished through additive multicultural education where teachers assign a biography about a diverse person without meaningfully integrating it into the curriculum. A truly inclusive curriculum presents different demographic groups' histories and cultural practices as both content to acquire and a lens through which to evaluate other content. Transformative multicultural education (Banks, 1994) teaches students multiperspectivity and opens their mind to different ways of being and knowing.

Transformational teaching that promotes social action requires that students utilize cultural lenses across subject matters and across time, at increasingly higher levels of rigor (D. Y. Ford, 2011). Traditional curriculum assumes that exposure to new material over the course of a week or two is enough for students to learn content when in fact, neuroscience suggests that at least three types of exposure over an extended period of time will ensure long-term retention (Whitman & Kelleher, 2016). Schools should therefore spiral curriculum within and across grades so that students engage with material at increasingly deeper levels (Bruner, 1960).

In fact, the Common Core Standards are designed to increase in complexity as the academic year progresses. They offer an excellent opportunity for teachers to revisit material but ask students to engage with it differently. For example, when first learning about the Revolutionary War, it is common for students to learn key battle dates, important historical figures, and the overall narrative (CCSS.ELA-LITERACY.

RH.6-8.3). A spiraled curriculum would ask students to revisit content later in the year by having them compare accounts of the Revolutionary War with those of the Civil War to ascertain differences in point of view (CCSS.ELA-LITERACY.RH.6-8.6). These standards can be enhanced by overlaying them with culturally responsive outcomes related to identity development and critical consciousness that ask students to understand how power, equity, and oppression are implicated in historical texts (Muhammad, 2020).

A spiraled curriculum increases OTLs for students who may have been absent when content was first covered, who didn't fully understand the first time, or who need more time to process. Spiraling also minimizes the likelihood that students will forget information as those neural pathways are reactivated throughout the school year. Finally, spiraled learning can also function as tutoring for students who do not have access to supplemental resources that help reinforce concepts.

The efficacy of a spiraled curriculum is dependent upon embedded assessments. Teachers routinely ask students to demonstrate their learning in ways that reflect low-level cognition and not the deep learning that spiraled curricula facilitate. For instance, the first-time students are assessed on new material it should measure their recall and comprehension. However, subsequent interactions with the same material should progressively move up Bloom's taxonomy (Krathwohl, 2002) and ask students to apply their knowledge, synthesize across content, and eventually create something new given their content mastery.

Assessments are arguably one of the more difficult aspects of teaching because they take a long time to design and, certainly, to grade. Equitable assessments can be even more tricky because they not only need to align with standards but they must also account for the myriad ways in which students process and produce information. Fortunately, the "ABCs of assessment" offer guidance:

- *Authentic.* Assessments should be connected to students' lives and offer a meaningful way for them to show what they learned.
- *Benchmarked.* Asset-based assessments are focused on students' growth. They should be designed to measure learning since the last assessment and to indicate progress toward future learning outcomes.

- *Choice.* Variations in students' learning preferences means they should be given choice in how they demonstrate their knowledge and skills. The assessment format should not predetermine the quality of students' work.
- *Structured.* Students should be given thorough rubrics and examples of different successful assignments as they choose between assessment options.

Evaluating students' work must also be done equitably, but grading is an inherently inequitable process. Teachers subjectively translate students' performance into an arbitrary number that is eventually translated into a letter grade. Students are rarely consulted about grading scales, so they may not fully understand what A-level work looks like. Further, grades are traditionally used to mark the end of a learning process and do not therefore offer students the opportunity to improve their learning.

More-equitable grading involves a dynamic exchange between teachers and students that evaluates students' learning formatively. Some schools have found success with narrative grading that allows students to score their own work and explain their evaluation process. This approach requires that students have a firm understanding of learning objectives, and that they be metacognitive about their learning to identify areas in which they need further study. Another alternative grading method is borrowed from standardized tests. Here, teachers score students categorically according to their proficiency level, with the lowest level framed as "not yet" rather than "below proficiency." Teachers provide substantive feedback on how students can get to the next level because students are expected to resubmit all "not yet" work. Official grades are not given until the end of the year and are based upon the percentage of assignments scored proficient across a student's collective body of work.

Getting rid of traditional practices that measure students' learning in finite individual chunks sends the message that learning is always in progress. Taking a "not yet" approach to learning encourages and supports students to rethink, redo, and reengage.

Schedule

Equitable assessment admittedly takes more time than traditional assessment, and time is among the top ranked variables teachers identify as an impediment to high-quality instruction. School leaders must design academic schedules so that students and teachers can optimize every learning opportunity. This requires balancing breadth and depth of content coverage with giving teachers and students ample planning and reflection time (Tables 3.1 and 3.2).

Table 3.1 Sample High School Student Schedule		
	A Day	**B Day**
8:00 A.M.–9:10 A.M.	Geometry	Biology I
9:20 A.M.–10:30 A.M.	English I	Art I
10:40 A.M.–12:00 P.M.	Band II	German I
12:10 P.M.–12:45 P.M.	Lunch	Lunch
12:55 P.M.–1:20 P.M.	Study Hall	Study Hall
1:30 P.M.–2:40 P.M.	Health and Physical Education	World Geography
2:50 P.M.–3:00 P.M.	Advisory	Advisory

Table 3.2 Sample High School English Teacher Schedule		
	A Day	**B Day**
8:00 A.M.–9:10 A.M.	Planning	English I
9:20 A.M.–10:30 A.M.	English I	Flex
10:40 A.M.–12:00 P.M.	English I Honors	Collaborative Planning
12:10 P.M.–12:45 P.M.	Lunch Supervision	Lunch Break
12:55 P.M.–1:20 P.M.	Lunch Break	Study Hall
1:30 P.M.–2:40 P.M.	Flex	English I Honors
2:50 P.M.–3:00 P.M.	Advisory	Advisory

The block schedules shown in the tables have four 70-minute classes each day for students and two 70-minute classes a day for teachers. Students have daily study hall sessions that can be used for tutoring or other supports, to complete group assignments, or to use school resources like the library or technology center. Teachers are given a planning period every day, alternating between independent and collaborative planning. They are given a flex period that can be used for professional development, to observe other classrooms, or to complete special projects. Teachers also rotate lunch supervision and study hall facilitation. Advisory is at the end of the day when students and teachers can decompress, share news, and plan for tomorrow. In large schools where teachers instruct five or six classes, flex periods and planning periods should alternate every other day, still making certain that teachers have almost 2 hours every day when they are not interacting with students.

These schedules communicate minimal expectations that students and teachers do schoolwork outside of school. Students can receive academic interventions and teachers can plan and grade during the school day. This will not be the case for 100% of people 100% of the time but this structure fosters educational equity by making sure everyone has the necessary supports for success within the school building.

Reflection Questions

1. How are diversity and inclusion conceptually related? How do they relate to one another in practice?
2. What elements of the school climate are most important to which student demographics when it comes to inclusion?
3. What existing school practices might be perceived as performative, and how can they be made transformative?
4. What is most important to the cultivation of positive teacher–student relationships? Does that change based upon students' sociocultural identities? Why or why not?
5. Beyond bias, what other in-school factors affect students' opportunities to learn?
6. Which of the ABCs of assessment contribute most to educational equity? What inequities do each of them address?

7. What costs do BISOC pay when school is inequitable that white students do not?

Recommended Reading

Milner, H. R., IV, Cunningham, H. B., Delale-O'Connor, L., & Kestenberg, E. G. (2018). *"These kids are out of control": Why we must reimagine classroom management for equity.* Corwin Press.

Oakes, J. (2005). *Keeping track: How schools structure inequality.* Yale University Press.

Schmidt, W. H., & McKnight, C. C. (2012). *Inequality for all: The challenge of unequal opportunity in American schools.* Teachers College Press.

St-Amand, J., Girard, S., & Smith, J. (2017). Sense of belonging at school: Defining attributes, determinants, and sustaining strategies. *IAFOR Journal of Education*, 5(2), 105–119.

Whitaker, M. C. (2016) *Learning from the inside out: Child development and school choice.* Rowman & Littlefield.

4 Developing School, Community, and Family Partnerships

In Chapters 2 and 3, we determined roles within the school and set the stage for educational equity. Now we turn our attention to the role *of* the school in the fight for social justice. Schools have long been the hub of most communities. They are where children spend most of their time and are often the nexus of neighborhood activities. Especially in lower income communities where resources are scarce, schools serve as meeting places for social events, as churches, as childcare centers, and as sites for adult learning. School choice policies have lessened community investment in neighborhood schools, but schools remain invested in their communities.

In this chapter we identify strategies for creating community partnerships and family* engagement *programs*. There are plentiful high-quality resources for school leaders searching for culturally responsive and equitable engagement *practices*. The focus here is on structuring partnership frameworks that are responsive to students', families', and the community's evolving needs.

* The terms *family* and *parent* are used to describe students' caregivers without respect to biological relation.

THOUGHTS FROM THE FIELD

We've closed off so much because we're so focused on test-ing. We've completely put up walls around the school and edu-cation, and the nation is dying as a result of it, because we've lost our communities. And schools used to be the center of the community. We've got to get that back. So we have to go into it with, "I have a school, but I really am building a com-munity here," and reaching out to parents and looking at that community-building capacity.

Mr. Barry

I think it starts with stepping outside of your building. So many of the teachers and staff don't live in the neighborhood, they don't shop in the neighborhood, they don't participate in any functions that the neighborhood is hosting. I think that genuine desire of, "We are here to service these students but we recognize our school is part of a larger community," and actually getting engaged with what's happening in the community is important.

Ms. Richardson

Schools as Community Members

Thus far we've used organizational role theory (ORT) to understand schools as organizations with internal structures and practices, but schools are also part of a larger organization, or system, of commu-nity functioning. Ecological systems theory (EST) (Bronfenbrenner, 1979) describes how children exist in nested environments that influ-ence each other and ultimately, influence children's development and achievement. This theory is useful for examining schools' potential to impact more than students and their academic outcomes.

Figure 4.1 depicts the varied levels of EST and interactions between children's different "organizations." The microsystem is at the core to represent children's immediate environments. School, home, family

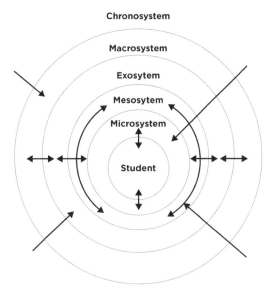

Figure 4.1 Model of Ecological Systems Theory

members, and peers are part of children's microsystem and have a direct effect on their development. The mesosystem illustrates how multiple elements within the microsystem influence one another and how that relationship further affects children. School relationships with community organizations and with families reside in the mesosystem as distinct factors that shape children's experiences. The exosystem, however, indirectly connects to children through someone in their microsystem. For example, parental employment affects children's daily lives as it predicts household income and the resources to which children have access. The macrosystem describes the cultural context (local values, attitudes, and belief systems) that determines how children experience each system and how the systems relate to one another. Finally, the chronosystem acknowledges that all these environments change over time, suggesting that what matters most to children's development and learning at a single time point is not always predictable.

The takeaway from EST is that educators must address more than what happens within their buildings if they are truly going to increase students' educational achievement. Yes, you want to build partnerships that support the school's vision and mission, but you must also understand the school's role in achieving the community's vision for the future. This requires consideration of students' nonacademic needs, ways the school can support families, and how the school can become an advocate for community causes. School leaders should reflect on out-of-school factors that relate to students' in-school capacities including:

- physical and psychological health (including access to quality food and medical resources)
- transportation
- recreation opportunities
- access to technology
- before and after school supervision
- parental education and employment

It is impossible for a school to independently meet all these needs and it would be inappropriate to attempt to do so without input from relevant stakeholders. Just as school members are education experts, community members are neighborhood experts.

Creating Community Partnerships

A community partnership is any formal arrangement a school has with an individual, a private or public organization or institution, or with an association. Partnerships are multidirectional, mutually beneficial, and grounded in shared or complementary needs. Table 4.1 suggests possible partnerships and their benefits.

Table 4.1 Examples of School–Community Partnerships		
Community Partner	**School Benefits**	**Partner Benefits**
Businesses	Donations, curricular enhancements, mentors, special-event support	Interns, use of school facilities, expanding potential customer base, advertising, tax credit
Childcare center	Childcare for students who are parents, research and observation site	Volunteers, sustained contact with families, resource support
Church or other religious institution	Before/after school care, extracurricular activities, resources, volunteers	Information about the broader community, support achieving mission
Colleges/Universities	Tutoring, mentoring, summer programming, professional development consultants	Practicum and observation site, research partner, community-based learning opportunities
Community groups/ centers	Before/after school programming, extracurricular activities, academic support, youth development initiatives	Support achieving mission, access to community members, use of school facilities, volunteers
Library	Donations, content expertise, curricular support	Access to patrons
Residents	Local expertise, volunteers, donations	Employment and education opportunities, supporting their child's learning, improving the school

Community partnerships can increase parent and family engagement, promote community trust in schools, encourage community service, increase students' opportunities to learn (OTLs), contribute to positive social and emotional development, and improve student attendance and academic achievement (Anderson-Butcher et al., 2010).

Types of Partnerships

Not all school–community partnerships are the same. There are multiple types of partners to address different school and community needs.

- *Affiliates* are partners who share a need or issue they cannot address individually. These relationships are designed to enhance the school's capacity around a focal area. For example, multiple schools often collaborate to jointly offer after-school programs or extracurricular activities because they do not individually have enough resources to run programs on their own.
- *Intermediaries* are organizations or people who act as brokers between the school and another external resource that can support school operations. A popular use of intermediaries is through school–university partnerships where universities supply schools with teachers, access to grant-writing services, or to professional development consultants.
- *Reform support organizations* are educational organizations that work with a school or district to comprehensively change school functioning. Such organizations can be locally, state, or nationally based. They might offer funding, advocate for policy changes, provide trainings and resources, or influence curriculum.
- *Community-based organizations* (CBOs) are nonprofit organizations within the community that improve community welfare by addressing problems such as poverty, food insecurity, and unemployment. The Boys and Girls Club, YMCA, and the Urban League are common CBO partners.

Each type of partner has potential benefits and drawbacks, but what it is most important is that partners share your vision for the school and believe in its ability to achieve it.

Identifying Community Partners

It is best to start locally when identifying potential community partners because they are likely to have a personal relationship with the school and consequently be more invested in its success. Local partners live and work in the community and are familiar with neighborhood needs, resources, and people. They will also have deep knowledge of the community's history and how the cultural context (or macrosystem) may or may not have changed across time.

The first step in finding a local partner is to identify neighborhood treasures: people or places that are well-known and highly regarded. These may be individuals whose family has been in the neighborhood for generations or nonprofit organizations that offer valuable services to the community. Other schools may also be local treasures if they are newer, have more resources, or if they have a different academic model.

The second step is to formally assess their position within the community. You should reflect on the following:

- How long have they been in the community?
- What are their core values, vision, and mission?
- Are their operational practices culturally conscious?
- Is their staff culturally competent?
- With whom do they partner?
- What is their past and present relationship to the school?

For potential partnerships with individuals, you will want to know what stake they have in the school and community, how they interact with other community members, and their capacity to work with the school. These answers are a good filter for measuring the likelihood that they would want to partner, the type of partner they may be, and the issues on which you could partner.

Third, you should review the resource assessment you conducted as part of the school-planning process in Chapter 1. Where are the gaps? Make sure you consider all aspects of school functioning including academic learning needs, staffing needs, and financial needs. Not all partnerships will be outcome-oriented; some partners may be good additions to the advisory board.

Finally, you will need to be honest about what you can offer a partnership. Where are their gaps? How can you support their vision? What will they gain from this relationship? This may require extensive research and multiple conversations, so it will be time consuming. However, it is critical that school leaders do the necessary legwork early on to ensure productive and positive partnerships later.

Developing Community Partnerships

Once you've identified potential partners, you need to decide who within the school organization is best positioned to establish a relationship with a new partner. The natural default is for a principal or community outreach coordinator to initiate the relationship, but that may not always be the best choice. You want to leverage existing social networks, so look for someone—a teacher, staff member, parent—who already has an in with the partner and ask for their assistance. They need not remain the point person for the partnership, but they can help with initial introductions.

The most important thing to remember when creating a partnership is to be clear about the purpose and goal of the partnership. Ground the first conversation in a proposal, not a problem. A request for a partnership should not be framed as a request for a solution, but as a collaboration around a shared value or issue of concern. Be sure to communicate your strengths and your weaknesses by discussing what you have, what you need, and how you can contribute to a mutual goal.

The second meeting is when you design the partnership using a memorandum of understanding (MOU) to record the details of the relationship. The MOU should indicate:

1. purpose and goal(s) of the partnership
2. respective resources that will be used to achieve goals
3. type of partnership
4. steps to achieve goals
5. timeline of activities
6. responsible parties for each activity
7. accountability methods
8. evaluation process

As you write the MOU, remember that partnerships are not transactional. There will be times when one partner appears to be getting more out of the relationship than the other. That is okay. Partnerships are about accumulating resources to invest in the school, not necessarily about enhancing school outcomes. You should therefore think about how you will bring the partnership into the school beyond specific MOU goals. For example, how does a relationship with a local restaurant extend past the provision of food for special events? Could this partner help you examine the value of culinary arts courses, or envision an internship program, or enhance your petition about the quality of school food? On the other hand, how will you further support the restaurant? Can their employees participate in the remediation and recovery programs designed in Chapter 3? Or perhaps they can use the cafeteria or gym to host large receptions and parties. School leaders must be strategic and imagine how a community partnership can address the needs of as many people as possible as frequently as possible, long after the MOU expires.

Connecting with Families

While you develop community partnerships, you should also be building a family engagement program within the school that welcomes and encourages families' participation in their child's education. As students' first teachers, families are the source of students' attitudes, values, beliefs, and behaviors and are the ultimate authority on their child. Educational equity is impossible without fully understanding students' needs, and families can help with that.

Decades of research reiterates the benefits of family involvement for students' behavioral and cognitive engagement, academic skills, and their overall achievement (Borgonovi & Montt, 2012; Chang et al., 2015; Dotterer & Wehrspann, 2016; Wilder, 2014). Strong family–school partnerships are positively related to students' motivation to learn, attitude toward school, self-esteem, and positive parenting practices (Christenson & Havsy, 2004; Patrikakou et al., 2005; Toldson & Lemmons, 2013). These outcomes are especially true for Latinx and Black adolescents who often experience barriers to academic success upon reaching high school (Jeynes, 2016, 2017).

Unfortunately though, minoritized families are frequently labeled "hard to reach" because of schools' inadequate engagement efforts. Parents may ignore schools' invitations to involvement because the requests are unreasonable, the timing is unfeasible, the communication method is ineffective, or the topic may be irrelevant. Research consistently reveals that working parents cannot attend school events during the day or evening but engage in a lot of at-home involvement activities (Stacer & Perrucci, 2013; Williams & Sánchez, 2012). It is therefore more likely that families are not hard to reach, but that schools are not privy to families' involvement practices. This is supported by research that found that although Black and Latinx parents are more often invited to workshops and asked to sign involvement contracts than white parents, they attend open houses, special events, and PTA meetings less frequently (Marschall & Shah, 2020).

The discrepancy between the number of opportunities and the level of involvement for different racial and income groups can be explained by reviewing parents' motivation for involvement. Hoover-Dempsey and colleagues (1997, 2005) proposed that parents' decisions about if and how they are involved in their children's learning are influenced by personal factors (role construction and self-efficacy), the invitations they receive for involvement, and their life context (knowledge and skills, time and energy, social capital).

Personal		Parent's Perceptions of Contextual Invitations to Involvement			Family Life Context Variables		
Parental role construction for involvement	Parental efficacy for helping the student succeed in school	General invitations from the school	Specific invitations from teacher(s)	Specific invitations from student	Parental knowledge & skills	Parental time & energy	Family culture; family social capital; family access to community social capital

It is easiest to focus on increasing invitations to involvement as a strategy for improving family engagement; however, school leaders must also consider families' beliefs about involvement. For instance, many Latinx parents respect teachers' expertise and do not always feel comfortable intervening in school practices. They view themselves as responsible for children's moral upbringing and the school as responsible for children's academic and cognitive development (Ceballo et al., 2014; Durand &

Perez, 2013; Ordóñez-Jasis & Jasis, 2004). Other cultural groups also have norms that influence their involvement behaviors. Research shows that Black and Asian parents believe that kids should be independent by the time they reach adolescence, so they tend not to "manage" their child's education but instead "structure" it through home-based involvement, academic socialization, and through intentional parenting choices (Chao, 2000; Sy & Schulenberg, 2005; Vincent et al., 2013).

An equitable family engagement program leverages the many ways parents understand their role in their child's learning while also minimizing the practical obstacles to family engagement. Racially minoritized and low-income families may not be involved because of language barriers, lack of knowledge about school functioning, inadequate academic skills, and certainly, limited time, energy, and resources. The COVID-19 crisis revealed just how many low-income and racially minoritized parents are frontline essential workers who are often forced to choose between their job and their child's education.

ADVICE FROM THE FIELD: BUILDING RELATIONSHIPS WITH FAMILIES

I think, first of all, it starts with honoring parents and respecting them and showing them that you value their opinion. I don't think we do enough of that as educators. Educators will say, "Oh, these families don't come in. They won't come into the school." No. Why aren't they coming into the school? They'll come if we build that strong relationship.

How we do that is, number one, we acknowledge that we value their culture and language. And we do that through our actions. We do home visits, translate publications, and when something negative happens, we're there to support them. When something positive happens, we're there to acknowledge them and be right alongside them. I think it's about building the relationship with families.

Then what you say is, "I know you're busy, but I really need you to come to this meeting for me. And I need you to tell

10 people what you heard at this meeting." So when they say, "Well, I can't," you say "but you've got to. I need you. I need you." They know I need them, and they know that I'm going to call them when I need them. We have that relationship where they know, well, he supported me during this and I have to have his back.

Principal Lewis

School leaders should leverage relationships and think outside of the box to engage parents beyond traditional means. Epstein (2018) provides a good starting point for designing a comprehensive engagement program that acknowledges the diversity of families' life contexts.

- Parenting: helping families construct a nurturing and supportive home environment
- Communicating: sharing information in accessible formats
- At-home involvement: offering suggestions for how parents can support students' learning
- Volunteering: structuring volunteer opportunities according to families' schedules and capacities
- Decision-making: including families in school governance
- Community collaboration: connecting families to community resources

This model extends past common family–school partnership frameworks focused on school-based (e.g., volunteering, open house, conferences) and home-based (e.g., homework help, reading with children) activities. It operates within the meso- and exosystems to center families, not just students. Equitable engagement programs should also meet the following criterion:

- *Data driven.* The entire program should be designed according to existing school, family, and community needs. These needs will determine the types and extent of partnership initiatives.
- *Results oriented.* Every engagement effort should be directed toward a clear outcome to ensure coherence and efficacy.
- *Theory and research supported.* Family engagement decision-making should be grounded in relevant theory and supported by research evidence. Best practices should be adapted to meet local needs.
- *Comprehensive.* Schools should simultaneously pull families in and reach out to them. Engagement initiatives should collectively address multiple needs through multiple strategies.
- *Integrated.* Engagement efforts should not be meaningless add-ons to school processes. They should contribute to the school's vision and mission, be in accordance with school policies, and yield meaningful outcomes.
- *Supported.* Job descriptions should include clear expectations of family and community engagement. Staff should be trained to effectively interact with diverse families.

Designing an effective family engagement program is similar to designing a curriculum. Each unit must build upon the last and contribute to an overarching outcome. The curriculum should include diverse perspectives and multimodal assessments. It should be delivered with fidelity and differentiated for various needs.

This is more complicated than it seems. Most family outreach follows a one-size-fits-all model that rarely aligns with minoritized families' interests or capacities. For example, parent–teacher conferences are standard across schools where families are expected to come to the school in the late afternoon or early evening to meet with two to eight teachers. This does not work for parents who don't speak English, work second or third shift, are caregivers for relatives and children, don't have transportation, or who can't fit this into their daily routine. How else might teachers consistently communicate with parents instead of relying on high-stakes meetings twice a year?

Even when involvement opportunities are accessible, they may not always generate desired results. The recent focus on trauma-informed teaching means many schools offer workshops to help parents understand how out-of-school factors affect their child's in-school learning. This is valuable information but it is not family centered. Informational workshops can be ineffective because they (a) assume families do not already know this information, (b) imply that families are able to act on this information, and (c) place the onus to change onto the parents rather than the school.

If the desired outcome of the workshop is for parents to decrease children's exposure to traumatic events, the initiative was bound to fail. Parents do not control the primary sources of chronic stress: poverty and neighborhood violence. A better engagement effort would include actionable steps parents can take to mitigate the effects of trauma on their child. These suggestions would ideally be given with parents' resources and life contexts in mind. Sharing the value of adequate sleep and physical activity goes further than lecturing parents about circumstances they cannot change.

Effective engagement programs take an asset-based approach and leverage families' knowledge while also building their capacities. All parents know the value of education and want the best for their child, but they may not always know how to support their learning. To increase family involvement, especially for parents with limited time and resources, schools must be strategic with their invitations. Recruiting and maintaining parent participation requires:

- tapping into familial and social networks
- explaining how their participation benefits their child
- making involvement opportunities interesting, enjoyable, and relevant
- ensuring parents experience success
- timing it when they are most likely to be available
- choosing an accessible delivery format

These guidelines apply to all types of family engagement, not just school-based activities. For instance, if you want to sponsor a health clinic once a month, you need to think through the types of services that are most needed, how to best tell families about the clinic, how they might get to the clinic, how long it will be open, and how to convince them to prioritize preventative health care over more pressing issues.

These problems cannot and should not be solved solely by the school. Family partnerships, like community partnerships, are about mobilizing collective assets to improve neighborhood well-being. Families and schools should share ownership and leadership of the engagement program such that families have input into how, when, and where they participate in their child's learning. But unlike community partnerships, there need not be an MOU because there is already a mutual understanding that we will do whatever it takes to support our kids.

Reflection Questions

1. What might be the outcomes of a community and family engagement needs assessment?
2. How do existing family involvement initiatives privilege certain demographics?
3. What types of partnerships are necessary to positively affect students across multiple systems?
4. How do the leadership models reviewed in Chapter 2 apply to developing community and family partnerships?
5. What professional development does school staff need to better engage with diverse families?
6. How can the equity action plan be extended beyond the school?
7. How would community and family partnerships enhance student outcomes?

Part II

Staffing for Equity

At the end of Shelby's first year, there is a lot to be proud of. Because of a partnership with a nearby university, teachers are no longer paying for materials out of pocket, and students have access to tutors after school and on weekends. They can also take advanced classes at the local high school, and the new academic skills center provides evening and weekend GED and remedial classes for anyone in need. As a result, achievement gaps have narrowed by half a standard deviation on average, which Shelby considers excellent progress for just one year. Shelby was able to accomplish her goals through a series of actions: creating an advisory board that helped develop a multi-year equity action plan, reallocating the budget, restructuring staff roles through a team-based organizational model, and developing school-community relationships.

But there is still work to do as the school planning process revealed major hurdles to educational equity. For instance, many staff reported that although the school promotes diversity and inclusion, it does little to ensure their existence. There is minimal effort to recruit a diverse staff, no acknowledgement or celebration of cultural holidays, and no attempt to differentiate according to students' cognitive, social, or emotional needs. Everyone agreed that equality—not equity—reigns supreme.

When asked why they don't engage in inclusive practices on their own, teachers and staff explained that it "never occurred to [them]." Further conversations revealed that most of the staff at Roger Gates have colorblind perspectives and truly believe that as long as they follow the curriculum, students will learn. Shelby is familiar with the "good teaching is good teaching" mantra, and knows that when teachers ignore students' identities, it is a sign that good teaching is in fact not happening.

Shelby found a ray of hope in the novice teachers who began their careers at Roger Gates in the last two years. Many of them graduated from teacher preparation programs that taught them the value of multicultural teaching and of viewing all students through an asset-based lens. But every one of the new and novice teachers described feeling "thrown in the deep end" when they arrived at Roger Gates. They did not receive any onboarding at the school, just the district-wide orientation. And when they ask colleagues for help, they are met with resistance and told they will eventually figure it out. The team-based model established in year 1 means that Shelby already has people in place to work on next year's priorities:

1. **Diversifying the staff.** The staff at Roger Gates is 91% white. Of the 3 BIPOC employees, one works in the cafeteria, one is a librarian, and one is a teacher. As a mixed-race woman, Shelby knows firsthand how it feels to be the "only" among colleagues, and more importantly, how it feels to be the go-to person for BIPOC students. She is committed to ensuring that students and staff get to learn with and from people with a multitude of identities.

2. **Creating a sense of community.** Diversifying the staff means that Shelby must be very intentional about creating a shared identity among school members. Just as the existing families feel resentment toward new families who have different backgrounds, interests, and values, the veteran teachers will feel some resentment toward new teachers. Shelby is aware that a lack of collaboration and feelings of exclusion are among the top reasons teachers and families leave schools, so she plans to work with current staff and families to create a school climate that welcomes new members.

Some of the most important decisions school leaders make occur during hiring processes, as research consistently reveals that teachers are the most important in-school factor that predict students' academic outcomes. They determine what students learn, when they learn it, and in what context the learning occurs. Teachers are truly the heart of any school and, as such, they must model and promote the school's vision and mission.

It is harder than people think to find teachers whose values and attitudes align with the school's organizational framework. So many teachers join the profession because they love working with children, because they love their content area, or because they want to give back to their community. These are all excellent reasons to be a teacher, and each rationale uniquely shapes a teacher's instructional style. A teacher who prioritizes building relationships with students is necessarily going to construct a classroom environment with very different expectations than a teacher whose primary goal is content delivery. It is therefore important for school leaders to be strategic when making staffing decisions. This part of the book uses social identity theory (SIT) as a framework to guide teacher hiring and onboarding processes.

Social Identity Theory

Social cognitive psychologists study how people's thinking shapes their behaviors. They are especially interested in antisocial behavior such as lying, aggression, and discrimination. For example, is lying motivated by good or bad intentions? How does one's religious beliefs affect their likelihood of lying? How does the possibility of getting a reward predict the frequency of lying?

To answer these questions, psychologists work backward by first examining the behavior and then examining the motivation for the behavior. The motivations are the most important aspect of study because they reflect our beliefs, values, and attitudes. We presumably only do things once we've thought about it and decided that a particular behavior will yield desired results.

This line of thinking is especially useful when attempting to understand why teachers make certain instructional decisions. A social cognitive psychologist would say, "they made that decision because they believe that _____ is what teachers should do." Similar to the notion of role construction discussed in Part I, social identity theorists believe that people's actions are guided by their social identities. Who we hang out with largely determines how we label ourselves, what we believe, what we say, how we dress, and certainly how we behave. And, what we say, how we dress, and what we do helps us define ourselves and choose appropriate friends.

Take for example, veteran teachers. One is deemed a veteran only after having taught for a certain number of years based upon school, district, or state standards. But once you become a veteran teacher, you must now behave as veteran teachers behave. The norms, or behavioral expectations, are what social groups use as a behavioral guide in relevant environments. These norms are enforced both within the group and also by nongroup members. Many novice teachers believe that veteran teachers have first choice of classes, of classrooms, and of committee assignments. As long as novice teachers believe this to be true, veteran teachers will behave accordingly. They will pick their classes, classrooms, and committees first because, as SIT states, different groups will always compete for status and resources.

This scenario is familiar to most teachers who've witnessed such conflicts at some point in their careers. We can predict who is going to say what when during meetings because we know who is on what side of an issue and which people have the strongest opinions. The leaders of any group are the ones who most reflect the group's values and most often behave according to the group's norms. The leader is also responsible for monitoring the group's health, meaning they are charged with making sure everyone in the group is behaving in ways that support the group's social position and that maintain its norms.

It is easy to think of a principal as the automatic leader, but SIT tells us that because there are so many subgroups in a school (e.g., novice teachers, veteran teachers, grade-level teachers, support staff, administrators), a principal is only the leader of the school at large. This means that a good school leader hires other leaders whose vision of their respective social groups aligns with that of the school's. If not, groups with competing interests will undermine the school's overarching mission.

This part of the book walks school leaders through the rationale and processes of hiring and onboarding equity-minded teachers. Because all school leaders want to hire effective instructors with strong commitments to all children regardless of social identity, I focus on the importance of teachers' beliefs, values, and attitudes—or dispositions—as an indicator of their multicultural worldview.

5 Limitations of Ethnic Matching and Multicultural Education

No one would argue that widening opportunity and achievement gaps are easily fixed. History tells us that educational inequities are incredibly difficult to resolve, especially given how interwoven public schools are with other social institutions. Changes in government, housing, health care, and the economy affect schools independently and jointly. It makes sense then that there is no single solution to educational disenfranchisement.

There are myriad promising interventions that can lessen, if not close, racial, economic, and linguistic education gaps. Two that dominate scholarship and discourse on educational equity are ethnic matching and multicultural education (ME). I present them together because there is an underlying assumption that the former facilitates the latter. In many cases this is true, but even so, they are insufficient to achieve educational equity without also considering the topics of other chapters in this book.

In this chapter, I overview the promises and perils of ethnic matching and multicultural education as elements of an educational equity action plan. I use social identity theory (SIT) to explain how the relationship between race, biases, stereotypes, and whiteness can disrupt teacher–student relationships despite ethnic matching. I then describe how regardless of racial identity, ME can be effective at improving students' achievement, before suggesting why it often is not. To be clear, I am not saying ethnic matching and multicultural education are ineffective paths toward equity. On the contrary, there is rich evidence that racial congruence and culturally sustaining instruction contribute to all students' achievement. The purpose of this chapter is to explore why, when schools have either or both of these elements, equity is not guaranteed.

Ethnic Matching

Discourse on teacher–student ethnic matching is complex because matching is not as simple as placing an Asian teacher in front of Asian students. Where do we find Asian teachers? How do we recruit them into predominately Asian schools? How do we ensure they have the relevant cultural knowledge to be effective? What do we do in multiracial classrooms? Answering these questions is necessary but is not the focus of this chapter (for a review see Easton-Brooks, 2019). Given the demographic realities of the teacher workforce and student population, I instead focus on understanding the psychology underlying ethnic matching in hopes that all teachers can activate the mechanisms that make ethnic matching effective.

Why Ethnic Matching?

The logic underlying ethnic matching is simple. If teachers and students share cultural backgrounds, It ought to be easy to develop teacher–student relationships grounded in similar life experiences. Those relationships inform the development of a culturally welcoming classroom environment and provide teachers insight into students' learning processes. That extra knowledge helps teachers expand students' opportunities to learn (OTLs) through cultural relevance and targeted differentiation.

This logic is supported by research demonstrating that ethnic matching is related to:

- higher engagement, motivation, and attendance (Rasheed et al., 2020)
- enrollment in more-rigorous courses (Quintero, 2019)
- higher representation in gifted programs (Grissom et al., 2017)

- positive teacher perceptions of students' academic skills, social and academic growth, and behaviors (Wright et al., 2017)
- higher expectations than white teachers (Gershenson et al., 2016)
- increased high school graduation rates (Gershenson et al., 2018)
- higher achievement and fewer discipline referrals (Lindsay & Hart, 2017)
- higher scores on standardized tests (Redding, 2019)

These findings make it clear there is something special going on between teachers and students when they are from the same racial or ethnic group. Pianta and colleagues (2012) proposed the teaching through interactions (TTI) framework as a guide for analyzing the elements of teacher–student relationships. They, like other scholars, argue that teacher–student relationships are a critical driver of student learning. But they further suggest deconstructing relationships into three domains: emotional, organizational, and instructional (see Table 5.1).

Table 5.1: Teaching Through Interactions Framework (Hamre et al., 2013)		
Domain	**Dimension**	**Description**
Emotional support	Positive climate	Reflects the overall emotional tone of the classroom and the connection between teachers and students
	Negative climate	Reflects the overall level of expressed negativity in the classroom between teachers and students (e.g., anger, aggression, irritability)
	Teacher sensitivity	Encompasses teachers' responsivity to students' needs and awareness of students' level of academic and emotional functioning

Table 5.1: Teaching Through Interactions Framework (Hamre et al., 2013)		
Domain	**Dimension**	**Description**
	Regard for student perspectives	The degree to which the teachers' interactions with students and classroom activities place an emphasis on students' interests, motivations, and points of view, rather than being very teacher driven
	Overcontrol	Assesses the extent to which the classroom is rigidly structured or regimented at the expense of children's interests and/or needs
Classroom organization	Behavior management	Encompasses teachers' ability to use effective methods to prevent and redirect misbehavior by presenting clear behavioral expectations and minimizing time spent on behavioral issues
	Productivity	Considers how well teachers manage instructional time and routines so that students have the maximum number of opportunities to learn
	Instructional learning formats	The degree to which teachers maximize students' engagement and ability to learn by providing interesting activities, instruction, centers, and materials
	Classroom chaos	The degree to which teachers ineffectively manage children in the classroom so that disruption and chaos predominate

Instructional support	Concept development	The degree to which instructional discussions and activities promote students' higher order thinking skills versus focus on rote and fact-based learning
	Quality of feedback	Considers teachers' provision of feedback focused on expanding learning and understanding (formative evaluation), not correctness or the end product (summative evaluation)
	Language modeling	The quality and amount of teachers' use of language simulation and language-facilitation techniques during individual, small-group, and large-group interactions with children
	Richness of instructional methods	The extent to which teachers use a variety of strategies to promote children's thinking and understanding of material at a deeper and more complex level

Why is Ethnic Matching Successful?

Combining the TTI framework with SIT reveals how ethnic matching permeates the many dimensions of teacher–student relationships to yield higher academic outcomes.

First, ethnic matching promotes sociocultural understanding between teachers and students. Because they are members of the same cultural group they are familiar with one another's norms. Some scholars call this cultural synchrony: when teachers and students have a common understanding of verbal and nonverbal language, manner of personal presentation, and learning methods (Irvine, 1990). Cultural synchrony also facilitates an awareness of, and empathy for, how students' social positionality affects their education.

In practice this means teachers can leverage shared perspectives to deliver culturally sustaining pedagogy. According to the TTI framework, this materializes as student-centered teaching, culturally responsive classroom management, personally meaningful instruction, accessible language, and culturally relevant instructional methods. Culturally informed teacher–student relationships are important for BISOC, who are often viewed through a lens of pity and contempt by white teachers who emphasize students' deficits and disparities in relation to white norms. Teachers whose race or ethnicity matches that of their students are more likely to view their students as bastions of cultural wealth, see their behaviors as cultural assets, and interact with them to develop their sociopolitical consciousness (Howell et al., 2019).

THOUGHTS FROM THE FIELD

I think it helps. It definitely helps to see someone like you during your day. Seeing someone that looks like you helps you fit in and feel like you're a part of it. And it also provides inspiration and connection because there are certain things that some cultures just don't experience. Having that one person or a couple of people that share the student's culture will help the student grow and mature in their own culture because they may have questions that they may not be able to ask Mom or Dad.

Mr. Barry

An asset-based perspective of students is a second explanation of why ethnic matching is successful. SIT tells us that people have personal investments in both the members of a community and in the welfare of the community itself. The metacontrast principle explains how in-group members work to ensure that their group is better off than other groups with whom they compete for resources. These resources range from school funding and access to highly qualified teachers to recommendations for placement in advanced education tracks. Thus, when teachers' well-being is linked to student success, the TTI model suggests they are more sensitive to students' needs and inclined to provide formative feedback that supports positive student outcomes. Indeed, research demonstrates that ethnic matching is associated with increased emotional and instructional support (Osei-Twumasi & Pinetta, 2019), as well as with high expectations for minoritized students, all of which helps students see themselves positively, despite negative societal messages about their cultural groups (Rojas & Liou, 2017).

Students' confidence is attributed to the third argument in favor of ethnic matching: the provision of role models with whom students can identify. SIT labels such teachers *prototypes,* who reflect the best characteristics of the group. Because the group leader is aspirational, students have more-favorable perceptions of same-race teachers (Cherng & Halpini, 2016), and higher levels of personal effort, happiness in class, and student-initiated communication (Egalite & Kisida, 2018). TTI attributes this to a warm and welcoming climate that sets the emotional tone of the classroom. Social learning theory (Bandura, 1977) confirms the necessity of models that affirm students' evolving academic and personal identities. When multiple identities align, students are more likely to see the utility of school, which improves their engagement and overall achievement (Vickery, 2016).

The fourth mechanism through which ethnic matching supports students' learning was discussed in Chapter 4. If students share their teachers' race or ethnicity, it is likely that their families do as well. As many of the barriers to effective family involvement are rooted in cultural differences, ethnic matching may strengthen families' participation in children's learning. Shared social identities increase parents' comfort speaking with teachers, their likelihood to advocate for their child, and decrease misalignment between home and school behavioral expectations (Markowitz et al., 2020). It is also likely that teachers can anticipate practical barriers to involvement such as language, cultural beliefs, and life context variables. Deep knowledge of students' out-of-school lives may, as depicted in the TTI framework, help teachers make more productive use of students' in-school learning opportunities.

Why Ethnic Matching Doesn't Always Work

Identities and their associated norms are shaped by much more than race and ethnicity. Identities are contextually bound such that what is most salient about yourself in one setting can be quite different in another. For example, it is unlikely that in an all-girls school, students would refer to themselves as "female." But if they went to a STEM school, it is probable that their gender would be prominent in self-descriptions. According to SIT, this is because we prioritize our most marginalized identities as a way to distinguish ourselves and our in-groups from other social groups.

In homogenous settings we will almost always advocate for the advancement of the in-group that is most oppressed in that context. Take for instance rural schools where approximately 90% of teachers and 73% of students are white (U.S. Department of Education, 2017a, 2017b). In a majority-white setting, rural teachers express the importance of community and local culture to teacher quality, not race (Whitaker & Valtierra, 2019). This is also true in predominately Black schools where Black teachers emphasize the importance of economic class in assessing cultural competence. For them, similar skin color does not supersede other social factors that shape educational experiences such as income, language, and nation of origin.

These sentiments are aligned with SIT that proposes three reasons why ethnic and racial matching may be ineffective at increasing students' academic achievement:

1. Teachers and students must view themselves as members of the same in-group, or intergroup conflict could emerge. The distinction between race and ethnicity offers a useful template for understanding the nuances of identity construction. Whereas race is a social construct based upon phenotype, ethnicity is related to cultural values and practices. For example, the racial group "Black" encompasses identities from across the racial diaspora. *Ethnicity* on the other hand distinguishes between African American, Ghanaian, Jamaican, Afro Brazilian and dozens of other cultural groups. The same is true of other broad racial groups such as Hispanic, Latinx, Asian, and white. Even when people self-identify as members of the same racial groups, social

bonding may center on other identity markers like religion, geography, or even skin tone. Race alone offers insufficient grounds on which to base cultural affiliation.

2. Teachers, as leaders of the in-group within a racially matched classroom, determine acceptable characteristics and norms of the group. It is possible for teachers to have biases against group members if they are perceived to embody undesirable traits or judged as not having the correct traits. A Black teacher may not like Black students with natural hair. A Spanish-speaking Mexican teacher may have negative feelings toward Latinx students who do not speak Spanish. Teachers' biases may prompt them to perceive students as lowering the group's social standing, which may lead them to treat students as out-group members. Conversely, in an attempt to maintain group prestige, teachers may demand that students acquiesce to their expectations. When teachers embrace "tough love" to prepare students for "the real world" they might mistakenly damage teacher–student relationships and more critically, students' self-worth.

3. Teachers may also inadvertently reinforce widely accepted negative stereotypes of their group. For instance, high-achieving Black students report that even Black teachers question the authenticity of their work, their academic aptitude, and comment on their exceptionality among their peers (Fries-Britt & Griffin, 2007). When students internalize negative stereotypes, they develop weak academic self-concepts that threaten their overall achievement (Okeke et al., 2009). Because beliefs guide behaviors, BITOC may interact with BISOC through a deficit lens that does not recognize students' full capabilities.

Each potential drawback of ethnic matching can be compounded by a lack of teaching competence that is unrelated to culture. BITOC are more likely than white teachers to enter the profession through alternative licensure programs with only a few weeks or months of training (U.S. Department of Education, 2016). They then choose to teach in urban schools where BISOC constitute 71% of the student body (U.S. Department of Education, 2017b). Taken together, while racially minoritized students in urban schools could potentially have a same-race teacher, that teacher is also likely to have fewer years of experience and less training than teachers in suburban and rural schools (Kalogrides et al., 2013). This conundrum poses an important question: Does culture or instructional skill matter more for student learning?

THOUGHTS FROM THE FIELD

I think the part we lose sight of is that at the end of the day, we have to have good teachers in the classroom. I've seen phenomenal teachers of color in classrooms, which I think is phenomenal for ethnic matching. I've seen some terrible teachers of color in a classroom who don't build relationships with kids, that are mean to them, and don't have an instructional background.

I'm not going to want them for the sake of ethnic matching. I'd recommend somebody else that doesn't look like them that's teaching and working their butt off and celebrating them, than somebody that looks like them. So, I think when we talk about ethnic matching, the qualifications should be that a teacher of color in front of kids who look like them should be able to teach and also celebrate kids. That's the piece that we leave off. You can't leave those pieces off because again, if you're not right for kids, I don't care what background you have.

Principal Lewis

Multicultural Education

Mr. Lewis is speaking against the assumption that teachers of color automatically know how to teach students of color because of their shared culture. Such thinking is problematic because it (a) frames multicultural teaching as a culturally based checklist of behaviors, and (b) undermines the hard work and commitment of effective multicultural educators. No racial group is a monolith with universal needs or interests. Every student brings a unique story into the classroom that only skilled teachers can access, celebrate, and leverage for students' benefit. Multicultural teaching requires a diverse tool kit of instructional strategies, an equity-oriented attitude, and a love of all children.

Defining Multicultural Education

Put simply, *multicultural education* (ME) is a broad term encompassing pedagogical practices that honor students' diversity. ME is a derivative of critical pedagogy that positions school as sites of resistance to oppression (Baldwin, 1963; hooks, 2014). According to critical pedagogues, schools should not reproduce the status quo but instead prepare students to participate in activism that ultimately transforms society. Teachers are expected to raise students' critical consciousness so they can examine the world, look for points of injustice, understand how they came to be, and feel empowered to change them. These lofty goals describe the purpose of ME but don't necessarily give us the "what" or "how" of it. For that, we consult decades of research about improving minoritized students' achievement, using culturally relevant teaching (CRT) as a starting point for ME practices.

In 1995, Gloria Ladson-Billings listed the beliefs that undergird multicultural teaching. In Chapter 6, we will explore the importance of teachers' multicultural dispositions, but for now, we overview four features of a multicultural teaching philosophy:

1. Purpose of school: to develop cultural competence, understand and critique the social order, and to experience academic success
2. Self-perceptions: teachers view themselves as doing important work alongside students as a member of their community
3. Conception of knowledge: knowledge is dynamic and culturally constructed
4. Instructional orientation: learning is a communal act that invites students' contributions by pulling knowledge out of them

Father of multicultural education James Banks (2010) captures these beliefs within five dimensions of multicultural education: an empowering school culture, prejudice reduction, knowledge construction, content integration, and equity pedagogy. Within each dimension are associated instructional practices that must be performed if teachers are truly educating for social justice. For example, an empowering school culture asks teachers to identify and explain the culture of power within the school (Delpit, 2006). Minoritized and marginalized students need to learn the norms of the dominant group if they are to be effective advocates for themselves and others. This is not to say that students should appropriate dominant norms, but that explicit conversation about them helps all students understand race and class-based power structures.

Critical dialogue can be facilitated by leveraging a decolonized curriculum to create assignments that require students to converse about hot-topic issues. Such conversations help students recognize the culturally constructed nature of knowledge. If teachers access students' funds of knowledge (Moll, 2019) they can demonstrate students' power to create new ways of understanding.

Why is Multicultural Education Successful?

Data linking ME and academic achievement are not as straightforward as what we know about ethnic matching. ME is complex, including aspects of teaching and learning that can't fully be pulled apart. It is hard to know if an empowering classroom climate, challenging material, an inclusive curriculum, or multimodal instruction is driving student success. The most likely answer is that all of them are contributing independently and jointly, which is why ME is most effective when all dimensions are actualized.

SIT attempts to explain the efficacy of ME through a social and emotional lens. ME affirms students' chosen identities and marks students' groups as distinct, and their beliefs and practices as valuable. ME also discourages competition between social groups that can derail learning. Finally, ME humanizes students who are too often treated as cogs in the education machine.

When students feel recognized and respected, they develop social bonds with classmates and their motivation rises (Zeqeibi Ghannad et al., 2018). They ask more questions, spend more time completing schoolwork, and demonstrate more on-task behaviors. We refer to these outcomes as increased academic engagement, but they can also be more simply understood as kids liking school.

Why Multicultural Education Appears Not to Work

I intentionally use the word *appears* in the section title because when done correctly, ME will boost students' achievement. The problem is that it is rarely implemented with fidelity.

ME is most frequently used superficially, as an add-on to "traditional" instruction or as a quick fix for a "diversity issue." This is true of most specialized pedagogies, including social and emotional learning (SEL) and trauma-sensitive teaching that see an uptick in use after school shootings, natural disasters, or other crises. The efficacy of these pedagogies is limited by how integrated they are into all aspects of teaching. For example, teachers tend to access the low-hanging fruit of ME by diversifying the curriculum but without also diversifying their assessments and utilizing equitable instructional strategies (Malo-Juvera et al., 2016). ME is further undermined by punitive discipline policies, a lack of family and community partnerships, and weak teacher–student relationships.

These missteps do not occur because teachers don't see the value of multicultural instruction. They occur because teachers don't feel as if they know how to engage in multicultural instruction. ME has four prerequisites: (1) the ability to take students' perspectives, (2) positive attitudes and beliefs about other cultures, (3) cultural knowledge, and, (4) the ability to employ culturally sustaining practices (Rychly & Graves, 2012).

SIT predicts that it will be difficult for out-group members to meet the first three criterion which are critical for the success of the fourth. Perspective-taking requires empathy for others' experiences, of which out-group members may not be aware. The development of positive beliefs and attitudes about other cultures assumes teachers are familiar with other cultures which is not often the case. Cultural ignorance fosters color-blind racial attitudes that reduce the likelihood of teachers recognizing a need for ME (Cadenas et al., 2020). And even when teachers feel comfortable building relationships with diverse students and want to implement ME, they admit to not having adequate cultural knowledge to properly do so (Abacioglu et al., 2020; Cruz et al., 2020).

What School Leaders Can Do

Teaching for social justice begins with school leaders who are responsible for disrupting the cycle of social reproduction and stratification in schools that reinforces the culture of power. It is essential that leaders challenge whiteness—the invisible structures that reproduce white supremacy—by engaging the principles of critical race theory (Ladson-Billings & Tate, 1995):

1. Accept that racism is embedded in the structure of U.S. schools and cultivate an anti-oppressive school culture.
2. Uncover implicit whiteness by analyzing school decision-making and reflecting on whose interests are being served.
3. Challenge the color-blind and power-blind notion of meritocracy.
4. Humanize teaching and learning by integrating people's histories and experiences into school functioning through job expectations, hiring practices, the curriculum, teacher evaluation, and community and family partnerships.

School leaders must establish educational conditions in which the potential of ethnic matching and ME can be maximized. It is not enough to hire diverse staff and host multicultural night. Teachers need to be willing and prepared to create community with kids who may or may not look like them. When teachers fall short in desire or skill, it is the principal's responsibility to bolster them. In Chapter 6, we will discuss how principals identify and hire equity-minded teachers with multicultural dispositions supportive of ethnic matching and ME. In Chapter 7, we discuss how principals can foster social cohesion among teachers before then reviewing how to enhance teachers' knowledge and skills for working with diverse students in Chapter 8.

Reflection Questions

1. We call it ethnic matching, but is that correct? Would racial or cultural matching move us closer to equity? How so?
2. How does racial tokenism relate to ethnic matching and multicultural education?
3. Beyond a lack of competence, why might white teachers be resistant to multicultural education?
4. Why is it important for white teachers to have BIPOC colleagues?
5. What role does anti-racist teaching play in the larger framework of multicultural education?
6. Rank order the five dimensions of multicultural teaching as they relate to educational equity. Which is most vital and why?

Recommended Reading

Easton-Brooks, D. (2019). *Ethnic matching: Academic success of students of color*. Rowman & Littlefield.

6 Identifying Equity-Minded Teachers

Chapter 5 discussed the need for highly qualified teachers regardless of their social identities. Here, I expand upon what is traditionally used to measure *teacher* quality by first distinguishing it from *teaching* quality.

When hiring new teachers, most school leaders focus on what teachers (will) do as indicative of their potential success in the classroom. Instructional skill should certainly be a priority during the hiring process because if nothing else, teachers should engage the following practices that research has proven effective:

1. Support and encourage students to learn (e.g., check for understanding, offer help without being asked)
2. Scaffold and differentiate instruction
3. Give positive feedback and celebrate small successes
4. Provide clear directions
5. Maintain high expectations
6. Employ multimodal teaching and assessment methods
7. Connect content to real life
8. Provide opportunities for hands-on learning (i.e., not just the textbook or lectures)
9. Teach at a developmentally appropriate level

Such strategies are excellent measures of foundational *teaching* quality, but they do not speak to the "why" behind teachers' pedagogical choices. A full assessment of a potential hire should also include an evaluation of the person behind the practice, or put differently, of *teacher* quality.

Teachers' dispositions refer to the cognitive (beliefs and values) and affective (attitudes) motivators of teachers' performance (Borko et al., 2007). One might imagine a list of desirable teaching dispositions to include:

Beliefs
 – school should be a place of joy
 – all students can learn

Values
 – caring about students as individuals, not just as students
 – relationship-building with students and families
 – continuing education
 – collaborating with colleagues

Attitudes
 – likes children
 – enjoys teaching

But this list is also incomplete because even if a teacher possesses these very good attributes, we have no evidence that these characteristics are reflected in their pedagogical practices, particularly when teaching diverse students. Social identity theory (SIT) tells us that in contrast to the saying "good teaching is good teaching," teachers' dispositions, and thus their teaching, will vary when interacting with people from social groups other than their own.

For example, teachers who otherwise report high teaching efficacy, altruistic teaching motivations, and positive perceptions of students also report not feeling prepared to teach culturally and linguistically diverse students (Simon & Johnson, 2015), particularly when students are also described as having learning differences (Chu & Garcia, 2018), or when they identify as members of the LGBTQIA community (Poteat & Scheer, 2016). We learned in Chapter 5 that even when teachers are the same race as their students, other social identities affect their perception of their students. Some teachers have been found to perceive students from lower- and middle-income families, as well as boys, as having lower cognitive skills and less motivation than higher income students and girls (Brandmiller et al., 2020; Sneyers et al., 2020).

Not-so-positive beliefs about students are not easily detected during interviews because teachers will likely present as people whom Castagno (2014) describes as educated in niceness. In her book *Educated in Whiteness*, Castagno argues that schools are structured to perpetuate inequities because they implicitly and explicitly require teachers and administrators to play "nice," or in other words, ignore how discrimination, prejudice, and bias permeate school processes. Nice people are afraid of conflict, don't want to hurt anyone's feelings, and when given the chance, will always look for the positives in a situation. When forced to engage in dialogue about cultural differences, nice people will emphasize intentions over outcomes, and in doing so, transfer the burden of conflict resolution to the victim who is deemed to be causing problems.

A politically correct approach to teaching necessarily endorses ideologies that ignore or reject the lived experiences of minoritized students. Many teachers report being color-blind because to acknowledge their students' racial or ethnic identities would be divisive and discriminatory (Russell & Russell, 2014). But in refusing to recognize students' cultural identities, teachers do not see how students' identities may shape their learning. Teachers educated in niceness are blind to how power operates in schools to benefit members of the dominant culture whose social norms (e.g., language, style of dress, religious practices) are accepted as standard. Social identity theorists explain egocentrism as necessary for upholding social hierarchies because to acknowledge someone else's social identity as linked to their positionality might threaten one's beliefs about their own unearned privileges.

Such denial encourages stereotyping out-group members to affirm their lower positionality. When teachers purport that students from low-income communities don't value education, or that urban students are scary, or that Black students are lazy, they will interact with students in ways that uphold those beliefs. Students will then internalize their teachers' beliefs and have lower expectations for their own education attainment (Carter Andrews & Gutwein, 2017; Gershenson et al., 2018).

Stereotypes reinforce the difference between teachers' in-group norms and the perceived norms of their minoritized students as out-group members. Group differentiation is evident when teachers' motivation is rooted in a desire to help students whom they perceive as disadvantaged in comparison to themselves. White teachers' savior complex and to a lesser extent, their desire to participate in cultural voyeurism, positions minoritized students as objects to acted upon and observed, rather than children to be educated.

Color blindness, power blindness, stereotyping, and cultural voyeurism undergird the myth of meritocracy in U.S. schools. When teachers fail to situate students' academic performance within the context of structural racism and classism and centuries-old prejudice and discrimination, students—not historically inequitable educational opportunities are to blame for underachievement. Students are said to not have tried hard enough, to not have sacrificed enough, or to not be resilient enough to overcome obstacles intentionally placed to ensure their failure. Teachers who insist that success relies solely upon student effort teach students that failure is the result of a lack of competence and willpower rather than a reflection of the systemic inequities that disadvantage certain social groups before they ever step foot in a school.

Prerequisites of Equity: Multicultural Dispositions

In 2021, the Council of Chief State School Officers updated the national teacher quality standards and learning progressions that require teachers to:

> recognize that all learners bring to their learning varying experiences, abilities, talents, and prior learning, as well as language, culture, and family and community values that are assets that can be used to promote their learning. To do this effectively, teachers must

have a deeper understanding of their own frames of reference (e.g., culture, gender, language, abilities, ways of knowing), the potential biases in these frames, and their impact on expectations for and relationships with learners and their families. (p. 6)

You will notice that the word *dispositions* is never utilized; however, it is clear that these standards imply certain multicultural beliefs ("all learners bring . . . assets"), values ("understanding . . . own frames of reference"), and attitudes ("potential biases in these frames") pertinent to teaching minoritized students.

Gary Howard (2007) more explicitly describes four dispositions (which he defines as "quality of personhood") of good teaching:

- Disposition for difference: being aware of and comfortable with how variations in race, gender, class, religion, language, and ability emerge in classrooms, sometimes in conflict with one another
- Disposition for dialog: possessing a desire to engage in meaningful and open-minded conversations with colleagues and students about cultural differences
- Disposition for disillusionment: a willingness to embrace cognitive dissonance and challenge one's own point of view
- Disposition for democracy: perceiving teaching as social justice work that facilitates student agency with an ultimate goal of "undoing those educational systems that have only favored a few and replacing them with institutional practices that will more effectively serve the many" (Howard, 2007, p. 7)

Teachers who possess these dispositional capacities are likely to develop a transformationalist teacher identity (Howard, 2006, 2016) through which teachers know themselves, know their practice, and know their students. This triumvirate underlies frequently cited multicultural instructional approaches such as culturally relevant teaching (Ladson-Billings, 1995), culturally responsive pedagogy (Gay, 2000), and culturally sustaining pedagogy (Paris, 2012)—all of which emphasize the importance of teachers' awareness of how their own identities intersect with those of their students. Such awareness has implications for how teachers conceptualize knowledge and the knowledge-building process, for how they develop and utilize curriculum, for pedagogical decision-making, and for how they view their professional role and responsibilities.

Teachers with multicultural dispositions as described by Howard are likely to cultivate their own and their students' *conscientização,* or *critical consciousness* (Freire, 1970, 1973). Teachers with well-developed critical consciousness understand that how one engages with the world is dependent upon social position. Further, they know how power works both structurally and interpersonally to maintain hierarchies between social groups. Multicultural teachers view themselves as change agents who develop students' ability to critically evaluate the world around them, to challenge their own and others' thinking, and to reject all forms of oppression.

Fostering critical consciousness requires that teachers be equity-minded and possess the following dispositions in addition to those listed earlier:

Beliefs
 – diversity is an asset and resource
 – knowledge is cocreated
 – if uninterrupted, schools are sites of social and cultural reproduction

Values
 – democracy
 – resistance
 – affective learning experiences
 – equity
 – authenticity
 – self-awareness

Attitudes
 – empathy
 – cultural humility
 – hope
 – love

When teachers operate through a lens of equity, they will:

- embrace counter narratives
- diversify the curriculum
- unveil the hidden curriculum
- explicitly teach the culture of power
- mine knowledge from children
- engage in critical reflection
- use dialogue as a primary pedagogical method
- problem pose
- invite critical (i.e., hot-topic) conversations

Collectively, these multicultural dispositions and their related ped-agogical practices speak to a teacher's willingness to give each student what they individually need to succeed in school. DuBois (1935) called this "sympathetic touch," that emerges when teachers use education as means to challenge oppression while simultaneously promoting students' cultural identities. Others label such teachers as "warm demanders" (E. Bondy & Ross, 2008; Ware, 2006) who balance high expectations with genuine concern for students' well-being.

Multicultural attitudes are at the core of teachers' ability to use a sympathetic touch when working with students whose social, emotional, and academic needs may not be met by traditional schooling practices. Being empathetic facilitates humane educational processes through which teachers take students' social and emotional perspectives and teach from a place of compassion instead of power (Bonner et al., 2018). Similarly, a teacher with cultural humility develops interpersonal relationships that acknowledge, respect, and value cultural differences, which increases their ability to notice inequities as embedded within schooling processes, not people (van Es et al., 2017).

In acknowledging that education is structured to reproduce inequities, teachers should also recognize what Freire calls the pedagogy of possibility (McLaren, 1999). What could happen if we were no longer constrained by oppressive social factors? Teachers should intend to disrupt inequities through their teaching and foster a sense of hope for students whom the systems consistently fails. Teachers with critical hope are committed to improving their craft so they can mitigate power imbalances and affect change at both the classroom and system level.

The final and most important attitude teachers must have is a spirit of love. Students bring their home lives to school every day in their dress, their mood, their behaviors. Deep knowledge about, and positive perceptions of, the neighborhood are prerequisites for asset-based teaching. Many teachers, particularly those in rural and urban schools, choose to live in other communities because the school neighborhood lacks amenities (e.g., gyms, cafes, parks, shopping), is perceived to be unsafe, and/or doesn't offer desirable housing (Boyd et al., 2011). When teachers are unfamiliar with, or worse, have disdain for the school community, it is almost certain that such negativity will carry over to the children who call that community home. When teachers take pride in being a member of the school community, they will view their students not only as pupils, but as neighbors with shared investment in school and community welfare.

THOUGHTS FROM THE FIELD

My job there was to make sure that we hired teachers that were in love with the community, in love with the kids, and of course in love with the content, but that was secondary. I would tell my teachers the first week, "Don't even go over content. Get to know your kids. Find out everything about your kids this first week. You need to know every kid by name and need, every kid." If I can find teachers that are in love with the community and love the kids, I can teach you content enrichment. If you can't connect with the kids, I don't care how much content you know, you're not going to do well. The kids will know it. You can't fake kids out. They know.

Dr. Houser

A communal sense of belonging is necessary for teachers and students to overcome the divides that social identity theory tells us are natural. When teachers and students view themselves as belonging to the same social group, they will develop mutually agreed upon social norms to guide their intragroup behaviors. We see this occur when white teachers of BISOC have positive teacher–student relationships grounded in a sense of trust reflected in students' behavior, their academic engagement, and their overall enthusiasm for learning.

When teachers have positive multicultural dispositions, they are more likely to utilize inclusive teaching methods, have positive self-efficacy for teaching diverse students, and have higher overall student achievement than teachers with absent or negative ideas about the intersection of social identities and schools (Emdin, 2016; Hachfeld et al., 2015; L. G. Kahn et al., 2014). Villegas and Lucas (2002) also found that multicultural beliefs were related to sociocultural consciousness, cultural and racial affirmation, and teachers' perception of their responsibility and agency for educational equity. It is clear all teachers, but especially those of minoritized students, must have positive multicultural dispositions if they are to be effective educators and change agents.

Interviewing for Equity

Research demonstrates that preservice teachers often possess negative beliefs about minoritized students (Kumar & Hamer, 2013), have low expectations for students of color (Glock, 2016), and don't believe in the value of culturally responsive teaching (Rizutto, 2017). It is prudent to spend time during the hiring process assessing teachers' multicultural dispositions as separate from the teaching practices they engender. You want to uncover the why behind their teaching, so you should develop a series of critical questions that reveal underlying cognitions. A single question about teaching diverse students cannot possibly yield enough information to assess a potential teacher's ability to diversify the curriculum, employ culturally responsive classroom management strategies, or build effective home–school partnerships with families.

Multicultural dispositions can be hard to accurately assess because teachers know that in a system where over 50% of students identify as culturally or linguistically diverse, they must at least appear to be open minded and welcoming of diversity when interviewing. But when teachers don't truly have positive multicultural dispositions, they will inevitably slip into "niceness" and describe themselves as fair, objective, and invested in equality.

Buzz words are red flags during the interview process. Fair does not exist in a schooling system that demonizes racially minoritized children as young as three years old. Fair cannot exist in a schooling system that privileges white, middle-class ways of being and knowing. Fair will not exist as long as schools maintain alleged neutral positions when it comes to issues of racism, classism, sexism, and ableism. Working toward equality only shifts the finishing line without attending to starting positions nor obstacles in the lane.

ADVICE FROM THE FIELD: HOW TO IDENTIFY EQUITY-MINDED TEACHERS IN AN INTERVIEW

What I do is look at equity through all of the responses that they give me. I look through the threads to say, if I ask them a question about data, did they ever say anything about disaggregated data and how to address data of special education or Black or Brown or white or free-and-reduced lunch students? They didn't say anything about that. That's a red flag for me. Or when I ask them about their lesson plans, they didn't really say anything about finding culturally responsive texts. They just said, "read it from the curriculum." And we all know the curriculum is not culturally responsive.

Additionally, I use scenario questions to see how they would process things. An example scenario question that we had is, "The power in your school goes out. You're in the middle of teaching a lesson. The principal gets on the intercom and says that students will remain in the building for the next three hours. What do you do?"

Some folks will just say, "Oh, well, we can play games." That's not the response I want to hear. We have an achievement gap.

Our Black and Brown kids aren't reading at the levels of anyone else, and we're going to play a game? We've got to teach through it. A lot of our folks that we've hired have said, "Okay. Well, I'm going to open up the blinds. I'm going to reassure my kids. We're going to pull out white boards and we're going to make it happen." Because our kids must have that. Our kids can't take wasted days. I don't care if there's power or not, or no water, we've got to continue to work. We've got to continue to have our kids achieve.

That's the biggest piece. That's that equity piece there, to be able to say, yes, our kids go through a lot in their lives. We're not making excuses for them and we're not going to say, "Oh, it's okay, baby." No, we're going to acknowledge the situation we're in and we're going to teach them how to navigate those problems. We're safe. We're moving forward.

Principal Lewis

A thorough interview such as the one just described will give teachers the opportunity to demonstrate their awareness of privilege and oppression, of how sociocultural differences emerge in classrooms, and of how they view their responsibility to disrupt inequitable schooling. Interview questions should be open ended so that teachers are not led to certain answers. Don't provide a rationale or context for questions as interviewees will interpret questions through their own cultural lens, which will provide deep insight into their multicultural teaching philosophy. For example, if you ask an applicant to define diversity, listen carefully to whom they describe as diverse and what characteristics make them diverse. Most people think of diversity solely in terms of race and language, but teachers must understand that students can possess many invisible minoritized identities including those related to gender, sexuality, religion, income, geography, and cognitive and physical abilities, among others.

How teachers speak about students can reveal their beliefs about students. When they talk about diverse students do they say "them" or "those"? Do they frame minoritized identities through a deficit lens and discuss what students lack instead of what they can contribute? Do they view diverse students as exotic beings from whom they can learn new things (particularly related to language, food, music, and other indicators of culture)? Here are a few suggestions that can help uncover a potential teacher's multicultural dispositions:

- Give scenarios and ask the applicant to explain what they would do in that instance. It is best to use a real scenario from your own school (while keeping people anonymous!) to assess how well an applicant's initial instincts align with existing policies and procedures. The scenario should be one that requires quick decision-making (something related to classroom management is a good idea). What would a teacher do if a student were sleeping in class, arguing with a classmate, or being generally disruptive? If their first instinct is to call a school resource officer or remove the student from the classroom, this teacher may not have a comprehensive understanding of the role teachers play in the school-to-prison pipeline.
- Ask questions that require them to take a minoritized student's perspective, such as "What types of struggles might students who are refugees experience in the classroom?" Questions like these provide insight into how much teachers know about students' out-of-school life contexts. It also speaks to their empathy and could possibly expose asset- or deficit-based attitudes.
- Encourage applicants to explain how they adjust their teaching depending upon the student demographic in the classroom. This gives them the opportunity to reject notions of color blindness and equality by explicitly describing their expectations for students' learning and their instructional approach when working with diverse students.
- Invite them to describe their personal attributes that will make them effective at your school. Their choice of adjectives will reveal how they view their teacher role *in relation* to students. Listen for the multicultural dispositions just listed. Don't be swayed by common descriptors such as "passionate" and "caring"; wait for

them to translate those adjectives to verbs during their teaching demonstration.

- Instead of asking why they want to teach, ask them to describe their pathway into teaching. Here you get information not only about their teaching motivations but also their dedication to becoming an effective teacher and their commitment to the profession. Teachers who invest in their own career development (e.g., through teacher preparation programs, by substitute teaching, as a paraprofessional) have deeper knowledge of what it takes to be an effective teacher than do those who choose to teach as a backup or stopgap job. Teaching is a difficult profession. Teaching for equity is impossible if you cannot anticipate the difficulties.

All of these questions do not need to be asked in a single ping-pong style interview (i.e., back-and-forth question and answer). Interviews should be scheduled for at least half a day to provide ample opportunity to assess an applicant as they engage with potential students and colleagues in different settings. The interview day should include:

- school tour
- a classroom observation
- lunch in the cafeteria
- teaching demonstration (at least 30 minutes in an existing class)
- meetings with school leaders, teachers, and support staff

If possible and age appropriate, candidates should spend time with students. There really is no better way to assess how well a potential teacher will interact with students than to observe them doing so. This can be an informal luncheon, a mock class session, or a formal student-led interview (be sure someone helps them write the questions). Children are comfortable giving candid feedback and will often say the very things adults are reluctant to say. Students can be your biggest asset in the hiring process if you integrate them meaningfully and take their feedback seriously.

Compare students' comments with your own and staff's perceptions of applicants. It is not uncommon for teachers to say and do things with students that they wouldn't say or do with colleagues. Pay close attention to how well their words match their teaching practices. A 30-minute teaching demonstration in someone else's classroom with unfamiliar students is not the best measure of a teacher's instructional potential. What it is however, is a decent measure of their interpersonal skills. Do they make an effort to learn students' names during their short demonstration? Do they share anything about themselves or just start teaching? Did they do any research on the school or neighborhood to make their lesson personally relevant to students?

As reviewed in Chapter 5, teacher–student relationships are at the core of inclusive instruction. A comprehensive interview must center teachers' ability to develop and sustain meaningful relationships with students, which will only be possible if they actually *like* their students. Integrating a careful examination of teachers' multicultural dispositions will help you determine if and to what extent, teachers believe their students are worth investing in.

Reflection Questions

1. Translate the dispositions reviewed in this chapter into concrete practices. How do these practices change based upon students' sociocultural identities?
2. What does having a transformationalist teacher identity mean to you?
3. How does niceness contribute to whiteness?
4. What is the purpose of school? How do you work toward that purpose in your daily duties?
5. How does sympathy differ from sympathetic touch?
6. Why is being empathetic toward students more equitable than being sympathetic toward students?
7. What is one question you could ask potential teachers to ascertain their multicultural dispositions?

7 Welcoming New Teachers

With the hard work of hiring equity-minded teachers behind you, the task now is to bring them into the school community efficiently and effectively. Just as students are nervous about making new friends, getting to know their teachers, and doing well in school, so are new teachers. Even veteran teachers with years of experience get anxious upon arrival at a new school because they are unfamiliar with the people, the practices, and the expectations. In other words, they are not a member of the in-group yet.

New teachers bring with them norms of prior schools or of their teacher preparation program that may not align with those of their new school. Do teachers arrive early and stay late? Do they share materials and collaborate on lesson plans? Are teachers truly friends or just colleagues? Teachers' experiences often conflict with what people say about a school, so instead of telling teachers what to expect in their new community, show them.

Welcoming new teachers occurs through two programs that are often conflated: orientation and induction. *Orientation* is when new teachers are introduced to the school. *Induction* is how they are integrated into the school. In this chapter I utilize social identity theory (SIT) and self-efficacy theory (Bandura, 1997) to inform the design of orientation and induction programs that support new teacher success and retention.

New Teacher Orientation

The first sign that new teacher orientation is actually new teacher instruction is when the district, not the school, hosts orientation. District-wide orientations occur at off-site locations during the week before school and consist of 2 or 3 full-day (8 a.m.–3 p.m.) presentations where teachers passively listen to lectures from district administrators whom they may or may not ever see again. There is a strict agenda of sessions guided by a district-provided checklist of how-to items (building access, purchase requests, technology use), information items (safety plans, class schedule, dress code, leave policies), expectation items (curriculum, state tests, evaluation procedures, supervision duties), and instructional practice items (lesson planning, grading, taking attendance, monitoring student progress). If teachers are fortunate to do anything active, it is filling out paperwork and participating in state-mandated trainings.

It is ironic that it is educators who design such a boring curriculum and who utilize ineffective instructional strategies. There is no way for a new teacher, who may also be a novice teacher, to process so much information in such a short amount of time. District-led orientations leave little space for teachers to meet colleagues, learn about their school, or to hear about the students they will soon encounter. They cannot familiarize themselves with the neighborhood, their building, or their classroom when they are sitting in a hotel ballroom 20 minutes away from their school.

A one-size-fits-all model is efficient but certainly not equitable. Teacher orientations must address teachers' specific needs as they relate to their position, their students, and their school. Orientation is the first part of a multiyear induction program and should therefore give teachers a broad overview of what they can personally and professionally expect in the next few years.

Effective Orientation Programs

The first point to clarify is that new teacher orientation is a program, not a training or a workshop. Trainings teach attendees about a new policy, process, or product, but without the opportunity to develop skills or utilize new information. They tend to be unidirectional, with information flowing from the presenter to the audience. A workshop is also a single session with an instructional purpose, but it is more interactive than a training, as it includes whole and small group discussions and activities. Most workshop time is spent in hands-on learning where participants work collaboratively to generate a final product (e.g., revised lesson plan, list of learning outcomes, ideas for engaging families).

A program is a set of structured activities over the course of days, weeks, months, or years. Each session within a program has its own format, goals, and participants. Program design is similar to curriculum design where participants' learning is scaffolded toward a larger outcome. Orientation programs are paced such that new teachers are not overwhelmed with information and can experience a good mix of activities that keep them engaged.

The difficulty in designing new teacher orientation is finding a balance between being too broad and too specific. Teachers should definitely hear about the school's vision and mission and be encouraged to reflect on how the core values emerge in their professional practice. They should learn about school policies and the logistics of their daily work. But all of that can be provided in a digital handbook for teachers to consult at their leisure. Orientation should be a time for interpersonal interactions so that teachers can *experience* the school culture.

When asked about the ideal orientation program, teachers want position-specific support, such as clarification about job expectations, suggestions for classroom management and family engagement strategies, advice on time management, and help with lesson planning (Algozzine et al., 2007; S. M. Johnson & Kardos, 2002). An effective orientation program meets these needs by building teachers' capacities, confidence, and sense of community.

Programmatic Elements. Orientation provides an annual opportunity for the school community to recommit to the vision and mission. Communicate to families that they are welcome at the school and encouraged to participate in their child's learning however they see fit. Show students that you are excited they chose your school and that you can't wait to get to know them better. Remind current staff of their accomplishments and contributions to the school thus far. Assure new teachers that their presence is an added value to the school.

It is the latter goal that is perhaps most difficult but most necessary to achieve. New teachers are understandably anxious and sometimes lack the self-efficacy beliefs that give them confidence to do their job. Self-efficacy describes what people think about their ability to perform certain tasks, which influences their willingness to do it and how well they do it. Positive (or high) beliefs yield successful task performance which then, through a feedback loop, further strengthens efficacy beliefs. Novice teachers sometimes have low self-efficacy for instruction, classroom management, and student engagement (Hoy & Spero, 2005). A carefully designed orientation program will increase teachers' efficacy via four sources:

1. Performance accomplishments: prior experience doing a task
2. Vicarious experience: watching similar others complete a task you haven't done before
3. Verbal persuasion: what knowledgeable others tell you about your ability to complete a task
4. Physiological arousal: your emotional state when thinking about doing a task

Each of these sources are methods of validating new teachers' presence in the school community. Orientation should include structured time for teachers to practice doing elements of their job, opportunities to observe other teachers, confirmation of their competencies, and emotional support. I suggest a four-pronged approach of capacity building, confidence building, and team building, which collectively facilitate community building.

Capacity building occurs through workshops where teachers are taught specific practices they will be expected to utilize in their position. Workshops could address the areas in which research reveals teachers feel inadequately prepared, such as social and emotional learning, multicultural teaching, trauma-informed teaching, assessment, and implementing 504s, IEPs, and BIPs (Ciganek, 2020; Dunks, 2018; J. L. Johnson, 2020; King & Butler, 2015). They might also address teachers' fears as they relate to interacting with students and families, creating a work–life balance, and avoiding professional burnout (Ozmantar, 2019). Specific workshop topics should be chosen in collaboration with new teachers given their job expectations and concerns. Table 7.1 contains workshop ideas labeled with an "L" for learning because workshops are where teachers learn the norms of the school through verbal persuasion.

Learning sessions are followed by working sessions (labeled with a "W" in Table 7.1) when teachers develop skills by practicing the strategies they learned in the workshop. Working sessions should immediately follow learning sessions so there is no opportunity for teachers to forget new information. Note that working sessions are facilitated by instructional coaches or mentor teachers in small groups or pairs because new teachers need to practice skills in low-threat environments where they can get feedback in a nonevaluative manner. Smaller groups also allow facilitators to differentiate according to each teacher's needs. Working sessions are perhaps the most important component of new teacher orientation because this is when teachers rehearse doing their actual job and develop confidence in their abilities.

Potentially high-stress working sessions should be balanced by more casual social sessions (indicated by an "S" in Table 7.1). However, these are not social in the sense that teachers are socializing with one another outside of school but in that they are building their social network within the school. Structured social sessions expose new teachers to colleagues who share advice and guidance. These interactions are the vicarious experiences new teachers need as they develop self-efficacy beliefs. Social sessions are team-building opportunities where teachers get to know one another and their working styles as a start to a collaborative professional relationship.

The Principal's Role in Orientation

The effectiveness of each session is largely dependent upon how the principal designs new teacher orientation and whom they choose

Table 7.1 Sample New Teacher Orientation Agenda			
DAY 1			
What	**Why**	**Who**	**When**
Speed-dating (S)	Meet and greet	Teachers, leaders, staff	8:30 A.M.–9:15 A.M.
Anti-oppressive teaching workshop (L)	Identify how power emerges in schools	Teachers, leaders, staff	9:20 A.M.–10:35 A.M.
Developing culturally responsive lessons (W)	Learn how to write equitable lesson plans and decolonize the curriculum	New teachers and instructional coach (small groups)	10:40 A.M.–12:00 P.M.
DAY 2			
What	**Why**	**Who**	**When**
Classroom management workshop (L)	Review PBIS, restorative justice, trauma-sensitive teaching	Teachers, leaders, staff	8:30 A.M.–9:45 A.M.
Classroom management practice (W)	Practice strategies	New teachers and mentor teacher (pairs)	9:50 A.M.–11:10 A.M.
Teacher panels (S)	Learn about school, students, and job expectations	Teachers, leaders, staff	11:15 A.M.–12:00 P.M.
DAY 3			
What	**Why**	**Who**	**When**
Strengths finders (S)	Identify individual and group working styles	Teachers, leaders, staff	8:30 A.M.–9:15 A.M.
Goal setting (W)	Draft a professional development plan	New teachers and mentor teacher (pairs)	9:20 A.M.–10:35 A.M.
Community resource scavenger hunt (L)	Get to know the community	Teachers, leaders, staff	10:40 A.M.–12:00 P.M.
DAY 4			
What	**Why**	**Who**	**When**

(Optional)	Preparation	Teachers, leaders, staff	8:30 A.M.–3:00 P.M. (flexible)
1:1s with Principal	Review/expand professional development plan	Teachers and principal	45-minute intervals
Open house	Meet students/families	All school	5:00 P.M.–7:00 P.M.

DAY 5 (SATURDAY)			
What	**Why**	**Who**	**When**
Open House	Meet students/families	All school	11:00 A.M.–1:00 P.M.

among current staff to participate. Table 7.1 illustrates a program that is spread over the course of a week of mostly half days to make sure teachers are not overwhelmed. Optional afternoons in addition to an optional full day give teachers freedom and flexibility to prepare for school as they'd like, concurrent with orientation. The program concludes with two open houses scheduled on separate days to accommodate families' schedules.

Sessions are short enough to sustain attention but long enough for appropriate breadth and depth of engagement. Learning and working sessions are longer than social sessions, which suggests to new teachers that praxis is a priority at this school. Content choices convey a social justice–oriented school culture, investment in professional development, and a commitment to community and family partnerships. One-on-one meetings with the principal demonstrate the principal's personal investment in the staff.

It is a good idea to ask teachers to prepare for these meetings by doing a self-assessment of their competencies and working style. Returning teachers should have meetings with other leaders such as the assistant principal or a department chair that are grounded in their most recent evaluation. In a 45-minute meeting with new teachers, principals should:

- explain the mission, vision, and core values in relation to day-to-day activities and processes
- review the school's organizational structure and reporting lines
- review job expectations
- highlight important policies
- explain evaluation processes
- set goals for the year
- create a long-term career map and professional development plan
- assign each teacher a role in the educational equity action plan
- explain the induction program
- determine personal preferences for coaches and mentors (e.g., gender, working style)

Effective one-on-one meetings can demystify school norms, clarify professional expectations, and communicate a belief in teachers' future success. These conversations should ultimately resolve teachers' fears and anxieties (i.e., decrease physiological arousal) and affirm their place in their new social group.

Each aspect of orientation supports new teachers' professional development while simultaneously building social cohesion. Orientation is the time for teachers to learn how the school defines itself, its priorities, goals, values, and most importantly, their personal role in, and responsibility to, the school community. At the end of orientation, it should be clear that in this school, teachers:

- have open lines of communication among themselves and with leadership
- can give feedback to leadership without fear of reprisal
- feel comfortable speaking up
- have the freedom to create their own professional learning communities that function autonomously
- know the principal supports them
- are invited to share ideas
- embrace a spirit of praxis through critical inquiry

- collaborate with one another
- care about and for one another

Integrating New Teachers

Novice teachers report feeling abandoned and isolated when orientation ends and the school year begins (Voss & Kunter, 2020). The enthusiasm and energy they experienced in orientation is redirected to students, often leaving new teachers on their own to sink or swim, experiencing emotional exhaustion and reality shock. This explains why on average, 10% of teachers leave the profession after their first year (Gray & Taie, 2015). The COVID-19 pandemic may temporarily inflate these numbers as two to three cohorts of novice teachers experienced at least some of their teacher training in a virtual environment. These teachers may be unaware of the full range of professional responsibilities of in-person schooling and may feel overwhelmed by job expectations.

Teacher attrition can be mitigated by a well-developed induction program that gradually increases teachers' independence over their first 2 years. Integrating new members into an existing group is complicated because of the nuances of intragroup functioning. The school culture, while driven by the vision and mission, is maintained by implicit norms that everyone seems to know but that no one talks about. Do teachers chat in the hallway between periods or use those 5 minutes to hastily prepare for the next class? Is the teachers' lounge a place for quiet work and relaxation or is it the social hub of the school? It may not seem like a big deal if a new teacher is never in the hallway between classes or chooses to eat lunch alone, but these nonprofessional metrics are often used to determine how well a new teacher "fits" in the school. If other teachers perceive their colleague as violating group norms, it is unlikely that they will invite professional collaboration or offer support.

A proper induction program anticipates these difficulties by scaffolding teachers' integration into the school. Most induction programs are 2 to 3 years as data suggests that teachers become "effective" in year 4 (Podolsky et al., 2019). A multiyear program makes sense as teachers spend their first 3 years developing and refining their instructional practices, familiarizing themselves with standards and the curriculum, and developing their professional identity. Even experienced teachers need a grace period to redefine themselves, given the social context of a new school. The ideal induction program would last 4 or 5 years: longer than the 3-year timetable in which many teachers leave.

Effective Induction Programs

Research demonstrates that high-quality induction programs that yield teacher retention are comprehensive, structured, rigorous, and closely monitored (Ingersoll, 2012). They often include mentoring and coaching, a focus on continued professional learning (discussed in Chapter 8), and the explicit cultivation of school belonging (Watkins, 2005; Wong, 2004). Vonk (1995) identified three dimensions of novice teachers' professional development that inform induction program design: ecological/organizational, personal/emotional, and professional knowledge and skills.

Ecological/Organizational. In Chapter 2 (organizational structure) and Chapter 3 (organizational practices), we discussed how a leader creates a school culture aligned with the school's vision, mission, and core values. In Chapter 4 (schools, communities, and families), we identified how the school operates within students' microsystems to shape learning and development. Teachers' professional practice is also shaped by elements embedded within the microsystem of the school including the broad structure and daily practices, as well as more-implicit factors like personal ideologies, interpersonal interactions, and even linguistic codes. SIT suggests that to successfully integrate into the group, new members must agree with, adopt, and adhere to group norms. But this does not always happen, as teachers may not be aware of group norms, they may conflict with personal norms, or they might not be able to enact norms.

Teachers may therefore choose to adapt to school norms, if only temporarily. New teachers are willing to change their instructional practices, use provided curriculum, and organize their classroom according to school norms. But they are less likely to change explicit behaviors (e.g., standing for the pledge of allegiance), utilize language (e.g., label minoritized students "at risk"), or embrace perspectives that conflict with personal values and beliefs (e.g., that lowering expectations will increase student achievement) (Whitaker, n.d. [in progress]). In some circumstances, teachers may be completely unwilling to acquiesce to job expectations, in which case they reject the school culture and often leave at the end of the school year.

Such a poor fit should have been detected during the hiring process designed in Chapter 6, but when it is not, it does not mean that teachers must leave the school. It takes time for teachers to learn the rationale behind organizational processes. They also need intentional support in finding overlaps between personal and professional identities. As part of induction, teachers should choose one committee on which to serve or one student group to coach or advise to help them find their niche within the school.

ADVICE FROM THE FIELD: HOW TO SUPPORT TEACHERS AND STILL HOLD THEM ACCOUNTABLE

A lot of it is being really clear about what the mission and vision of the school is. It is about giving them opportunities to be involved and helping everyone talk about the mission and vision so that we have the same understanding. Once we've done that work, if people are still saying, "No, I'm not with this," I'm going to give you a year. I'm going to give you a year with me constantly being about the [mission and vision]. So usually in that first year when I'm at a site, I'm listening to everybody, finding out what their experiences are of the school, rolling out the vision and mission based on what they've shared with me, what the data show, and doing that with the leadership team. And then the folks who are not with that vision, I might pull them into my office and have conversations because maybe there's something I don't know, and there often is.

Sometimes I've given people passes once I get to know them and find out what their skill set is. I might give them something that they can do to help develop the school. A lot of times that builds their buy-in. I often find that people are not into things because they have had negative experiences with their school leadership.

After that I can usually cut that number of teachers down to a few folks who are just not with the program. And then I make it really clear: "Look, this is what we're doing this year. You can be with us or you probably will want to find another home if you're not going to be with this." They have some thinking to do about that.

Ms. Fisher

Personal/Emotional Development. It is expected for new teachers to struggle to adjust to their new position. Novice teachers especially find it difficult to transition from the student role to the teacher role. They may overidentify with their students, want to be viewed as a friend, or be uncomfortable being an authority figure. They may also find that who they thought they'd be as a teacher is not who they actually are or can be, due to professional constraints. Many new teachers experience disidentification that requires them to consciously rebuild their professional identity in accordance with unforeseen expectations and responsibilities. This can be an extremely stressful process for teachers who may have spent years imagining, or for veteran teachers, building their professional identity.

Self-constructions are further complicated by how others perceive you. New teachers may feel like they don't fit in with their colleagues or that they aren't connecting with students as they'd hoped. If they are from a different cultural background, it may be difficult to find common ground in this new social environment. Many teachers are reluctant to share emotional and social concerns out of embarrassment or the belief that they need to manage things on their own. This often results in new teachers overcompensating by taking on extra responsibilities to prove their professional capability.

Such choices are concerning because teaching is a high-stakes career where small decisions can have disproportionate impacts on students. It is understandable, then, that new teachers might get overwhelmed by the weight of their responsibilities and the minutiae of daily tasks. Induction programs must include an emotionally supportive space where teachers can unpack their affective experience. Importantly, this space should be limited to new teachers who are having similar experiences that promote empathy and compassion, and decrease judgment.

Professional Knowledge and Skills. Traditional induction programs tend to focus on building teachers' professional capacities but without fully anticipating the breadth of their needs. Effective teaching requires content knowledge (including knowledge of child development), pedagogical knowledge, and pedagogical skills. The former is often erroneously assumed because of licensing requirements, especially for secondary teachers. But passing the praxis does not mean that teachers have extensive content knowledge, or if they do, that they understand their content from multiple perspectives. Most teachers are taught through a Eurocentric curriculum in K–12 as well as in their teaching training. If they have not taken steps to develop a multicultural understanding of their content, it is unlikely that they will have the breadth and depth of content knowledge to fill curricular gaps.

Teachers' pedagogical knowledge is also largely dependent upon what they experienced in their preparation program and during their teaching practicum. Many teacher preparation programs still frame teaching as a checklist of best practices that are universally acceptable and effective. Teacher educators and mentor or cooperating teachers often endorse trendy instructional methods that may be unrelated to child development and brain processing, or that are unfeasible given practical constraints (e.g., flipped classroom). The haste to graduate teachers who can fill national shortages further contributes to inadequate content coverage in teacher training where preservice teachers are introduced to instructional frameworks (e.g., Universal Design for Learning [UDL]), but are not taught how to implement them.

Pedagogical skills are the area in which novice teachers report feeling most deficient (Klassen & Chui, 2010), not because they necessarily are deficient but because what they learned in their teacher preparation program may not be aligned with what is expected of them in their new school. Knowledge and skill gaps can be addressed through coaching and mentoring programs that form the core of induction. However, research on the efficacy of teacher mentoring is varied, indicating that for most new teachers, mentoring is a hit-or-miss experience. Chief among mentees' complaints is that mentor teachers are unavailable, not in their content area or grade level, or that mentoring meetings are random and too often dependent upon the mentee's initiative (Wynn et al., 2007). Most mentoring programs lack structure and intentionality. Appropriate mentoring programs contain the following:

- a clear purpose
- specific roles
- commitments from all parties
- a schedule of interactions
- a guiding curriculum
- intentional mentor/mentee matches
- facilitated communication between parties
- flexibility

I further suggest multipronged mentoring where mentees are paired with more than one mentor with different expertise. For instance, new teachers are often assigned a mentor teacher who is expected to holistically support their mentee regardless of their own (in)abilities and professional responsibilities. Instead, new teachers should have a network of mentors who offer strategic support:

> Mentor: Provides global support by acting as a think partner and sounding board, assisting with career planning, providing encouragement and guidance; focused on short and long-term personal fulfillment.

> Instructional coach: Gives pedagogical support through teaching observations, oral and written feedback, assistance with curricular and lesson planning, and advice as needed; focused on short-term professional success.

> Teacher cohort: Offers emotional support through casual conversations; focused on short-term personal welfare.

> Principal: Supplies professional support through teaching observations, oral and written feedback, determining and

fulfilling professional development needs; focused on long-term professional success.

Mentor networks ensure that new teachers always have access to a resource and that they receive comprehensive support. Additionally, by connecting them to a variety of people, new teachers have entry into multiple social groups within the school.

The Principal's Role in Induction

Induction programs are critical to teacher retention because they are the filter through which teachers interpret their experiences. All teachers struggle in their first year at a new school, but teachers who receive support through induction are less likely to leave the school and the profession (Ronfeldt & McQueen, 2017). But it is not the mere presence of support that makes teachers stay; it is the breadth of support, their access to supportive resources, and the consistency of the support that maintains teachers' positive efficacy beliefs. Principals are responsible for creating the work conditions in which new teachers are inundated with supports. The leadership styles presented in Chapter 2 can help you think through how to activate the organizational structure to foster comprehensive care of and for new teachers.

Table 7.2 Sample Year 1 Induction Program Schedule				
	Quarter 1	**Quarter 2**	**Quarter 3**	**Quarter 4**
Instructional Coach	3 observations 1 meeting/week	3 observations 2 meetings/month (1 group)	2 observations 1 meeting/month (1 group)	2 observations 2 meetings (1 group)
Mentor	2 meetings/month	1 meeting/month	1 meeting/month	1 meeting/month
Principal	2 observations	1 observation	1 observation	2 observations
Cohort	3 meetings	2 meetings	2 meetings	2 meetings
Professional Development	2 sessions/month	2 sessions/month	2 sessions/month	2 sessions/month

Table 7.2 reflects a Year 1 induction program schedule where teachers routinely meet with their instructional coach, mentor, teacher cohort, and principal. There is also structured time for professional development and scheduled teaching observations, followed by small group and individual feedback meetings.

The utility of those meetings is largely dependent upon coaches' ability to provide constructive feedback and mentors' ability to cultivate strong interpersonal relationships. Choosing coaches and mentors for the induction program is one of the most important decisions a principal can make. Appropriate instructional coaches should, of course, be excellent teachers with high student achievement, deep pedagogical knowledge, good classroom management skills, and strong teacher–student relationships. But they should also be compassionate and positive, and have good communication skills as well as an interest in contributing to other teachers' professional growth.

Identifying good mentors is more difficult given the social and emotional nature of mentoring relationships. While doing your best to honor teachers' mentor preferences, keep in mind that SIT tells us that good matches are facilitated by cultural congruence, similar worldview, and mutual experiences. As discussed in Chapter 5, this does not necessarily mean that you should match people based upon race, language, or other cultural factors. What matters more for this relationship is shared beliefs about teaching and students, comparable ideas about the purpose of school, and overlap in professional experiences.

Mentor matches won't always be perfect, so they should be closely monitored in Year 1 of the program. Year 2 matches will be determined in consultation with teachers, who by then, will have preferences for coaches and mentors. The Year 2 induction curriculum should also be tailored to each teacher given their experiences during Year 1.

Across both years there are few things to remember to optimize program effectiveness:

- Make certain new teachers experience success (i.e., no out-of-field teaching assignments, especially challenging classes, or expectations of pedagogical innovation).
- Give teachers time to develop.

- Remain available and present for teachers, coaches, and mentors.
- Consistently evaluate program outcomes.

Perhaps the most important thing for you to remember is that teaching is cognitively, psychologically, and emotionally difficult. It is easy to address the former but more critical to remain cognizant of the latter. Effective teachers are happy teachers whose job satisfaction is largely driven by their perception of professional support (Carver-Thomas & Darling-Hammond, 2019). Taking the time to provide tailored orientation and induction programs early in teachers' careers goes a long way to increasing the longevity of their careers.

Reflection Questions

1. What does equity look like when applied to orientation and induction program design?
2. Building upon your answer to reflection Question 1 at the end of Chapter 6, which practices should be prioritized in new teacher orientation? Why?
3. Which of the four sources of self-efficacy are most important to address during a teacher's first 3 years to improve retention? Why?
4. Given what you read in Chapter 5, how important is it for new teachers to have colleagues with similar sociocultural backgrounds? What might happen if a teacher is "the only"?
5. How does this chapter apply to welcoming new families into the school community?

Part III

Sustaining Equity

STICKING WITH SHELBY

In year 2, Shelby was able to participate in a Grow-Your-Own teacher pipeline program through her continued partnership with the local university. The program recruits students from the local high school into the teacher preparation program at the university, with the goal of placing them in neighborhood schools upon college graduation. Additionally, Shelby worked with the district to secure a grant from a nonprofit organization that provides Black teachers with $10,000 of supplemental income for their first three years in the classroom. These partnerships allowed Shelby to hire three new staff members and replace three staff members who left the school at the end of year 1. The new employees included a Latinx school counselor, two Black teachers, one Asian teacher, one white teacher, and one Latinx community outreach coordinator.

While Shelby is excited by her diverse pool of new hires and knows they will bring much-needed equity mindsets to the staff, she is concerned about their longevity at Roger Gates. During orientation it became clear that these new teachers bring with them an awareness of equity considerations that her veteran teachers do not share. Finding effective mentor pairings and willing instructional coaches remains a hurdle in the induction program because despite liking one another personally, the novice and veteran teachers are not speaking the same professional language.

In fact, when ascertaining their interest in serving as mentors and instructional coaches, the veteran teachers explicitly stated that they probably couldn't help the newer teachers with inclusive practices because they do not truly understand what "inclusion" means in the context of their daily duties. They further explained that because there is no expectation for them to utilize multicultural teaching practices, they do not independently seek professional development in that area. Almost everyone agreed that because the school had been understaffed for the last 3 years, they feel overwhelmed with their current responsibilities and can't imagine having to learn something new on top of everything else.

Shelby feels bad that she's let something as important as inclusive classroom practices go unaddressed for two years, but she reminds herself that she needed the necessary structures to support inclusive instruction before she could implement it. Now, with the appropriate academic framework and at least some equity-oriented staff, she turns her attention to three things she knows will effect meaningful and lasting change at Roger Gates:

1. **Centering equity in instruction.** *While not surprising, it is alarming that veteran teachers at Roger Gates know so little about multicultural teaching. It is unreasonable to hold teachers accountable for expectations they clearly aren't prepared to meet, so Shelby begins to think through a professional development program that can equip everyone with the appropriate knowledge and skills to employ culturally sustaining pedagogical practices.*

2. **Redesigning the teacher evaluation processes.** *Despite an emerging PD program, the truth of the matter is that not everyone will effectively center equity in the classrooms. The teachers made it clear that unless equity is a part of their evaluation criteria, they have little motivation to change their teaching. Shelby hopes these negative attitudes will change as teachers experience their PD, but if not, she knows that she needs to revise the evaluation criteria if she is going to successfully identify teachers who should stay at Roger Gates and those who should move on.*

3. **Creating career pipelines.** *Already though, Shelby is thinking beyond annual evaluations. Teacher attrition is high nationally, and especially at schools like Roger Gates. It is not enough that Shelby hired diverse staff members; she must keep them. Toward that end, Shelby reflects on her own career path and the factors that encouraged her to stay in the profession. She soon realizes that*

in changing positions every 3–4 years, she always felt challenged and ener-
gized. Now, as a principal, it is her job to make certain her teachers have a simi-
lar professional experience.

Hiring and onboarding teachers, while challenging, is not the biggest staff-ing hurdle. The true difficulty comes in developing and retaining high-quality teachers. Teacher turnover is a serious problem that continues to fuel national shortages in special education, math, science, and English language instruction. Staffing gaps are most keenly felt in the South, in cities, and in high-poverty schools where 4 times as many teachers are uncertified than in non-Title I low-minority schools (Sutcher et al., 2016).

A dwindling teacher workforce is credited to an increased number of students in public schools, generational shifts in career interests, declines in teacher preparation program enrollment, and to an 8% national teacher attrition rate. Attrition is due to a variety of factors, some of which are beyond the principal's control (e.g., salary structures, testing and account-ability pressures, family demands), but many of which, such as professional learning opportunities, instructional leadership, time for collaboration and planning, and decision-making input, are determined by school leaders. This final third of the book uses cognitive role theory (CRT) to help school leaders proactively address turnover by explaining how teachers decide if they will be stayers, movers, or leavers.

Cognitive Role Theory

Cognitive role theory examines what happens after people assume new positions. Whereas organizational role theory (ORT) is about what others tell you your job is within a structure, CRT is about the evolution of people's own understanding of their professional responsibilities as they perform them. Theorists call one's understanding of their position a *role construction*, that is shaped by two factors: (1) the social context of the workplace that gener-ates implicit job expectations, and (2) people's assessment of the alignment between external and internal expectations.

We discussed how school norms can be implicitly communicated to new teachers in Chapter 7. CRT further explains teachers' decisions to adopt, adapt, or reject those norms through a four-step process:

Step 1) Role taking—When considering a new job, you must first interpret what others expect of the role before accepting the position.

Step 2) Role assessment—After starting a job, this is the process through which you evaluate if the job is what you thought it would be.

Step 3) Role conformity—A conscious decision to adhere to unanticipated role expectations.

Step 4) Role performance—The performance of professional duties according to reconciled internal and external expectations.

Each step represents a potential pitfall in a teacher's ability to effectively do their job. For instance, if a new teacher misconstrues job expectations, they will do their job incorrectly until otherwise directed. This can be as simple as failing to take attendance every day or as consequential as administering the wrong assessments. In busy schools where everyone is overwhelmed, such mistakes can go unnoticed until it is too late to correct. What starts as a misunderstanding can have severe long-term consequences if teachers' inaccurate role expectations are not adjusted.

Teachers must then reflect on why there were unforeseen professional responsibilities. Did they misread the job description? Why didn't anyone mention this during the interview or orientation? If there'd been consistent teaching observations, would this have been discovered? Oftentimes however, teachers realize their mistakes before a high-stakes evaluation and seek clarification and support. If the fix is easy, they will change their behaviors accordingly; but if it is not, they may decide against performing their role as externally expected, which can lead to role failure and ultimately, teacher attrition.

The bright side is that school leaders can proactively address each of these through ongoing professional development that promotes role consensus. In the coming chapters we will discuss how to design an equitable professional development program that provides teachers with explicit instruction, low-stakes practice opportunities, as well as formative and summative feedback on their use of newly acquired knowledge and skills. We then spend time determining how to evaluate teachers from an asset-oriented perspective that prioritizes their contributions to the school's vision and their enactment of core values. Following that, in Chapter 10, I challenge you to replace notions of teacher tenure with teacher advancement as we identify strategies for supporting teachers' career development. The final chapter encourages leaders to reflect on their progress toward educational equity through a six-step process for schoolwide assessment.

8 When Professional Learning Communities Aren't Enough (PLCs)

P roperly designed induction programs can keep new teachers from leaving the school within their first couple of years. But what about teachers who've been at the school for a few years, or veteran teachers who've been in the profession for a while? What keeps them from leaving? Reducing teacher churn requires school leaders to maintain a work environment where teachers experience job satisfaction through professional growth and personal happiness. In Chapter 10, we will take a long-term view of supporting teachers' career advancement, but in this chapter, I discuss how school leaders can create opportunities for teachers that can enhance their current effectiveness.

Linda Darling-Hammond and colleagues (2009) found numerous shortcomings of professional development (PD) models across the country, the most egregious of which was not having enough PD. More than half of all teachers who responded to the national Schools and Staffing Survey (SASS) reported receiving fewer than 16 hours of professional development in their content area over the course of 12 months. This is not to say that there weren't more PD experiences, but that teachers perceived those experiences as unrelated to their daily responsibilities. Darling-Hammond found that teachers dislike PD that is not specific to their content and grade, that is short and without extended opportunities for practice, and that does not go into enough depth.

Novice teachers especially struggle with front-loaded PD at the begin of the year that forces them to rebuild their role construction during an already stressful time (Whitaker, n.d. [in progress]). Scheduling problems are then compounded by practical constraints such as a lack of resources with which to implement new strategies, conflicts with existing practices and expectations, or irrelevance to teachers' professional duties (Wei et al., 2010). Even when teachers can utilize what they learned in a recent PD, there are rarely structured opportunities to get feedback or reflect on how well it went. If there is no follow-through, teachers may not perceive the new skill, information, or process as integral to their job expectations. In other words, if the principal or teacher leaders don't care enough to follow up, why should teachers? The answer is that many don't, as teachers report not changing their professional practices despite targeted PD (Fullan, 2007; Hill et al., 2013).

Lack of follow-through is unsurprising because changing behaviors implies that teachers have somehow restructured how they understand their role. But it is unlikely that teachers will do the hard cognitive work of revising job expectations if the PD does not clearly present new expectations, if new expectations conflict with existing expectations, or if the expectations are unrelated to their professional role. Further, if there is no accountability for additional expectations in an already overwhelming job, it makes sense that teachers will save cognitive resources and retain their initial role construction. If principals truly want to build teachers' capacities and effect positive change, PD must clarify, not confuse, role expectations.

Professional Development Models

There are many options when considering how to best reinforce teachers' job expectations while also supporting their ability to meet them. Conventional PD is transmission-based in that the goal is to give teachers new information, knowledge, and skills. In Chapter 7 we discussed the difference between trainings where teachers learn and workshops where they utilize their learning. These are the two most frequent PD formats because they are efficient and effective at conveying large bodies of information to a large group of people. On the downside, trainings and workshops can be too narrow if they prescribe pedagogical templates or too broad if they are not situated within the school and classroom context. Trainings and workshops are best when the goal is for teachers to learn about new resources (e.g., ClassDojo), a process (e.g., conducting three-way conferences), or an instructional strategy (e.g., reciprocal questioning) that they can utilize according to their needs.

The learning outcomes of trainings and workshops are further explored through professional learning communities (PLCs) where teachers engage in ongoing praxis. PLCs are groups of teachers who regularly meet to collaborate on improving their instruction. Oftentimes their meetings are focused on examining student performance data to identify content that needs to be retaught or reinforced, perhaps in new ways. These groups operate differently than the collaborative groups that might haphazardly form in a workshop to complete a directed task. PLCs are long-term, teacher-driven groups that are intentionally structured around a shared professional purpose and a sense of collective responsibility for student learning. Stoll and Seashore Louis (2007) suggest that PLCs include four components: professional learning, collective knowledge, cohesion, and an ethic of interpersonal care. PLCs are a natural extension of first and second year induction cohorts where teachers provide one another with continuing professional and personal support.

THOUGHTS FROM THE FIELD

People tend to think that if you just send somebody to development training then that's going to fix it. No, you need real time development.

That's how development looked. It was beyond going to a conference, it was beyond sitting in a library doing PD, it was real time coaching and mentoring and constant feedback. Even our professional development sessions on campus were geared towards staff needs, and we actually modeled instructional practices in our sessions. We put the objective up the way it's supposed to look in the classroom, and we would name, "Right now, we're going to use a multiple response strategy called concentric circle, and we're going to have a dialogue about X, Y, and Z." So teachers would *practice* new instructional strategies during that PD and get real time feedback from colleagues.

Dr. Carmichael

Dr. Carmichael is describing a whole-school PLC that blends mentoring and coaching with traditional PD sessions. In this model, PD is part of the school culture so it is integrated into daily routines. Teachers can request short-term coverage (often done by the principal or another administrator) so they can observe colleagues, attend nearby trainings, or meet with students and families. Teachers are expected to bring those experiences and insights into whole-school PD sessions for collective analysis. Teachers might also do 3–5 minute "flash" PD presentations during regular staff meetings to share effective strategies. Whole-school PLCs are effective at normalizing continued learning and setting an expectation for collaboration that honors everyone's expertise and empowers them to take ownership of their professional development.

Creative Approaches to Professional Development

Whole-school PLCs are a good way to expand PD beyond in-service days so that teachers can engage in the reflection and dialogue that is integral to learning. Traditional PD models are excellent for adding to teachers' tool kits, but they are not always the best way to actually *develop* teachers' skills. As school enrollments rise and professional demands increase, school leaders must think creatively about how to deliver consistent professional development in an equitable and budget-friendly manner. I suggest a more expansive and comprehensive approach to PD that includes individual, small group, and communal options for teachers.

Individual PD. The most impactful PD, especially early in teachers' careers, occurs at the individual level because teachers have unique strengths and weaknesses that are best addressed individually. In Chapter 7, we reviewed how to design induction programs where teachers receive intensive support from mentors, coaches, colleagues and the principal. While induction programs officially end after 2 or 3 years, the components should continue throughout teachers' careers, but it should be self-directed.

Licensure requirements dictate that teachers earn continuing education credits by attending courses, workshops, or trainings beyond the school. Meeting ongoing requirements is not always teachers' favorite thing to do because it is divorced from their professional context, making it seem like another box they must check rather than a meaningful learning experience. However, principals are well positioned to integrate state licensure requirements into school-based professional development programs.

Instead of sending teachers to random conferences, consider enrolling them in virtual professional development programs that offer webinars, consultations, and cross-school collaboration opportunities. There are many private and nonprofit organizations that provide virtual coaching that includes teaching observations, feedback, and trainings. Teachers can choose their coach based upon their expertise and get tailored support on a flexible schedule. Virtual coaching can be expensive, but it may be worth the investment given that teachers are more likely to change their instructional practice after receiving individualized, online coaching than after traditional school-based PD (Mixon et al., 2019).

You might find even more success with virtual coaching if teachers are then asked to engage in action research about their new teaching strategies. I do not mean that teachers should analyze student data and write a publishable paper, but they should carefully examine the effect of new instructional methods on student outcomes through self-study or narrative inquiry. Self-study asks teachers to examine a specific element of their professional practice by unpacking the "what" or explaining the "why" or "how." For example, a teacher might choose to evaluate the cultural relevance of a book or they may want to see how different types of questioning help students identify cultural factors within the book. The goal of self-study is to improve professional practice.

Slightly different, narrative inquiry is about understanding students' experiences in the classroom. Teachers invite students to share their educational story by asking them to reflect on what school has been like thus far. An open-ended prompt allows students to talk about what is important to them in their learning. When teachers know what matters to students, they can adjust their instruction to better engage and motivate them.

Studies suggest that action research yields improved teaching practice and intentional analysis of student outcomes (S. Bondy, 2001; Bozkus & Bayrak, 2019; Glanz, 2003). Action research forces teachers to pause and critically reflect on their daily behaviors, which can then help them identify where they need professional support.

Small Group PD. After completing their action research study, teachers should share their findings with colleagues because action research is ultimately about improving the profession, not just a single teacher's practice. I suggest that teachers create "work groups" of three to four people that serve as a professional support group for one another. Smaller than a PLC but slightly larger than a mentoring pair, work groups are places where teachers can discuss their profession and their professional practice.

Work groups can participate in book clubs where they dissect macro level education issues (e.g., school choice policies, tracking, school-to-prison pipeline) that inform how they respond to micro level issues in their classroom (Rodriguez et al., 2020). Of course, they could read books on their own, but a working group offers a space to dialogue about the implications of the national education landscape for their daily duties. This may not seem like a crucial element of professional development, but especially in instances of role confusion or cognitive conflict, teachers need a space to talk through professional challenges.

The group might also function as a study group when teachers want to try new instructional strategies. After induction it is rare for teachers to be observed outside of a formal evaluation, so members of the working group could take turns conducting formative observations of one another. These groups could also serve as the mechanism through which teachers practice and receive feedback about what they learned in trainings and workshops. Small group PD is a low-stakes personalized middle point between intensive coaching and whole-school (or district) PD.

Communal PD. Most PD is designed as if teaching were solely about content delivery and classroom management. But any teacher will tell you they spend a large portion of time serving as social workers, nurses, psychologists, and parents. Remedying that reality is far beyond the capabilities of a single principal, but acknowledging that reality is critical. Teachers need support for all of their other jobs in addition to their instructional responsibilities. Because principals are (usually) not also social workers, nurses, or psychologists, they need to create opportunities for their teachers to learn from experts in those respective fields.

Communities of practice (CoPs) are groups of people whose work overlaps in practices, goals, and/or audiences. Pediatricians, child psychologists, social workers, and coaches have unique insight into children's development and their out-of-school lives. Like teachers, they are committed to children's well-being, so they are the perfect people with whom to collaborate. CoPs engage in collective learning and resource sharing as they work toward a common goal. CoPs are not job-training mechanisms, but are structured groups where members contribute their knowledge and skills in the hope that it helps someone else be more effective in their job.

For example, it would be great if teachers were able to ask a medical practitioner about diagnoses indicated on IEPs and BIPs. Doing so would provide a rationale for the accommodations they are told to implement and give them someone to help determine how best to implement them. CoPs remind teachers that learning is dependent upon far more than what they do in the classroom. Communal PD can increase teachers' professional identity, broaden their engagement with stakeholders, and help them view children and their professional practice more holistically (Kirkby et al., 2019).

CoPs can also exist within the school. Sometimes called a *care team* in higher education, these groups are composed of people from across the school who monitor student progress and problem-solve acute crises. A CoP is slightly different in that it is not a response team when students struggle; rather, it is a proactive group that combines its knowledge to ensure high-quality, equitable student services. Unlike PLCs, in-school CoPs include nonteaching staff such as librarians, counselors, family engagement coordinators, after-school program supervisors, custodial and maintenance workers, and food service personnel. Each member interacts with students differently than teachers do and, therefore, may have alternative perceptions of students' needs.

CoPs, working groups, action research, and virtual coaching are professional development opportunities that create role consensus by providing a space for teachers to share perceptions of job expectations. Traditional PD is too reliant upon a single teacher's role assessment that subsequently determines their willingness and ability to independently improve their practice. School leaders must give teachers access to PD that encourages constant comparison of internal and external expectations, which then prompts teachers to make a conscious decision about accepting a revised professional role. In sum, every PD session restarts the role-taking cycle.

Guiding Principles for PD Design

An effective professional development program is not a teacher training mechanism. Especially in urban schools with large percentages of novice teachers, principals tend to use PD funds to fill teachers' knowledge and skill gaps. The administration might pay a more experienced teacher to be an informal mentor or send a struggling teacher to a 1-day workshop. These are quick fixes for difficult problems. Teacher *development* requires time and multifaceted interventions embedded within a program of support.

A well-designed program establishes an expectation of individual problem solving by providing a structure for critical inquiry. PD should model for teachers how to analyze why and for whom instructional strategies are or are not effective. Dialogue-driven sessions invite teachers to ask questions, interrogate realities, and challenge tradition. Within an inquiry-based framework, the "what" of teaching is the by-product, not the core, of PD. As teachers gain a deeper understanding of the context of their practice, it becomes easier to improve the substance of it when they have the agency to do so.

Teachers should feel comfortable experimenting with new pedagogies that may better meet their particular students' needs. Sociocultural learning theory (Vygotsky, 1978) suggests that knowledge is co-constructed, dynamic, and contextual, so teachers must adjust their instruction for each group of students. In this way, teaching truly is a constant experiment as students' needs and interests evolve and vary during and across academic years. Instead of following a prescribed menu of instructional strategies, equity-minded teachers identify what students know and can do on their own, what they can do with assistance—and then target their instruction between the two.

The same should happen for teachers during PD. Good PD is data driven so it can operate within teachers' zone of proximal development by building upon their existing knowledge and capabilities and providing supports to scaffold their learning toward independent mastery. This approach fosters motivation because teachers are learning something relevant, new, and attainable. Buy-in can be further increased if teachers are aware of the benefits of what they are learning. Will it make their job easier? Improve student outcomes? Every PD opportunity should be presented in the context of teachers' daily activities as well as within the framework of the school's vision and mission.

Darling-Hammond and colleagues (2017) further suggest that effective PD:

- is content focused
- utilizes models
- asks teachers to actively participate
- requires collaboration
- provides coaching and expert support
- includes opportunities for feedback and reflection

- is of a sustained duration

Following these guidelines for each PD opportunity creates a low-cost, high-impact experience for teachers. When the content is personally relevant, the format is engaging, and the timing is appropriate, PD can be enjoyable, empowering, and effective.

Principal Considerations

Designing individual sessions is in many ways the easy part of PD. Creating a comprehensive and equitable program is much more difficult because you must consider audience, format, timing, content, facilitator, and follow-through. Each of these needs to be thought through in the context of available resources (funds, time, people), organizational structure and practices, and district and state guidelines. Finally, you must keep equity in mind and attend to the diversity of teachers' affective and professional needs. Figure 8.1 offers a starting point for thinking through your multiple audiences and the types of PD they may require.

A teacher's will reflects their emotional connection to their job. High-will teachers are enthusiastic, excited, and intrinsically motivated to do well. Low-will teachers, on the other hand, have lost their passion for the profession and do not find satisfaction in their work. It is common for teachers to begin their career with very high will and for

Will

		Low	High
	Low	*Apathetic Teachers*	*Novice Teachers*
Skill			
	High	*Veteran Teachers*	*Master Teachers*

Figure 8.1 Framework for Professional Development

it to slowly wane if they do not have good working conditions, consistent support, or if they experience a lot of professional challenges.

Teacher skill is about their ability to effectively do all aspects of their job. High-skill teachers have both content and pedagogical knowledge, strong classroom management skills, positive relationships with students and families, and excellent student achievement. Low-skill teachers may be lacking in some or all areas of effective instruction. Their skills may also be misaligned to the school context and students' needs.

When designing a professional development program, you should make certain to address each typology of will and skill either through tracks (e.g., novice teacher PD series, Master teacher PD series) or by differentiating within PD sessions. It might also be that certain PD formats are better suited for affective (e.g., working groups) versus professional (e.g., communities of practice) support. Make sure that each audience will have access to all PD formats at some point during the year.

You should also think through the timing of PD opportunities. Working backward from district in-service days, where can you add additional PD sessions? Can you integrate PD into teachers' weekly schedules? Which type of PD is most easily integrated? Here, you must consider dosage and duration. *Dosage* speaks to how much PD a teacher receives and *duration* addresses how long. Work groups might only meet twice a quarter whereas PLCs may meet once a week. Be sure to keep in mind teachers' workflow during the year such that periods of high stress (beginning of the school year, testing) do not include too many PD sessions and that PD content is aligned with current job responsibilities. For example, a workshop on family engagement strategies is most useful at the beginning of the year as teachers are forming relationships. Similarly, it would not make sense to have virtual coaching sessions scheduled near the end of the academic year when teachers have little time to integrate feedback into their practice. Rely on your personal experience to predict when teachers will need what kinds of support.

Revisit the needs assessment you completed in Chapter 1 to inform PD curriculum design. Focus on the schoolwide PD as teachers will get individualized support through coaching and within their work group. Trainings, workshops, and PLCs should directly correlate with the outcomes and goals listed in the equity action plan. You will not be able to offer PD in every area, so reserve schoolwide sessions for the content with the most potential impact.

Consult your resource assessment to identify who within the school can facilitate PD. Carefully review your nonteaching staff as they too are members of communities of practice with expertise teachers may not have. Consider presenters' credibility among the staff (are they respected and trusted), their pedagogical skill (are they a good presenter), and their awareness of the school context (do they understand other people's professional roles). If you need to move outside the school, look to families and community partners first. The more integrated facilitators are into the school community, the deeper their investment in the PD's success.

Finally, and perhaps most importantly, is figuring out how to follow up with teachers after PD. Follow-ups can happen via work groups, but can also occur through PLCs, coaching, and if relevant, CoPs. You must create an expectation for praxis and provide a formal structure where it can occur. If teachers are expected to utilize new learnings, how and when will they be held accountable for doing so? How and when will you communicate this expectation to them?

You must be transparent about each decision you make when designing PD. Teachers should know your rationale for audience, format, scheduling, and content. Ask for their feedback on the program and invite their suggestions for change. Be strategic yet flexible, recognizing that PD must respond to teachers' evolving needs year after year.

ADVICE FROM THE FIELD: DESIGNING A MULTIYEAR PROFESSIONAL DEVELOPMENT PROGRAM

In the first year, I focus on strong systems and structures. Those systems are about celebrating kids, honoring kids, building relationships with families, maximizing time for kids, and professionally developing my teachers and my staff to make sure that they know the expectations of their role.

Year two is when I start sending out my key staff members— the ones who get the structures and systems—to external PDs about culturally responsive teaching because now they are ready to add that into the structures they have. They come back and help with our monthly data teams. In the data teams, we focus on disaggregating our data by looking at the different groups: Black, Hispanic, white, free-and-reduced lunch, special education, girls, boys. We look at all that data and we set priority students. Three to eight priority kids per month are selected in a particular desegregated group. So if we see that third grade is really struggling with our girls, we choose eight girls that we are going to intensively focus on, target, talk to their parents to try to get back on track.

Third year is where I really start to dive in, because I've built a relationship amongst my staff. They trust me. They understand that I care about kids and they understand that I can push them outside of their comfort zone. But now this is my cohort of folks that have been with me for three years. They understand what I stand for. They believe in me and they trust in me. That's when I start having those schoolwide professional developments and I use those folks that I strategically have sent at year two to start leading that development because they're teachers and they have the utmost respect across our building.

It's not me up there saying, "Read this book." No. It's our teachers that have been trained, that are your leaders in the school, that are up there talking to you about improving. We continue to have those folks present throughout the year, which I think has been really good.

Principal Lewis

You don't have to do what Principal Lewis does in his school. How you design PD should be dictated by your students, teachers, and your vision for the school. It should reflect your leadership style and align with your organizational commitments. You will know you've done a good job when your teachers look forward to PD, when they actively participate during PD, and when they consistently use what they've learned to improve their practice. Most importantly, you will see increases in teachers' self-efficacy, effective instruction, and student achievement (Darling-Hammond et al., 2009)—all of which increases teachers' likelihood of remaining in the profession and at their current school.

Reflection Questions

1. Given the national education landscape and lessons learned from COVID-19, why is PD especially critical in this moment?
2. How can you expand the induction program designed in Chapter 7 into a PD program?
3. Guided by social identity theory (SIT), what hidden difficulties may emerge within PLCs, work groups, and CoPs?
4. How will you and other school leaders hold yourselves accountable for modeling praxis?
5. What PD might nonteachers need? How will you identify their knowledge and skill gaps?
6. How can you integrate families into CoPs?
7. There is an erroneous assumption that veteran teachers don't need PD. How will you disrupt this narrative without offending experienced teachers who may believe they don't need to change or improve their practices?

9 Integrating Equity Into Teacher Evaluation

Ensuring teachers have accessible and responsive professional development (PD) implicitly clarifies role expectations and promotes the role assessment process. Cognitive role theory (CRT) suggests that school leaders now focus on role conformity and role performance. If you've consistently communicated to teachers your expectations and you've provided proper supports, your next steps are making sure they are actually doing what they are supposed to do and assessing how well they are doing it.

Teacher evaluation is not exactly fun for anyone, especially given how regimented it is by the state and/or district. The Every Student Succeeds Act (ESSA) loosened some of the testing and accountability restrictions but does not offer suggestions for how else to measure teacher effectiveness. Because of No Child Left Behind (NCLB), schools relied on high-stakes standardized test scores as the primary, and sometimes sole, evaluative measure. Twenty years later, it is clear that this approach does not accurately distinguish between high- and low-performing teachers.

More recent evaluation systems rely on multiple measures of teacher performance and are accompanied by PD supports and incentives. Most states require that principals use a specific framework or model to conduct evaluations, but with some freedom with respect to timing, evaluators, and additional performance standards. Despite built-in flexibility, almost all schools rely on a combination of the same three measures: students' standardized tests scores, teaching observations, and sometimes, student surveys.

Education discourse is rich with discussions of the utility of using student achievement data to measure teacher efficacy, but that conversation is beyond the scope of this book. Instead, I will focus on how principals can more equitably use test scores as a component of teacher evaluation because they do speak, at least a little, to teachers' instructional skills depending upon what you do with the data. The two most popular approaches for analyzing test score data are value added models (VAMs) and student growth percentiles (SGPs). Both use criterion-referenced standardized tests (i.e., tests that ultimately categorize students as below proficient, proficient, or advanced) to capture teachers' contributions to students' scores compared to the scores of their peers. The former compares students' performance to that of other students in their school and district, whereas the latter compares students' scores only to those of peers with similar prior achievement.

In both instances there are complex statistics involved where factors such as prior achievement, demographics, attendance, and even class size are controlled for in hopes of isolating a teacher's contribution to a student's test score. SGPs also measure how much students' scores have changed in a year to determine a growth percentile ranking that compares their progress to similar others'. The logic underlying these approaches is that more effective teachers will have students with higher scores and more growth, although research demonstrates that is not always the case (Chetty et al., 2014).

In fact, when combined with teaching observations and student survey data, it becomes even more unclear which teachers are meeting or exceeding role expectations and which are not, as different measures assess different aspects of teaching. It makes sense then to combine as many measures as possible, but how do you do so in a way that yields accurate and useful information about teacher effectiveness? This chapter focuses on creating equitable teacher evaluation processes that stimulate teacher self-improvement and help school leaders identify teachers' professional needs.

The Validity of Teacher Evaluation

The most glaring hurdle when it comes to teacher evaluation relates to validity because we don't actually know what it means to be a "good" or "effective" teacher, so how can we measure it? With no clear or uniform definition of a "highly qualified teacher," we are left to operationalize it for ourselves according to contextual demands and norms. If a teacher works with advanced placement (AP) students, they might assume that students taking and passing AP exams is an indicator of their success. Conversely, a teacher who works primarily with low-achieving students may view students earning passing grades as a professional win. Teachers' ideas about what counts as good teaching are also influenced by colleagues' professional practices as well as by students' and families' implicit and explicit feedback. Local and national education policies also give teachers hints about what is prioritized in teacher evaluation. When NCLB tied teacher pay to students' test scores (i.e., pay for performance), teachers felt pressured to make sure students scored highly, so much so that by 2018 there was documented evidence of widespread cheating scandals in seven states.

Cheating was inevitable as teachers understood that no matter how strong their instructional skills, they could not guarantee high scores because standardized tests do not account for extraneous and confounding factors that influence students' test performance. There has long been a concern with cultural bias embedded within standardized tests that affects students' question interpretation. Test-taking conditions, including access to testing accommodations, are also known to influence students' concentration and performance. Finally, tests don't account for personal and social factors such as students' effort and motivation, and the effect of peers and other teachers on students' academic achievement.

There are additional concerns about using test-based accountability metrics as data analyses do not account for the time between academic years when students experience a loss of learning (e.g., the summer slide). Learning happens in stages with periods of intense growth and development bracketing longer, flat maintenance periods. When students do not rehearse or use information and skills during the summer, they can lose achievement gains to the point of regressing as much as 4 months in math and reading (Kuhfeld, 2019). It is obviously unfair to hold teachers accountable for losses that happened prior to the start of the academic year.

Similar validity issues are present during teaching observations. Despite using rubrics that have strong face validity (i.e., they appear to measure teachers' instructional practices), there is still the issue of construct validity in that it is unclear what effective teaching looks like in practice. There are dozens of evaluation metrics that point to different elements of teaching as the primary indicators of teacher success. For instance, the Danielson framework for teaching suggests that high-quality teaching is evidenced through 22 elements embedded within six clusters: clarity and accuracy, learning environment, classroom management, intellectual engagement, successful learning, and professionalism. The Marzano Focused Teacher Evaluation examines 23 aspects of teachers' standards-based planning, standards-based instruction, conditions for learning, and professional responsibilities. Further still are teacher quality standards published by national organizations and accrediting bodies that determine if teachers meet credentialing qualifications.

Despite creating domains or clusters of instruction, rubrics derived from these frameworks fail to meet discriminant validity requirements as many elements of teaching are interrelated. For example, effective instruction is dependent upon good classroom management, and intellectual engagement predicts successful learning. Thus, when utilizing the Danielson framework to guide an observation, it is likely that you are double or sometimes triple counting the same competencies under different categories which could drastically inflate or deflate a teacher's observation score. Inaccurate scoring is also a result of undercounting important factors that may be missing from the rubric (i.e., a lack of content validity). Even the most comprehensive framework cannot include *everything* that matters in a classroom, especially because what matters depends on the students and the school context. Most rubrics are not designed with educational equity in mind, so criterion tend to be too broad and overlook culturally and linguistically diverse students' needs.

Even when rubrics explicitly include equity indicators, there are reliability issues with how the rubric is used. It is common for two people to give teachers different scores even when they conduct the observation together. Scoring discrepancies happen for two reasons. First, observers may not be trained to use a particular rubric and can misunderstand criterion and/or make mistakes when calculating scores. Second, and most common, is that teaching observations are open to bias. Observers view teachers who are professionally and/or personally similar to themselves more positively and thus, rate them higher than teachers they view as out-group members who may incite negative emotions (Floman et al., 2017; Park et al., 2015). To reconcile these differences, observation scores are averaged across observers, which does not address the root cause of the different scores.

Reliability issues are compounded by problems with fidelity. Time pressures sometimes mean that observations start late or are cut short, forcing observers to focus on certain elements of the rubric. The presence of an observer can influence the authenticity of classroom processes as teachers and students are aware of being watched. Finally, lesson content can affect the utility of the rubric when observing a single lesson.

Ideally these problems would be partially mitigated by triangulating observation scores with other performance measures such as test scores and student surveys. However, there are no standard guidelines for how to weight measures and then combine them into a composite performance rating. In some districts observation scores account for 40% of a teacher's final rating, whereas in other districts they are the sole measure. Student achievement data may not be weighed at all or may account for up to 50% of a teacher's rating (Steinberg & Kraft, 2017). Given the uncertainty within evaluation processes and the inconsistencies across them, it is unsurprising that teacher quality remains a pressing concern for school leaders who do not have an accurate mechanism to assess teacher effectiveness.

The Inequity of Teacher Evaluation

Evaluation systems are not only inaccurate—they are also inequitable. Holding everyone to the same standard despite all we know about what contributes to student outcomes is unfair. We know that students' prior achievement, along with their race or ethnicity and their income group can be used to (fairly accurately) predict their future achievement. As it is novice, racially minoritized women teachers who are most often assigned low-achieving, low-income racially minoritized students, it is these students who are most likely to have low standardized test scores. And, because it is low-income students who are most subject to the summer slide (Alexander et al., 2007), teachers at Title I schools are disproportionately impacted by evaluation practices that rely on student growth indicators.

Title I schools are also schools with high student mobility and absenteeism, which makes tracking student performance difficult. When students are missing prior year data, their test scores are removed from VAM and SGP analyses, creating a smaller pool of student scores upon which teachers are evaluated. This is troublesome as estimates drawn from smaller samples are less accurate than those from larger samples (E. L. Baker et al., 2010), meaning that teachers in high-mobility districts may be expected to reach unattainable performance levels.

Despite that, teachers are evaluated against one another as if they are teaching in similar conditions, which even within a single school is not the case. Around 70% of teachers teach in grades or content areas for which there are no state-administered tests, yet their students' achievement scores are compared to students' scores on standardized tests that differ in content, length, format, and timing (Watson et al., 2009). Even when students take the same test, comparisons are worrisome because they utilize criterion-referenced test scores in a norm-referenced fashion. In other words, we take what is supposed to be an intra-student assessment and turn it into an inter-student assessment, which violates principles of measurement design.

We make additional mistakes when we compare teachers across districts. Not only do working conditions drastically differ between districts but performance rating calculations also vary. When synthesizing evaluation measures, districts assign points to each measure and then calculate the percentage of points teachers earned out of the total available amount. That number determines teachers' final performance rating and their professional trajectory. The problem is that in some districts teachers need only earn 50% of available points to be classified effective/proficient whereas in other districts they need 75% of available points (Steinberg & Kraft, 2017). Teachers who work in districts with lower competency thresholds can appear to be more effective than teachers in districts with higher thresholds even if their overall evaluation scores are lower.

These inequities are cumulative and can follow teachers throughout their career. Teachers who enter the profession in high-needs schools are more likely to be overly penalized and score lower during evaluations and less likely to receive accompanying PD than teachers in high resource schools. Without school-provided supports, already overwhelmed teachers are expected to independently seek training and mentorship or risk another poor evaluation, which could lead to termination.

THOUGHTS FROM THE FIELD

Every teacher is in a different place. There are times when we know this is a new teacher who is struggling in this area, and some would say, "This person should be rated a two," but then the argument is, "Well, you want to rate this person a two, but over the course of three months, this person has improved drastically. Even though they're still struggling, I think they're a three because they're doing the things they need to do to get to the next level."

Teachers of color and leaders of color tend to be evaluated much lower than their white peers because the person typically doing the evaluation is a white leader. So evaluators say, "You look like me, that's the way I would do it, so you're going to be successful. The way [redacted] is doing it, that's not the way I would do that. That looks awkward for me, and I don't think that's going to be successful, so I'm going to rate them lower so I can get them where they need to be." But the achievement results are showing something different. Why is that?

Equitable evaluation and teaching and leadership to me means meeting the teacher where they are and coaching them to where they need to go. You do not evaluate people on something they have not been developed in. That is horrible. "I'm going to evaluate you on implicit bias, but I never gave you training in implicit bias." That's ridiculous to me. And then I need to make sure that the person doing the evaluating is trained too.

Dr. Carmichael

Equitable Teacher Evaluation

Dr. Carmichael is pointing out the many inequities embedded in evaluation processes that school leaders must anticipate. He identifies bias as a major contributor to unreliable evaluation metrics. He advocates for a growth-oriented approach to assessment that celebrates teachers' accomplishments and offers necessary supports for areas of weakness. I further suggest that principals think holistically about evaluation, acknowledging that teaching is influenced by a variety of personal, interpersonal, and environmental factors—all of which must be accounted for when contextualizing teachers' role performance. I argue for a multipronged evaluation process that examines teachers' professional practice across time, in addition to their "objective" performance snapshots.

Culture of Praxis
The climate of inquiry and experimentation cultivated by a strong PD program should be an element of a larger culture of praxis. The school leader sets the tone for evaluation, so it is their responsibility to integrate it into everyday school functioning. Observations should occur routinely throughout the year, students and families should be invited to give quarterly feedback, and assessment should be a natural component of data-driven instruction. Formal observations therefore become just another observation rather than an anxiety-inducing event. Both teachers and students will be so accustomed to formative assessments that even if the district attaches high stakes to students' scores, within

the school, state administered standardized tests should not be treated any differently than other assessments.

A culture of praxis views evaluations diagnostically, recognizing them as opportunities to improve. School leaders should communicate such by emphasizing the utility of evaluations for keeping teachers, not dismissing them. An asset-oriented framing removes the implied threat of failure and celebrates teachers' accomplishments instead. Such a small change may not seem consequential, but teachers who view evaluation as a professional development opportunity report more job satisfaction and changes to practice (T. G. Ford et al., 2018).

Content of Evaluation

Research suggests that teacher evaluation is often inaccurate because of poorly designed metrics (Gill et al., 2016; M. T. Kane, 2017). When districts require principals to use a one-size-fits-all evaluation framework, there is little likelihood of capturing the nuances in teachers' role performance that make them effective within a particular school. Instruction should absolutely be the bulk of what teachers are evaluated on, but what else is in their job description? What should you evaluate in order to get an accurate and complete picture of teachers' capabilities?

Equitable evaluation frameworks have construct and content validity within your school context. Remind yourself what good teaching looks like within your organizational structure and given your vision and mission. Be careful to avoid the pitfalls of other frameworks that double count the same performance standards by making a ranked list of teachers' professional responsibilities. You want to be thorough and include everything that is important to teachers' success, but you also want a manageable number of standards that coherently relate to one another. For instance, it would be unreasonable and impossible to assess teachers on 100 elements (or criteria) across 10 standards. Instead, limit the number of elements within each standard to five and the number of standards to six, yielding a total of 30 criteria on which teachers are evaluated.

Criteria must explicitly speak to educational equity. Most existing frameworks identify critical elements of effective teaching but they are not written with equity in mind. The Marzano model assesses how well teachers "help students revise their knowledge." An equitable evaluation would assess how well teachers "help students interrogate knowledge through sociocultural lenses." The former assumes that knowledge is stagnant and definitive with universal right and wrong understandings. The latter recognizes that knowledge is socially constructed and that culturally and linguistically diverse students may have different conceptions of knowledge. When written more inclusively, it becomes possible to assess if and for whom teachers are utilizing good and equitable instructional practices.

Because it is difficult to find equity-oriented evaluation frameworks, principals will likely have to adapt district-provided metrics for their purposes. Here, educational leaders share ideas for what you might include as equity indicators for teacher evaluation.

ADVICE FROM THE FIELD: EQUITY INDICATORS

I think about really assessing their ability to tie cultural competency into their lessons. So not just going off of the curriculum but being really able to enrich the curriculum and speak to, "Yes, we might be learning about Thomas Jefferson, but did you also know that the Memorial Day holiday was started by an African American youth?"

Family engagement is a huge way to evaluate because if that connection isn't there, it makes it that much more challenging to truly reach the student, especially if the student is in need of some extra support.

Measuring student progress on an individual level, not grouping the class as a whole, but asking, has this student who had behavioral challenges at the beginning of the year been able to adjust and better handle the situations in the classroom? Or, has this student's reading level improved? I think even gauging the student's level of excitement for learning is another way to evaluate a teacher's effectiveness.

Ms. Richardson

I don't think teachers are held accountable enough for disaggregated data. Are we growing SPED students? Are we growing Black kids? The school is, of course, rated on that piece somewhat, but our teachers aren't. So I think one thing that needs to be a component of evaluation is how we are growing within disaggregated groups.

Principal Lewis

How are they self-starting equity work? Because I think educational equity work needs to be deeply personal. It requires you to have introspection on your own identity and how you show up in the work, because if you don't do the individual work, you can't be culturally responsive. It's so inauthentic to ask kids to see themselves when you're not engaged in that yourself as a professional.

Is the teacher authentically showing up? Do they know the kids' names? Can they pronounce them? That sounds basic but it is the first place we start to see equity slip away.

Curriculum content is another factor. Those are choices you get to make. So when the media is like "Why don't we teach Juneteenth?" That's because we're making choices about what we're teaching and what we're not teaching. We're making choices about what reading passages we're using. We're making choices about what kind of word problem we're doing in math and science. Teachers need to be accountable for these choices.

Director Nash

Our experts make it clear that educational equity demands that you examine teachers' performance *in relation to* students' needs. This means that every criterion must be able to be disaggregated by student subgroups. Consider another example from the Marzano model that measures if teachers "[lesson] plan to close the achievement gap using data." This element is easily disaggregated by students' demographics, which would tell you whose needs a teacher is prioritizing in their instructional planning. Table 9.1 uses the InTASC teacher quality standards as an example for how you can add equity to existing evaluation metrics.

Table 9.1 InTASC Standards Equity Additions		
	InTASC Standard	**InTASC Equity Additions**
Standard #1 Learner Development	*The teacher understands how learners grow and develop, recognizing that patterns of learning and development vary individually within and across the cognitive, linguistic, social, emotional, and physical areas, and designs and implements developmentally appropriate and challenging learning experiences.*	*The teacher mitigates hegemonic power structures that privilege certain developmental skills particularly as they relate to language and behavior.*
Standard #2 Learning Differences	*The teacher uses understanding of individual differences and diverse cultures and communities to ensure inclusive learning environments that enable each learner to meet high standards.*	*The teacher possesses an asset-based view of learner differences as opportunities to improve their professional practice. The teacher establishes performance expectations that are aligned with students' learning capacities and needs.*
Standard #3 Learning Environments	*The teacher works with others to create environments that support individual and collaborative learning, and that encourage positive social interaction, active engagement in learning, and self-motivation.*	*The teacher creates a physical and emotional environment that respects, values, and celebrates students' identities and life experiences. The teacher actively fosters a sense of belonging among a community of learners.*

Table 9.1 InTASC Standards Equity Additions *continued*		
Standard #4 **Content** **Knowledge**	*The teacher understands the central concepts, tools of inquiry, and structures of the discipline(s) he or she teaches and creates learning experiences that make the discipline accessible and meaningful for learners to assure mastery of the content.*	*The teacher acknowledges that knowledge is socially constructed and integrates multiple sociocultural perspectives into the curriculum.*
Standard #5 **Application of** **Content**	*The teacher understands how to connect concepts and use differing perspectives to engage learners in critical thinking, creativity, and collaborative problem solving related to authentic, local, and global issues.*	*The teacher utilizes learning materials that are relevant to students' cultures that help them bridge in-school learning to their out-of-school lives.*
Standard #6 **Assessment**	*The teacher understands and uses multiple methods of assessment to engage learners in their own growth, to monitor learner progress, and to guide the teacher's and learners' decision making.*	*The teacher ensures every student has the opportunity to experience success by giving students choice in how they demonstrate their knowledge and skills in culturally relevant and personally meaningful ways.*
Standard #7 **Planning for** **Instruction**	*The teacher plans instruction that supports every student in meeting rigorous learning goals by drawing upon knowledge of content areas, curriculum, cross-disciplinary skills, and pedagogy, as well as knowledge of learners and the community context.*	*The teacher plans instruction to access students' and the community's funds of knowledge.* *The teacher plans instruction with full awareness of students' access to resources.*

	InTASC Standard	InTASC Equity Additions
Table 9.1 InTASC Standards Equity Additions *continued*		
Standard #8 Instructional Strategies	*The teacher understands and uses a variety of instructional strategies to encourage learners to develop deep understanding of content areas and their connections, and to build skills to apply knowledge in meaningful ways.*	*The teacher employs instructional practices that align with students' social and cultural norms including non-Western practices that emphasize social interaction.*
Standard #9 Professional Learning and Ethical Practice	*The teacher engages in ongoing professional learning and uses evidence to continually evaluate his/her practice, particularly the effects of his/her choices and actions on others (learners, families, other professionals, and the community), and adapts practice to meet the needs of each learner.*	*The teacher is aware of their sociocultural positionality within the school and community and how it intersects with others' to shape power dynamics.* *The teacher is open to feedback.*
Standard #10 Leadership and Collaboration	*The teacher seeks appropriate leadership roles and opportunities to take responsibility for student learning, to collaborate with learners, families, colleagues, other school professionals, and community members to ensure learner growth, and to advance the profession.*	*The teacher invites student input into learning processes and class functioning.*

Performance standards are just one part of equitable assessment. You also need to consider how you measure a teacher's performance. The Marzano model uses a proficiency scale of Not Using (0), Beginning (1), Developing (2), Applying (3), and Innovating (4). In the former example, this scale is not particularly useful as the indicators don't align with the criteria. A better scale might be Never (0), Rarely (1), Sometimes (2), Frequently (3), and Always (5) to reflect how often a teacher uses data to design lessons to close the achievement gap. A more appropriate scale would yield useful information about the frequency with which a teacher targets different subgroup needs.

Creating performance indicators (i.e., measurement scales) is tricky but necessary because without a detailed scale you invite individual interpretations. Most indicators are categorical (below expectations, met expectations, exceeds expectations) or numerical (1–4), each of which tells a different story. Nominal scales that place people into distinct groups do not have numerical equivalents, so it can be hard to compare across the labels. How does a teacher in the "meets expectations" category differ from a teacher who "exceeds expectations"? What is the breaking point between "below expectations" and "meets expectations"? If you choose nominal indicators, be certain to thoroughly detail what teachers have to do and how many criteria they must meet within each classification.

Ordinal scales that numerically rate teachers' performance facilitate comparisons better but still not perfectly. Is a teacher who gets a 4 in classroom management twice as better as a teacher who gets a 2? If you want to rank teachers, use an interval scale that has equal distance between each indicator or a ratio scale that has the added benefit of a meaningful zero point, which would indicate the absence of a behavior or skill. It is okay to have different indicators for different standards or even for different elements within standards. Equity will not be achieved through a standardized template.

Principals also need to move beyond traditional measures of teacher effectiveness to ensure a comprehensive analysis of a teacher's role performance. Here I borrow from higher education to think of teacher evaluation as constructing a dossier that represents all facets of teachers' professional practice, which requires determining what data you should collect to best measure each standard. Teaching observations are an excellent way to assess instruction, but they are not the only way. Student surveys can capture elements of instruction that are not included in rubrics or that observers overlook. For instance, the Tripod survey asks students if their teacher encourages and values student input. Parent or family surveys might similarly ask parents about the frequency, substance, and outcomes of their interactions with teachers.

If you really want details, invite colleagues, students, and families to submit letters about their interactions with teachers. Narratives will tap into the complexity of a teacher's work much better than too-short observations or perfunctory surveys that are subject to bias (T. J. Kane et al., 2013). Further, when it is time for feedback, letters offer specific evidence of teachers' impacts, which is not always the case with observations.

External evaluations should be balanced by teachers' self-assessment. Teachers should construct a portfolio of their work that they think best reflects their role performance. It might include lesson plans, samples of student work, and examples of communications with families and community partners. Teachers should also video record themselves teaching and use the observation rubric to self-evaluate. The final component of their portfolio should be a written reflection of their teaching in which they name their accomplishments and identify areas in which they'd like more support. When teachers have input into their evaluation, they perceive the process as more authentic and are less likely to become demoralized and disengaged (Bradford & Braaten, 2018).

Process of Evaluation

With the "why" and "what" of teacher evaluation clearly defined, you must now attend to the "how." What does teacher evaluation look like in your school? How are evaluation metrics synthesized? What are the implications of final performance ratings? Novice teachers especially need clarification about what counts most in their teaching evaluations, to whom they will be compared, and what happens after evaluations. These are important questions that deserve careful attention if you are to minimize validity and reliability concerns and ensure the utility of teacher evaluation processes.

We've already discussed the value of multiple observations throughout the year for a culture of praxis. But routine evaluations by multiple people have the additional benefit of improving the reliability of observation scores, identifying growth over time, and of scaffolding teachers' role construction toward role conformity. Informal observations are formative assessments that help leaders consistently monitor teachers' progress and, consequently, develop equitable expectations for their role performance prior to formal evaluation processes.

You will need to be attentive to the applicability of performance standards and criterion across teacher subgroups. I am not suggesting that you develop individualized evaluation frameworks for each teacher, but that you create reasonable expectations given what you know about teachers' training, experience, content, and class assignment. Most principals do this automatically, but such adjustments should be clearly communicated to teachers so they fully understand their job expectations.

Equally as important is how different metrics are weighted in the final performance rating. States and districts often make this decision, but if you have flexibility within the metrics (i.e., "student achievement" could mean standardized test scores, GPAs, or capstone projects) or in how you analyze data, there are a couple of things you can do to create a more equitable process.

First, choose metrics that best align with teachers' daily responsibilities. If you want to or must use teacher-designed assessments to measure student achievement, be sure that teachers (a) know how to design effective assessments, and (b) know to do so as part of their professional practice. If your state or district requires test scores be factored into teacher evaluations, see if you can use SGPs rather than teachers' value added scores. Student growth percentiles are easier for teachers to interpret and they emphasize teaching processes over product, which increases teachers' work engagement (Zeng et al., 2019). Disaggregate test scores to look for areas of success that may have been buried within the aggregate group by looking at class-level medians, not means, which are very sensitive to outlier data. It is also important to note the spread of scores to ascertain the variability of students' performance across and within classes and demographic groups. Such a detailed analysis of student achievement facilitates targeted feedback that promotes instructional change (Amrein-Beardsley & Holloway, 2019).

Second, be aware of how different metrics relate to one another. It is not only the individual weighting that matters to teachers' performance rating but also how much two performance metrics are correlated with

one another. Teaching observations and student surveys should measure the same overall construct of effective teaching, but they should ask
about different elements of a teacher's practice. If the survey is another
version of the rubric, these elements will highly correlate and make a
joint contribution as well as individual contributions, ultimately double counting in the final evaluation score.

If there is appropriate discriminant validity between measures,
you can use the different measures to triangulate data. Observation
scores should be supported by survey data, which should be contextu-
alized and expanded upon through letters and within a teacher's portfolio. When an overall narrative is inconsistent, one of the metrics is
flawed and should be removed from the dossier if possible. If it cannot
be removed, at the very least, triangulation helps detect issues with
role conformity by identifying what element of professional practice
is lacking. If a teacher has strong instructional skills as indicated by
observations and surveys, they might still have weak professional skills
as reflected in colleagues' letters. Each data source helps paint the overall picture that adds nuance to performance ratings.

Principal's Role in Teacher Evaluation

In addition to designing performance standards and indicators, determining evaluation timelines and processes (including who conducts
observations throughout the year), principals also play a vital role after
evaluations. Many evaluation processes do not lead to teacher change
because no one facilitates teachers' interpretation of feedback (Firestone & Donaldson, 2019). As the person who uses performance ratings
to make decisions about teachers' professional trajectories, it is important that you are the one with whom teachers meet to review and process through evaluation outcomes. It is common for master and mentor
teachers or instructional coaches to do this but feedback is most meaningful when it comes from the school leader.

Review meetings should be grounded in teachers' evaluations but
framed broadly to discuss the individual's place within the school
community. Like parent–teacher conferences, these are two-way conversations during which you jointly reflect on the evaluation process,

explicitly identifying areas of strengths and weakness. It is a good idea to revisit the professional development plan created during induction to adjust their current role expectations and determine possible future roles. A successful meeting leaves teachers feeling supported and motivated to take on new challenges that are aligned with their interests and evolving skills (Tuytens & Devos, 2017).

However, in situations where there is an unsuccessful evaluation, you have decisions to make. It is rare for principals to rate teachers poorly but when they do, they tend to be teachers with less experience, male teachers, and teachers of color (Drake et al., 2019). That these groups are already minoritized within schools suggests that the first step when reviewing evaluations is to ensure the absence of bias. Did this teacher have a particularly difficult class assignment? Were their skills upon hiring aligned with their class assignment? Who conducted observations and what is their relationship with the teacher? How might student-level factors have affected standardized test scores?

Once bias has been accounted for in the composite rating, isolate those performance standards that the teacher struggled to meet and see if they agree with the scores. If they do not, a larger conversation about their role construction may be necessary. You should also carefully review the criterion within each standard and ask the teacher to reflect on how and when they met that criterion. It is very possible that an observer overlooked something or that other artifacts (beyond what is in the dossier) better demonstrate teachers' competencies. The conversation should be aimed at finding areas of success, not harping on areas of difficulty.

After reaching consensus, what are the next steps? You should not assume a teacher wants to remain at the school or in their current position within the school. Ask them what their professional goals are and invite them to make suggestions for how to better reach them. If they choose to stay in the school and you agree, it may be prudent to revise their role expectations given their current skill level. It is unfair to continue to ask teachers to perform duties that they've demonstrated they cannot perform without additional support.

Such support should be documented in a collaboratively written improvement plan. Not unlike IEPs, a professional improvement plan should target specific standards and specify the timeline for reaching proficiency. It should be so detailed that it indicates the exact instructional strategies or professional practices they are expected to perform. The plan must also include clearly identified supports and details about the reevaluation process. As most formal evaluations occur near the end of the academic year, it is unlikely that you or anyone else can follow up with teachers in the near future. It is therefore vital that an improvement plan begin with professional development during the summer for which they will be held accountable at the start of the new year. It might also be a good idea to invite struggling teachers to participate in orientation to reinforce job expectations and give teachers another, albeit short, development opportunity.

Not all teachers will agree to work over the summer, but like any other service profession, teaching requires a commitment to continuing education. If teachers do not want to engage in PD over the summer or are asking to be paid to do so, you should prompt them to reassess their teaching motivation. It is not unreasonable to ask teachers to attend school- or district-sponsored conferences, trainings, or to participate in webinars. If they believe it is, they may not be a good fit for the profession and you should agree to part ways. Effective school leaders don't shy away from letting ineffective teachers go. In fact, one sign of a good leader is that they have low turnover for high-performing teachers and high turnover for low-performing teachers (Grissom & Bartanen, 2019). In the next chapter we will discuss how to keep high performers engaged and satisfied with their professional role, even if it means changing the role.

Reflection Questions

1. Review last year's teacher evaluations and disaggregate by subgroups. Who are your low performers and who are your high performers? Are there racial or gendered patterns?

2. Write a definition of "highly qualified" given your school context. Brainstorm performance standards that support your definition.

3. Teaching and learning are linked processes and should have linked outcomes. How are teacher performance standards mirrored in student expectations and assessments?

4. Why are BITOC disproportionately affected by invalid and unreliable evaluation measures?

5. Cultural bias is clearly embedded within current evaluation processes. What about gender and age bias? How might they emerge in teacher evaluation?

6. Where can you integrate equity standards into existing metrics?

7. Equitable evaluation requires that teachers be held accountable for shared expectations. How closely is your PD program aligned with your evaluation process?

10 Improving Teacher Retention Through Career Advancement Opportunities

With evaluations done, improvement plans written, and accompanying PD scheduled, we turn our attention to teachers with high evaluation scores. How do you make certain these great teachers—regardless of experience—remain at the school and maintain their effectiveness? What can you do to promote high will and reward high skill? Cognitive role theory (CRT) explains that successful role performance is dependent upon the accuracy of teachers' role expectations as well as on their willingness and ability to comply with them. Most teachers leave their school or the profession within their first 2 years during a prolonged role-assessment process (Day & Gu, 2010). By year 3, teachers begin to develop positive self-efficacy beliefs and by year 5, their role performance starts to flatten. Now that they've built their teaching tool kit and are comfortable in their role, teachers more closely attend to the context of their work and the factors that restrict their role performance (Vagi & Pivovarova, 2017).

Chief among perceived barriers are a lack of administrative support, too few PD opportunities, too much bureaucracy, and not enough agency (Glazer, 2018; Newberry & Alsop, 2017; Santoro, 2021). Ingersoll (2001) identified additional reasons teachers leave the profession:

- student discipline problems
- lack of student motivation
- large class sizes
- inadequate preparation time
- no input into school policies
- lack of community support and family engagement
- unsafe working conditions
- too little instructional time
- ineffective colleagues
- poor salary

If you've followed the book thus far, many of these factors will be nonissues in your school. The organizational structure should ensure that teachers feel like members of the school community whose input is highly valued. Their teaching schedules should include sufficient time for PD, planning, and instruction. Your community and family outreach strategies should encourage extensive and meaningful partnerships. In this chapter we address salary and career advancement as the remaining components that research suggests matters in teachers' career planning (Bland et al., 2014). We will also discuss additional factors like classroom assignment, job security, and teachers' well-being as you work to retain effective educators.

Understanding Stayers

Teachers who remain at their school are often called "stayers." They have chosen not to switch schools ("movers") or exit the profession all together ("leavers"). But why? Teachers stay at their school because they love their students, they feel effective, and because they perceive themselves as making valuable contributions to the school (Kelchtermans, 2017; Smith & Ulvik, 2017; Towers & Maguire, 2017). Furthermore, teachers who participate in induction programs, receive consistent PD, and who are given appropriate time and resources report more job satisfaction because of a balance between job demands and support (Geiger & Pivovarova, 2018).

Retaining good teachers should be among your top priorities as the school leader. Teachers who spend multiple years in the same school can build lasting relationships with students and families that enhance the overall sense of community. These teachers develop an understanding of the neighborhood and students' out-of-school life contexts that shapes their instructional practice. Consistent staffing also means that you can gradually build teachers' abilities, which creates a leadership pipeline to ensure that students are not repeatedly taught by novice teachers—who themselves benefit from having more-experienced colleagues (Jackson & Bruegmann, 2009).

Retaining novice teachers also requires that they experience success early in their career. Beginning teachers need less demanding classes, support and feedback, and opportunities for collaboration. More experienced teachers need challenges that keep them engaged and invested in improving their craft. Be cautious when changing working assignments across school years as teachers must accumulate experience in the same content and grade to build their competencies. Ensuring proper teacher development is essential as after year 3, teachers are eligible for tenure and it may become difficult to dismiss them if they prove unsuccessful in their role.

Rethinking Tenure

Debates about the value of tenure are more thoroughly discussed elsewhere, but given the tension surrounding teacher tenure it is worth examining its relation to educational equity. At its core, tenure is reasonable: After a brief probationary period during which teachers presumably demonstrate their teaching potential, they gain the protection of due process, which guarantees they are given reason, documentation, and a hearing prior to being fired. Teachers argue that such protections allow them to make decisions in the best interest of students—even if such decisions go against parent, principal, or school board wishes. There are also related arguments for academic freedom so that teachers are not bound to a standard curriculum that they may perceive as limited or at times, inaccurate. These concerns are not trivial in schools serving culturally and linguistically diverse (CLD) students whose academic, social, and emotional needs may differ from those prioritized in "traditional" instruction. Teachers must have assurances that they won't lose their job if they implement the culturally responsive practices educational equity necessitates.

Equally as important is that tenure protects teachers from being terminated for things unrelated to teaching such as "fit," which is often employed to mask bias and discrimination in teacher evaluation. Tenure protections are valuable to minoritized teachers (i.e., BIPOC, male, queer, differently abled, neuroatypical, immigrant, non-heritage English speaking) who are likely to experience hostile work environments and disrespect from parents and colleagues that may influence evaluation decisions (Bristol & Goings, 2019; Dykes & Delport, 2018).

Tenure also protects teachers from being immediately fired if they do receive a negative evaluation. Especially in Title I schools where achievement can fluctuate greatly from year to year, it is likely that teachers' evaluation scores will be similarly unstable if tests are heavily weighted. In states with rigid evaluation systems a teacher could be fired if after three "proficient" ratings they receive two "below proficient" scores. Without due process, high-quality teachers may avoid working in lower income schools because it would mean that students' lower (than wealthier students') test scores may jeopardize their employment, which contributes to large numbers of novice teachers and high-turnover rates in low-income, racially minoritized schools.

Tenure opponents argue otherwise, suggesting that it is not the absence of tenure in low-income schools that fuels teacher turnover, but the presence of it. They point to tenure as a teacher retention problem rather than an opportunity. Because dismissing teachers who have tenure can take up to 6 years and cost over $300,000, most principals don't bother (Griffith & McDougald, 2016). Many states have tenure laws that do not include performance as an indicator for dismissal so there would be no point in initiating termination proceedings. According to a 2020 report by the Education Commission (Rafa et al., 2020), 30 states and Washington, D.C., do not require performance to be considered in layoff decisions. Coupled with the fact that only nine states consider teacher performance ratings when awarding tenure (and even then it may not be the primary factor), teacher tenure does not necessarily correlate with teacher effectiveness.

The absence of performance standards in tenure decision-making suggests that if principals want to improve the overall teaching quality at their school, they must place their hope solely in novice teachers who can be removed if they prove ineffective. Weeding out low performers fuels a rotating door of teachers as principals attempt to hire, develop, and evaluate new teachers before they become eligible for tenure. As most staffing shortages and consequent job openings are in low-income schools with diverse students, it is they who have the highest churn as teachers' inexperience clashes with principals' aspirations.

School turnarounds are further limited by tenure-driven financial constraints. Because you cannot easily fire tenured teachers, you are stuck paying them an increasing salary every year despite little to no evidence of increased performance. Tenure necessitates long-term financial investments in teachers that may prevent fiscal flexibility, even in the case of declining enrollments. Schools with the most needs often have the smallest budgets, so keeping ineffective teachers on the payroll disproportionately affects schools with heterogenous student populations who most require equitable education opportunities but can least afford them.

As tenure timeline and eligibility criteria are determined by the state, you cannot mitigate the inequities it creates across and within schools. Your work as the school leader is to ensure that when a teacher applies for tenure, they receive a fair and equitable review and that your recommendation reflects their long-term potential for career success.

Tenure Reviews

The goal of tenure review is not to get rid of bad teachers but to retain good ones. The problem is that most review processes are not thorough and do not accurately identify teachers whose accomplishments warrant long-term job security. In 2018, a statistically improbable 90% of teachers in the United States had tenure (U.S. Department of Education, 2019e). Such a high percentage speaks to a lack of rigor in tenure standards. In fact, 81% of teachers confess that they know at least one tenured teacher in their building who should not be in the classroom (Farkas et al., 2003).

Because teachers are well positioned to be aware of colleagues' professional strengths and weaknesses, it makes sense that they should have input into tenure decision-making. Peer review is common among physicians, lawyers, and professors but is very rare in K–12 where principals often solely make a recommendation to the district or state. The problems with having a single person responsible for such a serious decision are obvious, but the benefits of peer review are more subtle.

A review committee distributes the labor across multiple individuals, so the principal is not encumbered with reviewing tenure applications in addition to their regular duties. Shared work leads to a more careful review than what may happen if principals feel rushed to complete yet another task. Multiple reviewers also make it possible to have a more comprehensive review that assesses numerous aspects of teachers' practice. If committee members are assigned carefully, you can align individual expertise to various facets of teachers' applications. Multiple perspectives also broaden the context for evaluation as different committee members may look for different indicators of achievement. As tenure often travels across districts and sometimes states, it is vital that a review process determines a teacher's value to the profession, not just to a particular school.

It is therefore very important that you are strategic about what you include in the review process. Although the state likely has tenure performance standards, unlike evaluation standards, they may not detail specific elements, criteria, or performance indicators. For example, New York asks principals to review teacher effectiveness with respect to student learning, teacher practice, and professionalism. But the specific artifacts teachers present as evidence of their accomplishments are determined by the principal. If you have similar agency, consider aligning evaluation and tenure processes such that teachers submit a portfolio of work that reflects their long-term achievements. In addition to assessing instructional practices, you should look for steady improvement in student outcomes, increasing engagement with families and the community, a commitment to continued education, and a deepening understanding of, and investment in, equity.

Salary

Successful annual evaluations should be accompanied by a salary increase; however, the two are not related to one another in most districts. The most common compensation model in the United States is experienced-based (also called back loaded or seniority pay) such that teachers' salaries correlate with the number of years they've been teaching. The salary schedule is predetermined so a beginning teacher has a pretty good idea of what they will be making in 5 years. This knowledge may negatively impact teacher retention as salary raises in education do not keep pace with those in comparable fields nor with comparably educated professionals (Allegretto & Mishel, 2019). A recent college graduate may be okay with a small salary early in their career, but once they gain experience and become more effective they will understandably want commiserate compensation.

The logic underlying experience-based salary structures doesn't always align with reality. While teachers do improve as they acquire experience, the gains are largest early in teachers' careers. By year 6, teachers' performance becomes much more stable and may even temporarily dip by year 10. A salary structure that is solely based on experience may reward ineffective teachers whose outcomes aren't as good as those accomplished by less experienced teachers. One study found that high-performing teachers left districts with seniority pay in favor of performance pay, but low-performing teachers stayed (Biasi, 2019). If tenure reduces the likelihood of dismissal despite poor performance, and a raise is guaranteed either way, teachers may become complacent and apathetic.

You can't change the district's base salary structure, but you can advocate for equitable models of additional compensation tied to job performance and job context. Determining an equitable model will be tricky as various models benefit teachers differently based upon their assignment, years of experience, and prior performance. Table 10.1 overviews which compensation models are best for whom. Here I provide more details about each option:

- *Merit pay*: Individual teachers receive bonuses based on improvements in their performance. These improvements are not necessarily tied to students' test scores but can be evidenced through observations or other principal-determined factors. Merit pay can increase teachers' motivation, but it is not consistently related to higher student outcomes (Shifrer et al., 2017).

- *Performance pay*: Teachers earn salary increases tied to improvements in students' performance on standardized tests or other achievement measures. Performance pay became popular after NCLB required stronger teacher accountability, but has waned since the passing of ESSA. While performance pay is associated with modest increases in students' test scores, it can also create competition among teachers for a limited pool of funds (Pham et al., 2020).

- *School-based performance pay*: All professional staff in a school earn a bonus if students meet certain goals. This model is more effective at raising student achievement than performance pay and can increase collaboration (Pham et al., 2020). However, it might create conflict between teachers if they feel like everyone is not working equally as hard toward shared goals. There is also the added risk of masking individual teachers' outcomes within school outcomes.

- *Knowledge- and skills-based pay*: Teachers earn permanent salary increases for acquiring and applying new skills. This model is fairly rare as it asks principals to develop metrics for assessing teachers' use of skills, which will require some form of observational follow-up. Principals must also consider what happens to the school culture if you monetize PD instead of including it in job expectations.

- *Market-based pay*: Teachers in hard-to-staff schools and shortage areas receive annual stipends. Market-based pay is most applicable upon hiring and is unrelated to teachers' performance once in the position. It can be used as an incentive for teachers to get additional endorsements and move into a new position within their current school.

- *District-sponsored loan forgiveness*: Teachers in hard-to-staff schools and shortage areas receive annual stipends to be applied to education loans. Different from federal loan forgiveness programs that eliminate remaining debt after a period of time in the profession, district-sponsored loan programs are short-term, meant to help teachers manage their monthly finances. Research suggests that this program is effective when annual payments range from $500–$2500 (Feng & Sass, 2018).

Table 10.1 Compensation Targets		
Compensation Model	**Whom It Advantages**	**Whom It Disadvantages**
Experience-based pay	Veteran teachers	Novice teachers
Merit pay	Novice teachers	High performers
Performance pay	High performers	Teachers with difficult assignments
School-based performance pay	Teachers with difficult assignments	N/A
Knowledge- and skills-based pay	All teachers	N/A
Market-based pay	Teachers with difficult assignments	N/A
District-sponsored loan forgiveness	Teachers with difficult assignments	N/A

Ideally, you'd have all of these models at your fingertips to use as necessary. In reality, districts tend to adopt one or two of these, leaving you to decide if there is space within the budget for additional compensation. Given your district's model, your job is to fill the gaps and make certain that those who may be disadvantaged by existing salary structures have alternative opportunities for compensation.

Professional Advancement

One way to retain teachers that gets around salary constraints is by moving high performers into higher paying positions. Not only does this acknowledge and reward their talent but it also has the added benefit of reengaging teachers who may have become complacent in their current role. A new position will restart the role-taking process as teachers learn new expectations, develop new self-efficacy beliefs, and begin role assessment. As teachers' cognitive engagement rises, so will their effort as they adjust to more rigorous job expectations.

Early-career teachers and teachers who may not be top performers can also benefit from new professional challenges. Everyone gets bored in their role at some point, so as school leader you must have structures in place to reignite passions and keep teachers committed to the profession. Maintaining teachers' investment in the school requires creative thinking about professional opportunities teachers may not even know to ask for. What positions does the school need to fill to enact the equity plan? What positions would enhance student outcomes?

THOUGHTS FROM THE FIELD

I think education has really antiquated ideas about what the career ladder needs to look like. I'm really annoyed that we think that in order to get to system level leadership you basically need to be old and experienced. As administrators, you can create these leadership positions. That's the authority that you have. Are you creating a building leadership team? Are you creating grade level leads? Are you creating spaces for people to explore?

I also think you have to give grace because I've had people who get their admin credential and they're like, "You know what, that's not for me." That's awesome. It is equally important and valid to stay a classroom teacher. We need more powerful, great classroom teachers so I support that. In those cases I tell them, "You can be an informal teacher leader in this way. You can be a formal teacher leader in this position. But if you want to be a building administrator, here are some of the things that you might want to read. Here are some of the things that you might want to explore. Here are some people that you might want to talk to."

When I'm coaching people, I'm very explicit about, "I think you've got some real leadership potential. Have you ever thought about this?" Administrators should explicitly amplify, reinforce, and tap talent, and then help people see what the pathway is to get from A to B.

Director Nash

Director Nash is advocating for more equitable leadership models—where everyone has an opportunity to do more and earn more, including beginning teachers who may be barred from leadership early in their careers. New roles should also be available to teachers who may not want to be in the classroom forever and for those who want to teach but perhaps desire more challenge. While you certainly want great teachers to remain in the classroom, the larger goal is to keep them in the profession. But if you want to maximize the likelihood that they stay at your school, you must provide as many professional avenues as possible.

Think of this as creating career lattices—not ladders—that allow teachers to move laterally and vertically into new positions. By not tying roles to experience but rather to expertise and achievements, you expand teachers' potential impact on the school. For instance, a second year teacher may not be suited for an instructional leadership position but they could have deep knowledge of curriculum development or extensive data analysis skills. How can you leverage teachers' hidden talents in mutually beneficial ways?

I suggest tracks between which teachers can move as their career goals change. Each track targets a different area of school functioning within which teachers can apply for different roles. Some roles will necessarily be tied to prior performance, but others may ask teachers to demonstrate their competency through credentials or previous work experience. Some positions may completely replace a position, whereas others may be integrated into a teacher's current role. You will need to revisit the organizational structure to clarify how new or revised positions fit within the school. I encourage you to resist the notion of hierarchy within and between tracks and to design positions that make unique and necessary contributions to the school. Table 10.2 suggests possible tracks and job opportunities.

Table 10.2 Career Tracks			
Potential Positions			
Administrative Track	School policy advisor	Induction and PD coordinator	Department chair
Content/ Curriculum Track	Data coach	Curriculum development director	Curriculum coach
Instructional Track	Instructional coach	Lead teacher	Master teacher

The nuances of leadership positions will depend on your school needs. For instance, an instructional coach may work with teachers who have improvement plans. A lead teacher might be the go-to person for preservice teachers looking for a practicum placement. A master teacher may conduct teaching observations and be on the tenure review committee. No matter the positions you choose, established tracks serve the dual purpose of keeping talent in the school while also helping teachers advance their careers.

Innovative thinking about educational careers is vital to increase workforce diversity. There are too few BIPOC in the field of education and even fewer in leadership positions. Many BITOC leave the profession before gaining enough experience to assume leadership roles, so the leadership pipeline consists primarily of white women in instructional and curriculum tracks and white men in administrative tracks. In Chapter 5, we discussed the value of having diverse teachers for students' outcomes, but there are also benefits to the profession. BITOC who move into leadership positions are socioculturally situated to understand how CLD students' needs have been systematically ignored through history. Their multicultural worldviews contribute new perspectives that enhance problem solving, particularly around issues of equity. Improving education for our most vulnerable youth will require the creative thinking that diversity facilitates.

Teacher Thrival

If you can get teachers through year 5, consider that a success because 44% percent of teachers leave the profession within their first 5 years (Ingersoll et al., 2018). A national survey conducted by the American Federation of Teachers (2017) found that 61% of teachers reported that their work is always or often stressful and 58% describe their mental health as "not good." Teachers also reported poor health and sleep deprivation because of chronic stress, which can result in poor cognition and difficulties with emotion regulation (Katz et al., 2016). Inevitably, teachers begin to feel hopeless, cynical, and ineffective as their effort never satisfies job requirements (Spittle et al., 2015). Teacher burnout is among the top contributors to teacher turnover (Perrone et al., 2019) and is arguably the most concerning.

Skaalvik and Skaalvik (2017) investigated the dimensions of teacher burnout and its contributing factors. They found that emotional exhaustion, depersonalization, and reduced personal accomplishment were three primary facets of burnout. Further, they discovered that discipline problems, time pressure, low student motivation, and value dissonance contributed uniquely to each dimension. They concluded that providing supports will go a long way to helping teachers feel valued and efficacious, but the emotional toll that teaching takes must be more strategically managed.

Teachers' emotional well-being is becoming increasingly important with the surge of school shootings, economic crises, and the COVID-19 pandemic—all of which have drastically increased work demands. Teachers in Title I schools, special education (SPED) teachers, and school psychologists have historically been those who report compassion fatigue from interacting with individuals exposed to prolonged trauma (Sacco et al., 2015; Thieleman & Cacciatore 2014). But now, almost all teachers are likely to experience the physical and emotional turmoil characteristic of secondary traumatic stress (Hamid & Musa, 2017).

While you don't want these teachers to leave the profession, you also don't want them to remain in the classroom under emotional duress. It is perhaps more worrisome that teachers continue in the field despite feeling worn out, apathetic, and pessimistic. Valtierra (2016) termed this phenomenon teacher "burn in," which leads to survival, not thrival. Thriving teachers are resilient, passionate, and find joy in their work (Nieto, 2014; Palmer, 2007). As the school leader, you must send the message that teachers' emotional well-being is a prerequisite to their professional success. Here are a few things you can do to encourage emotional awareness and self-care:

- Be cognizant of the national education landscape, which is often the source of teachers' concerns about job security, accountability, and compensation.
- Monitor the overall tenor of the school, especially during stressful times of year. It is okay to cancel a meeting or reschedule a PD.
- Set a standard for self-care. Make it clear that teachers can request short-term coverage if they need to take a break during the school day or be absent for a mental health day.
- Prioritize connection over content. Begin staff meetings with check-ins.
- Integrate mindfulness trainings into the PD program. Encourage teachers to share these strategies with students.
- Respect teachers' downtime. Do not ask them to respond to email, meet with parents, or prepare lessons during breaks. There should be no expectations of evening and weekend work unless contracted or agreed to.
- Maintain communication. Consider an open-door policy or weekly office hours so teachers know you are available outside of formal meetings.
- Build community. Create or encourage participation in district-wide affinity groups for minoritized teachers who may experience

additional stress and professional pressure pertinent to their sociocultural identities.

• Be authentic. Don't be afraid to share your vulnerabilities, anxieties, and dreams; in doing so you model how to bring your whole self to work. Teachers should know that their school is an emotionally safe space to be themselves.

THOUGHTS FROM THE FIELD

Culture or climate is so important. Leadership is so important. I tell people, "People don't leave schools. They leave leaders."

Dr. Houser

The truth is that many of the factors that make teachers leave are beyond your control. But, as Dr. Houser says, teachers don't leave schools, they leave leaders. The best you can do is to advocate on teachers' behalf for equitable compensation, support their career advancement, and provide positive working conditions. Teachers will recognize and appreciate your investment in their professional and personal selves and hopefully reciprocate by remaining at the school.

Reflection Questions

1. How can you leverage the factors that motivate teachers to join the profession (reviewed in the introduction) to help keep them in the profession?
2. Review your staffing assessment and equity action plan. Where are leadership opportunities?
3. Compile the highly qualified evaluation standards you wrote at the end of Chapter 9 to create a list of tenure standards. How many current teachers qualify for tenure using these standards?
4. Do students benefit from teacher tenure? If so, which students? If not, why not?

5. Which salary models benefit what demographic of teachers?
6. Data shows that BITOC leave the profession at faster rates than white teachers. Why? What factors may disproportionately contribute to BITOC burnout?
7. Why is it important for students and families to see diverse leadership at their school?
8. How can you integrate self-care into your PD program?

11 Conducting Schoolwide Equity Assessments

I
f you've stuck with me this long, you will be happy to hear that we've made it to the end . . . or really, to a new beginning. Way back in Chapter 1, you conducted a needs assessment to identify educational inequities throughout the school. You determined what needed to be assessed, who would do the assessment, and how data would be collected. You then used those outcomes to backward design your core values, vision and mission statements, and your equity action plan. Since then you'll have put much thought into your organizational structure and practices, family and community outreach programs, teacher hiring and onboarding processes, and into how best to integrate professional development and teacher evaluation to promote retention. It's now time to see if all your hard work has met the intended goal of enhancing educational equity.

I diverge from common practice here and suggest that you conduct a schoolwide equity *assessment*, rather than the traditional equity *evaluation* or *audit*. The distinction is important because it speaks to purpose, procedure, and implications. Assessment in this situation is formative, in that it provides information about in-process practices so you can make proactive adjustments. Evaluations are used to judge outcomes at the end of a predetermined period and are beneficial for future decision-making. Audits are a blend of both but are narrow in scope as they deeply investigate a single aspect of school functioning.

I suggest conducting audits after you've completed the equity assessment and have identified a specific process or practice that is not producing desired outcomes. Equity audits on teacher quality, student achievement, and even on program design are fairly common (Skrla et al., 2009). Principals work with district personnel to assemble a team of external reviewers who spend 1 day at the school gathering and synthesizing data that informs a written report with recommendations for increasing equity in the target domain.

Districts will sometimes conduct equity audits to ascertain systematic differences in equity across schools. Audits usually happen after the implementation of a new policy that has potentially large impacts on student achievement. For example, NCLB required schools to include students with disabilities in state assessment and accountability systems, which resulted in much lower student achievement scores in most schools, but not all. A district might conduct an equity audit of special education student achievement to identify schools with good SPED outcomes in hopes of replicating their practices.

The goal of a schoolwide equity assessment is also to bolster what is working and to quickly change what is not. Because the exact inquiry areas will be determined by your action plan, in this chapter I review the six-step process of conducting a school equity assessment. I pay special attention to potential pitfalls that may derail the process or produce unconstructive outcomes.

Step 1: Choosing Assessment Domains

The action plan has a list of SMART goals (Specific, Measurable, Agreeable, Realistic, Time-framed) with relevant objectives for each. It is tempting to simply review the objectives and identify which have been met and which haven't, but that would be an evaluation, not an assessment. You want to understand the process through which a goal was achieved and the impact of that goal on educational equity. All teachers may have reduced discipline referrals by 25%, but does that truly matter to student outcomes? Which demographic of students had fewer referrals? Did teachers meet the accompanying goal of implementing restorative justice practices? How do those two goals, if both were achieved, jointly enhance equity? Those are the questions a school discipline equity assessment will answer.

But that can't be the only domain you assess. What other areas of school functioning are related to discipline that may have been affected by the implementation of restorative justice? Perhaps the needs assessment revealed a negative correlation between absenteeism and work completion, so another SMART goal might have been "teachers should check in with absent students once every 2 days they are absent." Following up with absent students was a good goal when written, but if fewer suspensions have eliminated the majority of absenteeism, this goal is no longer needed. It might be more useful to switch domains entirely and examine another important area such as family engagement.

Again, you don't want to rely solely on the goals and objectives in the action plan to guide your assessment. You need to synthesize and expand upon small goals to create a guiding purpose statement. For instance, a purpose statement for a family engagement equity assessment might be, "The family engagement assessment team will examine which parents and families are involved at the school, the type of involvement, the extent of their involvement, the perceptions of their involvement, and the impact of their involvement on students, teachers, and/or the school." Note here that this purpose statement details what to assess but it doesn't indicate the driving factor underlying those facets of family engagement.

For that, you need to have a clear problem of practice (PoP) that illuminates the behavior motivating outcomes that can be changed if the assessment finds it to be ineffective. A good PoP should be chosen based upon research or available evidence. For instance, you may focus on invitations to family involvement as you conduct the family engagement equity assessment because parents' decision-making about when and how they are involved is dependent upon their perceived invitations to involvement (Hoover-Dempsey & Sandler, 1997; Walker et al., 2005). If the assessment demonstrates that only parents from a particular income group attend school events, you will want to understand how school practices influenced that finding. According to City and colleagues (2009), a "rich problem of practice focuses on the instructional core; is directly observable; connects to a broader strategy of improvement; is high-leverage" (p. 102).

The PoP should then be used to create a research question that will inform your data and choice of measures. In this example, a good research question is, "How can we ensure that families have equitable and impactful opportunities to participate in their child's education?" You should be able to answer this question at the conclusion of the assessment.

Step 2: Building the Assessment Team

Building the assessment team is a strategic process. The team will not actually work together to conduct assessments, but each team member will spearhead an assessment of a particular area. Because assessment is such a detailed process that can take many months, it is best to simultaneously assess domains that are unrelated to one another so that data collection in one area does not influence another. You also want to align people's expertise with the identified domain (think back to our conversation about team-based leadership in Chapter 2), so if you are assessing multiple goals and objectives within the same domain, you may need a single person to lead both processes. Because it is unreasonable to ask them to conduct two assessments simultaneously while also doing their regular job, you will have to create a detailed assessment timeline that takes into consideration individual people's capacity to lead such an important initiative.

Assessment team leads will create task forces of four to five people to help manage the additional work. Any smaller and there won't be enough members for a comprehensive review; any larger and the assessment will become unwieldy. Task force members should have deep familiarity with the assessment domain and collectively offer multiple perspectives on the topic. For example, if you are assessing equity in advanced course enrollment, you will need teachers who teach advanced classes to be on the team and perhaps the curriculum coach or others with knowledge of differences between academic tracks.

Keep team membership internal. While external reviewers bring objectivity, that is not necessary at this stage. Formative assessments are more valid when team members have the institutional knowledge to know whom to include in the assessment, what to ask them, and most importantly, how to contextualize findings. It is best to staff assessment task forces with members of the action plan implementation team, but to assign them to different domains to prevent bias. Keeping the same group of people improves consistency and means that you already have structures in place to support their additional work.

Finally, leave one spot open because once you choose data sources, you may need to add someone to the team. For instance, if you decide to do student focus groups as a part of the advanced course enrollment assessment, you will need someone who has a good relationship with identified students to facilitate those conversations. That person may or may not be on the assessment team already.

Step 3: Making an Assessment Plan

Go back to your purpose statement, problem of practice, and research question. Who is explicitly named in the purpose statement? Who utilizes the identified practice? Who can best answer the research question? In our family engagement example, parents and families are named in the purpose statement, teachers and students extend invitations to involvement, and anyone related to the school may have valuable insight into the research question.

You will want to include multiple perspectives so that you can triangulate your data by comparing one group's perception to another's. Research demonstrates that teachers and parents have different perceptions of invitations to involvement (Bakker et al., 2007; Wong & Hughes, 2006) so it is necessary to think through all possible stakeholders and how their positionality within the school may influence their experiences. A good rule of thumb is to have at least two sources of data, but three is better. It is okay, and probably more efficient, if one of those sources is data or artifacts that can objectively illustrate a phenomenon.

Including data and artifacts in the assessment has the added benefit of determining your timeline for you. The assessment should begin by reviewing concrete facts that will inform what you ask participants. If document analyses show that invitations to families are descriptive and not persuasive, you will want to ask families about their perception of the value of attending school events. Conversely, if invitations describe the benefits of their participation, you might ask them to indicate how relevant those benefits are to them.

When you develop the overall timeline, give yourself plenty of space between data collection events to do this kind of mini analysis. Combing through documents and watching videos will take longer than glancing at achievement data. Once completed, you will need additional time to develop or locate measures for consequent data collection. Don't forget to factor in the time it takes to schedule and conduct interviews and to distribute and collect surveys. How you collect data will also affect this timeline. In-person data collection can engender more substantive and accurate information because participants can seek clarification if necessary. But online data collection is faster and can reach a broader audience. Once you choose your measures in Step 4, you may need to revise the assessment plan.

Step 4: Choosing Measures

A measure is simply the method for collecting data. Common measures include surveys, interviews, and focus groups. Schools also rely heavily on data and educational artifacts (e.g., samples of students' work, videos of instruction) during assessments. Determining which of these will best answer your research question is paramount because some measures are better for certain types of questions (see Table 11.1).

You also need to consider the individual and collective utility of each measure because not all measures generate credible data to the same extent. Issues of objectivity versus subjectivity aside, when selecting measures, you will want to attend to their validity, reliability, and if pertinent, fidelity. As a reminder from Chapter 9, *validity* describes the extent to which a measure assesses what it is supposed to assess. A test about the American Revolution should include questions about the Boston Tea Party but not questions about the Battle of Gettysburg. It should also assess students' knowledge of the Stamp Act, the Battles of Lexington and Concord, and the Treaty of Paris as pivotal events of the war. Measures that are on target (face validity) and all-encompassing (content validity) will yield accurate information about the domain under examination.

Reliable measures are data collection methods that produce consistent findings no matter how you ask questions or the amount of time between collection periods. Surveys are notorious for being unreliable unless they've been used many times with various people under differing circumstances. Published surveys will almost always have undergone some type of reliability assessment, so you can be fairly certain they are acceptable measures. However, I caution against developing your own survey because you will not be able to preemptively guarantee that questions are worded clearly, are not repetitive, and are easily understood by everyone. If a measure has low reliability, you will likely get incoherent information that may diminish the value of the findings.

Reliability has a different name when assessing behaviors rather than beliefs and attitudes. When doing observations for example, you want observers to adhere to the observation protocols and correctly use the rubric. This is called *fidelity*. You may have heard this term in relation to teaching practices or with respect to curriculum. In both cases the intent is for educators to use instructional tools as they were designed to be used. Diverging from the curriculum may mean that students have knowledge gaps at the end of the year. Similarly, using measures without fidelity will generate incomplete data.

Data Analyses

The final consideration when choosing measures is what you will do with the data once you have it. Data analyses can get very complex very quickly, so you want to choose measures with easily managed data. Table 11.1 describes each measure's research focus, type(s) of data, and time estimates for data collection and analyses.

As noted in Table 11.1, some measures are more time consuming than others, but they also generate more comprehensive data than do measures with minimal time investments. Rich data sounds great but remember that the more data you have, the more complicated the analyses. Further, the type of data will also dictate the analysis process. Quantitative data provides numerical snapshots but very little

	Research Focus	Type of Data	Time for Data Collection	Time for Analyses
Table 11.1 Data Collection Considerations				
Data	Facts	Quantitative	Minimal	Minimal
Surveys	Beliefs/ Perceptions	Quantitative Qualitative	Minimal	Minimal
Observations	Behaviors	Quantitative Qualitative	Moderate	Moderate
Interviews	Beliefs/ Perceptions	Qualitative	Considerable	Considerable
Focus Groups	Consensus	Qualitative	Moderate	Considerable
Documents	Evidence/ Examples	Qualitative	Minimal	Considerable

context for the numbers. You will likely be interested in the overall distribution of data as reflected by measures of central tendency such as the mean, median, standard deviation, and range. Quantitative data is easily disaggregated by subgroup, so while it may not provide a lot of detail about what influenced data points, it does facilitate intergroup comparisons.

But not all quantitative data is the same. Achievement scores are objective indicators of student performance, but accompanying survey data might reflect people's perceptions of students' performance. Parents may think their child's performance is similar to that of other students, or teachers may not realize that their immigrant students are performing a full standard deviation below the class average. Survey data is most useful when you identify average perceptions among groups that can be further examined through other data collection methods.

Observational data is even more limited because it is drawn from a small sample and cannot (or rather, should not) be generalized to a larger population. The family engagement task force may choose to observe teachers' interactions with parents during parent–teacher conferences. However, it is impossible to observe every teacher in every conversation so the team must randomly choose (or perhaps their research question promotes purposive sampling) a sample of teachers to observe. Ideally there would be two observers per exchange, but in reality it is more efficient for each observer to conduct two or three independent observations. A well-designed observational rubric used with fidelity will allow the team to compare (but not average) observational scores (quantitative data) and summative notes (qualitative data). Observers would then jointly write a synthesized summary of teachers' interactions with parents, focusing on the problem of practice and research question.

Quantitative data is often supplemented with qualitative data to explain numerical findings. This is why you should wait to develop interview and focus group questions until after you've analyzed quantitative data. Individual and group interviews require that you create an interview protocol with scripted questions to ensure reliability across interviews. Interview questions should also have face validity in that they directly relate to the problem of practice and research question. However, they may not have content validity because you won't be able to discuss everything important about family engagement in a 30–45 minute interview. Draft questions that explain, not repeat, quantitative findings. For example, if parents indicate on surveys that they only get two invites a year from teachers, you know to directly ask interviewed teachers how many invitations they send to parents. Similarly, if students report that their parents help with homework every day, you may ask interviewed parents how comfortable they are helping with homework. Make sure someone else reviews your interview protocol with an eye toward reliability and validity. Double-barreled questions, negatively worded questions, and multipart questions can confuse interviewees and decrease reliability. You should use simple, clear, accessible language and avoid educational jargon including the acronyms we love so much.

The content of interviews will be the first source of data, but you should also take running notes during the interviews that will help make sense of responses later. Running notes attend to tone, body language, speaking volume, and pace. In focus groups, be sure to note who speaks the most, the order of responses, and how often people make conflicting and affirmative statements. Interviews and focus groups result in a lot of information that will require careful analysis of patterns within and across conversations. The goal is to identify over-arching themes that reveal general perceptions and beliefs about the topic of inquiry.

Broad themes should be supported by evidence. If, on average, parents discussed feelings of exclusion during their interviews, it is prudent to locate copies of invitations sent to parents to identify possible sources of those emotions. When analyzing documents, pay attention to language, legibility, formatting, and tone. Compare across documents to ascertain consistency in messaging (for example, across invitations to involvement) and consistency in quality (for example, across student work). It may be that parents feel excluded because invitations are only sent in English or because teachers are not uniformly inviting parents' participation. Perhaps the invitations are missing critical information or parents' involvement is solicited in ways that implicitly prevent them from participating. Remember that documents do not tell the full story so they should not be analyzed in the absence of other data sources. But when used correctly, documents can provide concrete examples of abstract phenomena.

Step 5: Interpreting Findings

Interpreting findings is the most difficult part of assessment because there are so many things that might have happened to influence outcomes. This is why it is extremely important that task force members are able to contextualize results using their knowledge of how other school factors interact with their target domain in ways that may skew outcomes. The task force also has knowledge of the assessment process itself, so members are aware of procedural missteps that could affect findings. Here are a few things to ask yourself before making conclusions:

- Was the timing of the assessment appropriate? What else was happening at the school that might have affected the assessment process?
- How might bias have emerged during assessment?
- Were the measures valid, reliable, and used with fidelity?
- How did the choice of measures affect findings? Would different measures have facilitated different outcomes?
- Were the correct participants chosen to share information? How might other people have answered questions? Would a random sample have been better?
- Was data analyzed using appropriate methods? Was data disaggregated in meaningful ways?

If you feel confident that there were no practical errors, the next step is to situate your outcomes within your school framework. What unique elements of your school may contribute to outcomes in ways not present at other schools? For instance, if parents are asked to sign an involvement contract, it is likely that you already had higher than average levels of parent participation. Or, perhaps most families are upper income and therefore have more resources to devote to their child's learning. Both scenarios would skew outcomes in ways that make it difficult, though not impossible, to identify inequities.

Once you've considered local influences, think about confounding factors that might have been at play. Parents may have reported receiving few invitations to involvement but teachers reported extending numerous invitations. The disconnect may have nothing to do with the content, timing, or method of invitation. It may be that students did not give their parents the invitations. You discovered at the beginning of this process that invitations to involvement predict family engagement; however, you did not account for the fact that the quality of parent–child relationships also affects parents' motivations for involvement (Mo & Singh, 2008). In this case, parent–child relationships would be a confounding variable that explains your findings.

Lastly, turn your attention beyond the school. How do your findings compare to those of similar schools in your district and state? The goal of such comparisons is not critique or judgment, but information. Looking at other schools' outcomes will provide insight into the efficacy of family engagement strategies that may also be effective at your school. You might also discover alternative explanations for findings that you didn't consider.

Step 6: Determining Implications

Your findings are pretty useless if you don't do anything with them. The point of doing equity assessments is to gather information you can use to make changes in school practices, but not all findings suggest change is warranted. If a disaggregated analysis of survey data demonstrated no significant differences between parents' involvement rates based upon income, race, or student grade level, there is probably nothing for you to do. Or it could be that despite consistent rates of involvement as indicated on surveys, teachers' interviews suggested that the impact of parental engagement differs depending on student achievement. This would mean that survey findings may not matter for high-achieving students but they do for low achievers. But how?

The tricky part of assessment is determining the implications of findings by synthesizing findings to make conclusions. If everyone has the same rate of family involvement but the impact of involvement matters more for low-achieving students, then there actually *are* inequities in family engagement. Low-achieving students may not be experiencing adequate amounts of parent participation given their academic needs. So, how can you make sure that students who benefit most from their family's involvement get it?

This is the point at which the assessment team leaders reconvene to share findings with one another and to make a plan to publicly share outcomes with the school community. Transparency is critical to maintaining communal trust and for ensuring the efficacy of the equity action plan. It is likely that the advisory board will need to revise the action plan, but only after receiving input from relevant stakeholders. Families will have great ideas about how the school can increase involvement rates. Teachers will have suggestions for increasing the impact of parents' involvement. Students, too, may have preferences for how their parents are involved in their education.

Effective and equitable leadership is inclusive and forward thinking. Teaching and learning are dynamic processes that change according to the evolving needs of students, teachers, and families. If your goal is to improve educational access and opportunity for all students, keep in mind the oft-cited adage that you can't teach what you don't know and you can't lead where you won't go. Equity assessments ensure that you have the knowledge and vision to lead for justice.

Reflection Questions

1. How do evaluations and assessments work together to improve equity?
2. Why are counternarratives important when conducting equity assessments?
3. Should students and families be members of an assessment task force? Why or why not?
4. Among the possible data collection methods, which are most inclusive? Which have the highest potential for bias?
5. Problems of practice are the actionable behaviors that facilitate or impede equity. How will you identify the problems of practice underlying abstract action plan goals?
6. What other schools in your district have an equity focus? How might you collaborate with them to conduct assessments?

Final Thoughts

It is nearing the end of Shelby's third year and she is hastily reviewing the outcomes of her equity audit. Not all components are complete, but her contract ends in a month and the state wants to know if Shelby has been successful at turning Roger Gates around. The state seems pleased with Shelby's test scores from her first two years, and hopeful that in year three, achievement levels will rise even more. Shelby thinks that moving from 32% to 7% below proficiency in just two years is evidence enough, but apparently it is not.

So, Shelby decides to assemble a portfolio of progress that demonstrates growth beyond test scores. In it she includes: a list of grants Roger Gates has been awarded; community partnerships; family engagement initiatives; attendance and discipline rates; enrollment numbers in advanced courses, survey data from people who've used the academic skills center; quotes from families garnered from the equity audit interviews; and samples of teachers' lesson plans and students' work.

She writes a cover letter that describes how she:

- *created an advisory board that co-wrote a strategic plan*
- *brainstormed new positions, policies, and practices that would increase student outcomes*
- *spent weekends hanging out at neighborhood hotspots to create goodwill between the school and the community*
- *actively recruited new families and encouraged existing families to give her a chance to restore Roger Gates*

- *cultivated the most diverse staff in the school's history—one that reflects the increasingly heterogenous student body*
- *developed orientation, induction, and career advancement programs that sent attrition rates to an all-time low*
- *kept equity at the core of everything she did*

She concludes her letter with a simple request: she'd like to remain at Roger Gates middle school not as a turn-around principal, but as the principal.

While Shelby waits for members of the school board to arrive for their "observation," she thinks about a conversation she had with an 8th grade parent yesterday. When she asked him why he decided to enroll his rising 6th grader at Roger Gates despite the school's recent struggles, he replied, "Because once you got here and I saw what you were trying to do to make the school better, I realized that change isn't bad as long as you have someone who cares leading the charge."

Conclusion

Titles have never been my strength. I tend to name things exactly what they are. My course names include Educational Psychology, Urban Education, Diversity and Equity in Education, and Education Reform. I do slightly better with journal articles and much worse with books. This book was no different.

I wait until a project is complete to create a title because that's when I truly know what the work is about. But still, it's difficult to capture everything important about a text in a few words. My publisher and I eventually landed on *Public [School] Equity: Educational Leadership for Justice* after a lot of back and forth, during which I realized what was most important for me to convey to readers. I was convinced (kind of) to drop the brackets, but I include them here to emphasize permutations of the three words I chose for the short title.

Public School. This is a book about schools, but specifically, public schools. Fifty-one million children attend public schools in the United States, be they traditional, charter, or magnet. Included in that 51 million are 27.6 million racially minoritized students, 12 million students attending high-poverty schools, 7 million students with IEPs, and 5 million English language learners—all of whom are the focus of conversations about educational access and opportunity. I also included the word *public* as a reminder to us all that schools are a public good and a civic institution.

School Equity. This is also a book about equity and how we can achieve equity within a single school. I intentionally focus on school equity because schools are where the work happens. State and district entities are too far removed from the day-to-day of school life, so I've never understood why we expect reform to originate there. After three quarters of a century of ineffective policies, we should know that if schools are going to change, we are going to have to change them from the inside out.

Public Equity. Hence my emphasis on public equity. Private investment in public equity (PIPE) is a common phrase in the financial world but it applies to education as well. We the people must take ownership of our children's futures by investing our collective resources into our neighborhood schools. And we need leaders to manage those resources.

Educational Leadership for Justice. The long title of this book makes it clear that I am speaking to education leaders including principals, assistant principals, master teachers and instructional coaches, community organizers, education advocacy organizations, superintendents, lobbyists, and policy writers. I am asking education leaders to lead *for* justice because that is the end goal. Justice. Other book titles ask that we lead *with* justice, but that phrasing centers the work without acknowledging the spirit of the work. Leading for justice requires that you advance the liberation of our youth from oppressive policies and practices within schools, so that they can one day transform the world beyond the school.

An early reader of this book asked me what it would look like if just one education leader in just one school lead for justice. Here is my vision.

Picture This

New Orleans, Louisiana: No longer a school district composed entirely of charter schools operated by charter management organizations (CMOs) led by white businessmen in other states. Chapters 1 through 3 imagine what schools might look like if we didn't outsource leadership and if we keep equity at the core of policies, practices, and pedagogies:

- schools are locally owned and operated; a school for the people, by the people, with the people
- achievable vision and mission statements, supported by a concrete action plan
- responsive and anticipatory decision-making
- courses aligned with students' interests and life goals, be they college, career, or family focused
- a collaborative school culture with communal investment in equity
- manageable teacher workload
- no student homework
- credit recovery
- enhanced opportunities to learn
- no academic tracks
- active student participation in their learning, affirming that they are their own best advocates

Detroit, Michigan: The 24% of children who left their neighborhood school return to schools strengthened by the family and community partnerships described in Chapter 4, resulting in:

- coalition building
- families being included in school decision-making
- families regularly in the school
- home visits
- positive family contacts
- full community participation in school board elections
- the school is a hub for community events
- robust student mentoring program
- student internships at community businesses
- after-school programs led by community leaders
- graduates stay in the area
- active alumni engagement

Washington, D.C.: The capital city still has the highest number of racially diverse students in the nation, but they are now taught by a teacher workforce that mirrors their demographics. Chapters 5 and 6 ask us to envision a school with rich sociocultural wealth. Such a place would have:

- an affirming school climate
- asset-based perceptions of students
- an explicit recognition of the culture of power
- culturally sustaining pedagogies
- anti-racist teaching
- anti-oppressive teaching
- curricula that reflect students' sociocultural identities and experiences

Arizona: This southwestern state is lauded for having the lowest, not the highest, teacher turnover rate in the country. Chapters 7 through 10 argue that reducing annual attrition rates from 24% to below 10% could happen if a school:

- maintained a culture of praxis
- implemented a multiyear induction program
- overwhelmed new and novice teachers with supports
- determined teaching assignments based on teachers' skills and interests
- offered consistent and relevant professional development opportunities
- challenged teachers
- respected teachers
- provided career advancement pathways
- promoted self-care and emotional well-being

The Big Picture

I ended the Introduction with an admission that centering equity one school at a time would not result in large-scale reform in the near future. But what about the distant future? How might that look?

In my dream of dreams, neoliberalism and free-market capitalism would have no place in our schools. We would not be competing with one another to make certain our children receive a quality education. Those with the most capital would not be privileged on the school choice market. In fact, there would be no market. Middle- and upper-income families would not choose their homes based upon school district, so mixed income (and consequently, mixed race) neighborhoods would be commonplace. Children would happily attend the school down the street that is just as good as the school across the tracks because they each do what is best for their students.

Teachers could then use factors other than student race and income to decide where to work. A highly qualified teacher would be understood as someone with the skills, knowledge, and cultural competence to effectively work with *these* kids in *this* school, regardless of their own sociocultural identities. Acknowledging that some teachers are more effective with some students would not be taboo or politically incorrect. It would be right. And Just. Expanding the notion of teacher–student matching beyond race and ethnicity would help us view students holistically, as more than their most oppressed identity. We might then humanize education—and change the purpose of school from learning, to learning how to learn. If we focus on the process and not standardized products, kids will see school as a joyful space to (be)come.

I truly believe that if students want to be there, teachers will too. So much of what pushes teachers out of the profession relates to student engagement. Yes, we must properly compensate teachers, but we should do that *and* make certain that they too experience joy at school. Teacher churn sustains the narrative that teaching is a stopgap job on the way to a more prestigious career. Increasing retention by improving working conditions and expanding advancement opportunities will send the message that teaching is a profession that requires adequate preparation.

Enrollment in traditional teacher preparation programs might therefore rise to their pre-Race to the Top levels. We will no longer need alternative licensure programs to hastily fill staffing shortages in racially isolated and high-poverty schools as those schools would no longer exist. And if they did, fully licensed teachers would be there to utilize anti-racist and trauma-informed teaching practices.

At the end of Chapter 1, I asked leaders to think through building equity up, building equity out, and building equity in. That is what I am describing. We must create equity in a single school, apply equitable models to other schools, and then make certain we have the capacity to sustain equity across all public schools. Education reform necessitates a chain reaction that begins with repurposing schools as the place where justice begins, not ends.

After all of that, my short answer to the reviewer would be: One leader in one school leading for justice looks like freedom.

ADVICE FROM THE FIELD: HOW TO LEAD FOR JUSTICE

First and foremost would be to meet the parents. Day one, send an email or a letter, open lines of communication, give everybody your email address because you want them to know they can reach you. You can't be equitable if you don't know what the inequities are. And the only way to know that is to get in touch with families. I really think there is a big system versus parent conundrum going on, and reaching out, a simple, "Hey, how are you?" or a "What do you need?" could break that. Just send out a quick survey, and ask, "What are the needs in your community?"

Mr. Barry

If you're going to lead for equity and justice, you need to start in the interview. You need to make it very clear during the interview that you're coming in to lead for equity and justice. That way, if that's not what they want, they won't hire you. Don't go in and try to get a job and then pull the okie-doke and say, "No, I'm a social justice warrior." No. During the interview, make it clear that, "When I come in, these are the things I'm hoping to accomplish." And when they hire you, remind them that that's what you said, and start to talk to the district, your boss, and the superintendent about the things you need to make that happen. And then when you meet with staff early on, make it clear that, "This is what we're doing, and this is where we're going." That way, anyone who's not on board can transfer. That simple. If not, you'll never reach that goal of equity.

Dr. Carmichael

Establish a need. Start off with data so that when you're proposing that the staff get out there and transform the school in these ways that are more socially just, the request can be based on something other than opinion. Begin with real clear, low-hanging fruit changes. You want things you can get some quick wins early on because that deep work, that's cultural work, right? Usually inequity is about the culture. That's a three to five year job. So you want to give them something early that they feel like, "Oh my God, this really made a difference. I can trust my principal." And then keep going deeper and deeper. Build the buy-in through relationships. I have them look at literature together. Maybe the whole school reads a book or an article or something. I would say they should do this work over the course of a year together and reexamine at different points. How are we doing?

Ms. Fisher

Definitely read what's going on. Read the research. Use what you can, don't try everything. Just use what you can. Always carry a list of 10 things your school needs. A list. I need 25 computers in the computer lab. The cheerleaders need new uniforms. The band needs new equipment. Always have a list. Because you are going to be on an elevator with someone or at an event and they will ask what you do. That's your in. You say "I'm a principal at so and so school and I love it but we have needs." You will be surprised how many people want to help. You have to be ready to ask.

Dr. Houser

Establish your priorities, share them with everyone, and then align all resources to those priorities. You have to be proactive. You have to be proactive with funding, with staff, and with the ability to take on needs as they come. You have to recognize that you are going to receive students that are all different, all unique, all special, all from different walks of life, that all need something different. And us, as the leaders, we've got to ensure that we are putting things in place, whether it be differentiating our instruction, whether it be providing one-on-one interventions or small group interventions, or paraprofessionals or check-ins, or a mentor or financial assistance. We've got to put things in place to make sure everyone has resources. That's crucial for equity work.

Principal Lewis

In your first year, don't do anything. You need to observe your surroundings. You need to see how ripe certain issues are before you start pushing it, and you need to build certain capital. So my practical advice for administrators, is that in your first year, you should just listen, do empathy interviews, just try to understand where the power bases are. Make sure that if you see something that you hate, make sure you really understand the history of that, because there's history and there's politics that you won't know about. Start to understand your context, build the relationships, do technical things that get you credibility, so that when you want to do this kind of equity work in a big way, you can calculate the risks on some of the projects that you want to take on.

Director Nash

Do your research. Create authentic connections with people that look like your students and get out there. There are so many ways that you can connect, and support and uplift communities. If you have the funds, you can fund a campaign, you can sponsor an organization, you can literally go volunteer your time. Don't look for your students or your community to educate you. Remember that the most good that you can do is to help dismantle oppressive systems. You have to lead for justice.

Ms. Richardson

References

Abacioglu, C. S., Volman, M., & Fischer, A. H. (2020). Teachers' multicultural attitudes and perspective taking abilities as factors in culturally responsive teaching. *British Journal of Educational Psychology*, *90*(3), 736–752.

Acosta, M. M. (2015). "No time for messin' around!" Understanding Black educator urgency: Implications for the preparation of urban educators. *Urban Education, 53*(8), 981–1012. https://doi.org/10.1177/0042085915613545

Albert Shanker Institute. (2015). The state of teacher diversity in American education. Retrieved November 11, 2020, from http://www.shankerinstitute.org/sites/shanker/files/The%20State%20Teacher%20 Diversity%20Exec%20Summary_0.pdf

Alexander, K. L., Entwisle, D. R., & Olson, L. S. (2007). Lasting consequences of the summer learning gap. *American Sociological Review*, *72*(2), 167–180.

Algozzine, B., Gretes, J., Queen, A. J., & Cowan-Hathcock, M. (2007). Beginning teachers' perceptions of their induction program experiences. *The Clearing House: A Journal of Educational Strategies, Issues and Ideas, 80*(3), 137–143.

Allegretto, S., & Mishel, L. (2019). The teacher pay penalty has hit a new high: Trends in the teacher wage and compensation gaps through 2017. *Economic Policy Institute*. Retrieved January 10, 2021, from https://files.epi.org/pdf/165729.pdf

Allen, J., Gregory, A., Mikami, A., Lun, J., Hamre, B., & Pianta, R. (2013). Observations of effective teacher–student interactions in secondary school classrooms: Predicting student achievement with the classroom assessment scoring system—secondary. *School Psychology Review, 42*(1), 76–98.

American Federation of Teachers. (2017). *2017 Educator quality of work life survey.* Retrieved January 11, 2021, from https://www.aft.org/sites/default/files/2017_eqwl_survey_web.pdf

Amrein-Beardsley, A., & Holloway, J. (2019). Value-added models for teacher evaluation and accountability: Commonsense assumptions. *Educational Policy, 33*(3), 516–542.

Anderman, E. M. (2002). School effects on psychological outcomes during adolescence. *Journal of Educational Psychology, 94*(4), 795–809.

Anderson-Butcher, D., Lawson, H. A., Iachini, A., Flaspohler, P., Bean, J., & Wade-Mdivanian, R. (2010). Emergent evidence in support of a community collaboration model for school improvement. *Children & Schools, 32*(3), 160–171. https://doi.org/10.1093/cs/32.3.160.

Baker, J. A. (1999). Teacher-student interaction in urban at-risk classrooms: Differential behavior, relationship quality, and student satisfaction with school. *The Elementary School Journal, 100*(1), 57–70.

Baker, E. L., Barton, P. E., Darling-Hammond, L., Haertel, E., Ladd, H. F., Linn, R. L., . . . Shepard, L. A. (2010). Problems with the use of student test scores to evaluate teachers. *Economic Policy Institute.* Retrieved January 4, 2020, from http://www.epi.org/publications/entry/bp278

Bakker, J., Denessen, E., & Brus-Laeven, M. (2007). Socio-economic background, parental involvement and teacher perceptions of these in relation to pupil achievement. *Educational Studies, 33*, 177–192.

Baldwin, J. (1963). The Negro child—His self-image. *The Saturday Review.* Retrieved August 12, 2020, from https://richgibson.com/talktoteachers.htm

Bandura, A. (1997). *Self-efficacy: The exercise of control.* Freeman.

Bandura, A., & Walters, R. H. (1977). *Social learning theory* (Vol. 1). Prentice-Hall.

Banks, J. A. (1994). *Multiethnic education: Theory and practice* (3rd ed.). Allyn & Bacon.

Banks, J. A. (2010). Multicultural education: Characteristics and goals. In J. A. Banks & C. A. M. Banks (Eds.), *Multicultural education: Issues and perspectives* (pp. 3–30). Wiley.

Bhabha, H. (1994). *The location of culture*. Routledge.

Biasi, B. (2019). *The labor market for teachers under different pay schemes*. NBER Working Paper No. 24813. National Bureau of Economic Research. Retrieved January 10, 2021, from https://www.nber.org/system/files/working_papers/w24813/w24813.pdf\

Biddle, B. J. (1979). *Role theory: Expectations, identities, and behaviors*. Academic Press.

Bland, P., Church, E., & Luo, M. (2014). Strategies for attracting and retaining teachers. *Administrative Issues Journal, Education, Practice, and Research, 4*(1). Retrieved from http://www.eric.ed.gov/fulltext/EJ1058481.pdf

Bondy, S. (2001). Warming up to classroom research in a professional development school. *Contemporary Education, 72*(1), 8–6.

Bondy, E., & Ross, D. D. (2008). The teacher as warm demander. *Educational Leadership, 66*(1), 54–58.

Bonner, P. J., Warren, S. R., & Jiang, Y. H. (2018). Voices from urban classrooms: Teachers' perceptions on instructing diverse students and using culturally responsive teaching. *Education and Urban Society, 50*(8), 697–726.

Borko, H., Liston, D., & Whitcomb, J. A. (2007). Apples and fishes: The debate over dispositions in teacher education. *Journal of Teacher Education, 58*(5), 359–364.

Borgonovi, F., & Montt, G. (2012). Parental involvement in selected PISA countries and economies. *OECD Education and Working Papers, 73.* Retrieved December 7, 2020, from https://www.researchgate.net/publication/241764302_Parental_Involvement_in_Selected_PISA_Countries_and_Economies

Boyd, D., Lankford, H., Loeb, S., Ronfeldt, M., & Wyckoff, J. (2011). The effect of school neighborhoods on teachers' career decisions. In G. J. Duncan & R.J. Murnane (Eds.), *Whither opportunity* (pp. 377–396). Russell Sage.

Bozkuş, K., & Bayrak, C. (2019). The application of dynamic teacher professional development approach through experimental action research. *International Electronic Journal of Elementary Education, 11*(4), 335–352.

Bradford, C., & Braaten, M. (2018). Teacher evaluation and the demoralization of teachers. *Teaching and Teacher Education, 75*, 49–59.

Brandmiller, C., Dumont, H., & Becker, M. (2020). Teacher perceptions of learning motivation and classroom behavior: The role of student characteristics. *Contemporary Educational Psychology.* https://doi.org/10.1016/j.cedpsych.2020.101893.

Bristol, T. J., & Goings, R. B. (2019). Exploring the boundary-heightening experiences of Black male teachers: Lessons for teacher education programs. *Journal of Teacher Education, 70*(1), 51–64.

Bronfenbrenner, U. (1979). *The ecology of human development: Experiments by nature and design.* Harvard University Press.

Bruner, J. (1960). *The process of education.* Harvard University Press.

Cadenas, G. A., Cisneros, J., Spanierman, L. B., Yi, J., & Todd, N. R. (2020). Detrimental effects of colorblind racial attitudes in preparing a culturally responsive teaching workforce for immigrants. *Journal of Career Development.* https://doi.org/10.1177/0894845320903380.

Carter Andrews, D. J., & Gutwein, M. (2017). "Maybe that concept is still with us": Adolescents' racialized and classed perceptions of teachers' expectations. *Multicultural Perspectives, 19*(1), 5–15.

Carver-Thomas, D., & Darling-Hammond, L. (2019). The trouble with teacher turnover: How teacher attrition affects students and schools. *Education Policy Analysis Archives, 27*(36), 1–32.

Castagno, A. E. (2014). *Educated in whiteness: Good intentions and diversity in schools.* University of Minnesota Press.

Ceballo, R., Maurizi, L. K., Suarez, G. A., & Aretakis, M. T. (2014). Gift and sacrifice: Parental involvement in Latino adolescents' education. *Cultural Diversity and Ethnic Minority Psychology, 20*(1), 116–127. https://doi.org/10.1037/a0033472

Chang, M., Choi, N., & Kim, S. (2015). School involvement of parents of linguistic and racial minorities and their children's mathematics performance. *Educational Research and Evaluation, 21*(3), 209–231. https://doi.org/10.1080/13803611.2015.1034283

Chao, R. K. (2000). The parenting of immigrant Chinese and European American mothers: Relations between parenting styles, socialization goals, and parental practices. *Journal of Applied Developmental Psychology*, *21*(2), 233–248.

Cherng, H. Y. S., & Halpin, P. F. (2016). The importance of minority teachers: Student perceptions of minority versus white teachers. *Educational Researcher*, *45*(7), 407–420. https://doi.org/10.3102/0013189X16671718

Chetty, R., Friedman, J., & Rockoff, J. (2014). Measuring the impacts of teachers: Evaluating bias in teacher value-added estimates. *American Economic Review*, *104*(9), 2593–2632.

Chiu, M. M., Chow, B. W. Y., McBride, C., & Mol, S. T. (2016). Students' sense of belonging at school in 41 countries: Cross-cultural variability. *Journal of Cross-Cultural Psychology*, *47*(2), 175–196.

Christenson S. L., & Havsy, L. H. (2004). Family–school–peer relationships: Significance for social, emotional, and academic learning. In J. E. Zins, R. P. Weissberg, M. C. Wang & H. J. Walberg (Eds.), *Building academic success on social and emotional learning: What does the research say?* (pp. 59–75). Teachers College Press.

Chu, S. Y., & Garcia, S. B. (2018). Collective teacher efficacy and culturally responsive teaching efficacy of inservice special education teachers in the United States. *Urban Education*. https://doi.org/10.1177/0042085918770720

Ciganek, L. A. (2020). *Novice teachers' perceptions of their preparedness to teach students experiencing trauma: A mixed methods study*. [Doctoral dissertation, Southeastern University]. ProQuest Dissertation Publishing.

City, E. A., Elmore, R. F., Fiarman, S. E., & Teitel, L. (2009). *Instructional rounds in education*. Harvard Education Press.

Civil Rights Project. (2020). *Lost opportunities: How disparate school discipline continues to drive differences in the opportunity to learn*. Retrieved December 1, 2020, from https://www.civilrightsproject.ucla.edu/research/k-12-education/school-discipline/lost-opportunities-how-disparate-school-discipline-continues-to-drive-differences-in-the-opportunity-to-learn/Lost-Opportunities_v12_EXECUTIVE-SUMMARY.pdf

Council of Chief State School Officers (CCSSO). (2021). *InTASC model core teaching standards learning progressions for teachers 1.0*. Retrieved

May 17, 2021, from https://ccsso.org/resource-library/intasc-model
-core-teaching-standards-and-learning-progressions-teachers-10

Cruz, R. A., Manchanda, S., Firestone, A. R., & Rodl, J. E. (2020). An examination of teachers' culturally responsive teaching self-efficacy. *Teacher Education and Special Education, 43*(3), 197–214.

Darling-Hammond, L., Hyler, M. E., & Gardner, M. (2017). *Effective teacher professional development*. Retrieved December 27, 2020, from https://static1.squarespace.com/static/56b90cb101dbae64ff707585/t/5 ade348e70a6ad624d417339/1524511888739/NO_LIF-1.PDF

Darling-Hammond, L., Wei, R. C., Andree, A., Richardson, N., & Orphanos, S. (2009). *Professional learning in the learning profession*. Retrieved December 27, 2020, from https://outlier.uchicago .edu/computerscience/OS4CS/landscapestudy/resources/Darling -Hammond,%20Wei,%20Adnree,%20Richardson%20and%20 Orphanos,%202009%20%20(1).pdf

Day, C., & Gu, Q. (2010). *The new lives of teachers*. Routledge.

Delpit, L. (1988). The silenced dialogue: Power and pedagogy in educating other people's children. *Harvard Educational Review, 58,* 280–298.

Delpit, L. (2006). *Other people's children: Cultural conflict in the classroom*. The New Press.

Dixon-Román, E. J. (2017). *Inheriting possibility: Social reproduction and quantification in education*. University of Minnesota Press.

Dotterer, A. M., & Wehrspann, E. (2016) Parent involvement and academic outcomes among urban adolescents: Examining the role of school engagement. *Educational Psychology, 36*(4), 812–830. https:// doi.org/10.1080/01443410.2015.1099617

Drake, S., Auletto, A., & Cowen, J. M. (2019). Grading teachers: Race and gender differences in low evaluation ratings and teacher employment outcomes. *American Educational Research Journal, 56*(5), 1800–1833.

DuBois, W. E. B. (1935). Does the Negro need separate schools? *Journal of Negro Education,* 328–335.

Dunks, J. (2018). *Ready for literacy instruction: A case study of initial educators' perceptions of their teacher preparation program* [Doctoral dissertation, Concordia University]. ProQuest Dissertation Publishing.

Durand, T. M., & Perez, N. A. (2013). Continuity and variability in the parental involvement and advocacy beliefs of Latino families of young children: Finding the potential for a collective voice. *School Community Journal, 23*(1), 49–79.

Dykes, F. O., & Delport, J. L. (2018). Our voices count: The lived experiences of LGBTQ educators and its impact on teacher education preparation programs. *Teaching Education, 29*(2), 135–146.

Easton-Brooks, D. (2019). *Ethnic matching: Academic success of students of color.* Rowman & Littlefield.

Eccles (Parsons), J., Adler, T. F., Futterman, R., Goff, S. B., Kaczala, C. M., Meece, J. L., et al. (1983). Expectancies, values, and academic behaviors. In J. T. Spence (Ed.), *Achievement and achievement motivation* (pp. 75–146). Freeman.

Egalite, A. J., & Kisida, B. (2018). The effects of teacher match on students' academic perceptions and attitudes. *Educational Evaluation and Policy Analysis, 40*(1), 59–81.

Emdin, C. (2016). *For White folks who teach in the hood . . . and the rest of y'all too: Reality pedagogy and urban education.* Beacon Press.

Epstein, J. L. (2018). *School, family, and community partnerships: Preparing educators and improving schools.* Routledge.

Farkas, S., Johnson, J., Duffett, A. (2003). *Stand by me: What teachers really think about unions, merit pay and other professional matters.* Public Agenda.

Farrington, C. A. (2014). *Failing at school.* Teachers College Press.

Feng, L., & Sass, T. R. (2018). The impact of incentives to recruit and retain teachers in "hard-to-staff" subjects. *Journal of Policy Analysis and Management, 37*(1), 112–135.

Firestone, W. A., & Donaldson, M. L. (2019). Teacher evaluation as data use: What recent research suggests. *Educational Assessment, Evaluation and Accountability, 31*(3), 289–314.

Floman, J. L., Hagelskamp, C., Brackett, M. A., & Rivers, S. E. (2017). Emotional bias in classroom observations: Within-rater positive emotion predicts favorable assessments of classroom quality. *Journal of Psychoeducational Assessment, 35*(3), 291–301.

Flores, B. B., Claeys, L., & Gist, C. D. (2018). *Crafting culturally efficacious teacher preparation and pedagogies.* Rowman & Littlefield.

Ford, D. Y. (2011). *Multicultural gifted education* (2nd ed.) Prufrock Press.

Ford, T. G., Urick, A., & Wilson, A. S. (2018). Exploring the effect of supportive teacher evaluation experiences on U.S. teachers' job satisfaction. *Education Policy Analysis Archives, 26* (59), 1–36.

Freire, P. (1970). *Pedagogy of the oppressed.* Seabury Press.

Freire, P. (1973). *Education for critical consciousness* (Vol. 1). Bloomsbury Publishing.

Fries-Britt, S., & Griffin, K. (2007). The Black box: How high-achieving Blacks resist stereotypes about Black Americans. *Journal of College Student Development, 48*(5), 509–524.

Fullan, M. (2007). *The new meaning of educational change* (4th ed.). Teachers College Press.

Gay, G. (2000). *Culturally responsive teaching: Theory, practice and research.* Teachers College Press.

Gay, G. (2013). Teaching to and through cultural diversity. *Curriculum Inquiry, 43*(1), 48–70.

Geiger, T., & Pivovarova, M. (2018). The effects of working conditions on teacher retention. *Teachers and Teaching, 24*(6), 604–625.

Gershenson, S., Hart, C., Hyman, J., Lindsay, C., & Papageorge, N. W. (2018). *The long-run impacts of same-race teachers* (No. w25254). National Bureau of Economic Research.

Gershenson, S., Holt, S. B., & Papageorge, N. W. (2016). Who believes in me? The effect of student–teacher demographic match on teacher expectations. *Economics of Education Review, 52*, 209–224.

Gill, B., Shoji, M., Coen, T., Place, K. (2016). The content, predictive power, and potential bias in five widely used teacher observation instruments. *Mathematica Policy Research.* Retrieved January 5, 2020, from https://ies.ed.gov/ncee/edlabs/regions/midatlantic/pdf/REL_2017191.pdf

Gist, C. D. (2014). Interrogating critical pedagogy: Teachers of color and the unfinished project of justice. In P. Orelus & R. Brock (Eds.), *Critical pedagogy for women and students of color* (pp. 46–59). Routledge.

Glanz, G. (2003). *Action research: An educational leader's guide to school improvement* (2nd ed.). Christopher-Gordon Publishers.

Glazer, J. (2018). Learning from those who no longer teach: Viewing teacher attrition through a resistance lens. *Teaching and Teacher Education, 74*, 62–71.

Glock, S. (2016). Does ethnicity matter? The impact of stereotypical expectations on in-service teachers' judgments of students. *Social Psychology of Education, 19*(3), 493–509.

Goffman, E. (1959). *The presentation of self in everyday life.* Anchor Books.

Goldhaber, D., Quince, V., & Theobald, R. (2017). Has it always been this way? Tracing the evolution of teacher quality gaps in U.S. public schools. *American Educational Research Journal, 55*(1), 171–201. https://doi.org/10.3102/0002831217733445

Gray, L., & Taie, S. (2015). *Public school teacher attrition and mobility in the first five years: Results from the first through fifth waves of the 2007–08 beginning teacher longitudinal* study. Retrieved December 22, 2020, from http://nces.ed.gov/pubsearch

Grier, B. (2019). *An examination of teacher characteristics by school locales in Georgia elementary schools* [Unpublished doctoral dissertation]. Valdosta State University.

Griffith, D., & McDougald, V. (2016). Undue process: Why bad teachers in twenty-five diverse districts rarely get fired. Thomas B. Fordham Institute. Retrieved January 11, 2021, from 1208-undue-process-why-bad-teachers-twenty-five-diverse-districts-rarely-get-fired0.pdf

Grissom, J. A., & Bartanen, B. (2019). Strategic retention: Principal effectiveness and teacher turnover in multiple-measure teacher evaluation systems. *American Educational Research Journal, 56*(2), 514–555.

Grissom, J. A., Rodriguez, L. A., & Kern, E. C. (2017). Teacher and principal diversity and the representation of students of color in gifted programs: Evidence from national data. *The Elementary School Journal, 117*(3), 396–422.

Hachfeld, A., Hahn, A., Schroeder, S., Anders, Y., & Kunter, M. (2015). Should teachers be colorblind? How multicultural and egalitarian beliefs differentially relate to aspects of teachers' professional competence for teaching in diverse classrooms. *Teaching and Teacher Education, 48*, 44–55.

Hamid, A. A., & Musa, S. A. (2017). The mediating effects of coping strategies on the relationship between secondary traumatic stress and burnout in professional caregivers in the UAE. *Journal of Mental Health, 26*(1), 28–35.

Hamre, B. K., Pianta, R. C., Downer, J. T., DeCoster, J., Mashburn, A. J., Jones, S. M., . . . & Hamagami, A. (2013). Teaching through interactions: Testing a developmental framework of teacher effectiveness in over 4,000 classrooms. *The Elementary School Journal*, *113*(4), 461–487.

Hill, H. C., Beisiegel, M., & Jacob, R. (2013). Professional development research: Consensus, crossroads, and challenges. *Educational Researcher*, *42*(9), 476–487.

hooks, B. (2014). *Teaching to transgress*. Routledge.

Hoover-Dempsey, K. V., & Sandler, H. M. (1997). Why do parents become involved in their children's education? *Review of Educational Research*, *67*, 3–42.

Hoover-Dempsey, K. V., Walker, J. M., Sandler, H. M., Whetsel, D., Green, C. L., Wilkins, A. S., & Closson, K. (2005). Why do parents become involved? Research findings and implications. *The Elementary School Journal*, *106*(2), 105–130.

Howard, G. R (2006). *We can't teach what we don't know: White teachers, multiracial schools* (2nd ed.). Teachers College Press.

Howard, G. R. (2007). Dispositions for good teaching. *Journal of Educational Controversy*, *2*(2), 1–6.

Howard, G. R. (2016). *We can't teach what we don't know: White teachers, multiracial schools* (3rd ed.). Teachers College Press.

Howell, D., Norris, A., & Williams, K. L. (2019). Towards Black gaze theory: How Black female teachers make Black students visible. *Urban Education Research & Policy Annuals*, *6*(1).

Hoy, A. W., & Spero, R. B. (2005). Changes in teacher efficacy during the early years of teaching: A comparison of four measures. *Teaching and Teacher Education*, *21*(4), 343–356.

Ingersoll, R. M. (2001). Teacher turnover and teacher shortages: An organizational analysis. *American Educational Research Journal*, *38*(3), 499–534.

Ingersoll, R. M. (2012). Beginning teacher induction: What the data tells us. *Phi Delta Kappan*, *93*(8), 47–51.

Ingersoll, R. M., Merrill, E., Stuckey, D,, & Collins, G. (2018). Seven trends: The transformation of the teaching force: Updated October 2018. CPRE Research Report# RR 2018-2. Consortium for Policy Research in Education. Retrieved January 12, 2021, from https://repository.upenn.edu/cgi/viewcontent.cgi?article=1109&context=cpre_researchreports

Irvine, J. J. (1990). *Black students and school failure. Policies, practices, and prescriptions.* Greenwood Press.

Jackson, C. K., & Bruegmann, E. (2009). Teaching students and teaching each other: The importance of peer learning for teachers. *American Economic Journal: Applied Economics, 1*(4), 85–108.

Jeynes, W. H. (2016). A meta-analysis: The relationship between parental involvement and African American school outcomes. *Journal of Black Studies, 47*(3), 195–216.

Jeynes, W. H. (2017). A meta-analysis: The relationship between parental involvement and Latino student outcomes. *Education and Urban Society, 49*(1), 4–28.

Johnson, J. L. (2020). *Early career elementary teachers' perceptions of their preparation during their teacher preparation program.* [Doctoral dissertation, Piedmont College]. ProQuest Dissertation Publishing.

Johnson, S. M., & Kardos, S. M. (2002). Keeping new teachers in mind. *Educational Leadership, 59*(6), 12–16.

Kahn, L. G., Lindstrom, L., & Murray, C. (2014). Factors contributing to preservice teachers' beliefs about diversity. *Teacher Education Quarterly, 41*(4), 53–70.

Kahn, R. L., Wolfe, D. M., Quinn, R. P., Snoek, J. D., & Rosenthal, R. A. (1964). *Organizational stress.* Wiley.

Kalogrides, D., Loeb, S., & Béteille, T. (2013). Systematic sorting: Teacher characteristics and class assignments. *Sociology of Education, 86*(2), 103–123.

Kane, M. T. (2017). Measurement error and bias in value-added models. *ETS Research Report Services, 2017*(1), 1–12.

Kane, T. J., McCaffrey, D. F., Miller, T., & Staiger, D. O. (2013). Have we identified effective teachers? Validating measures of effective teaching using random assignment. Bill & Melinda Gates Foundation. Retrieved January 5, 2020, from https://files.eric.ed.gov/fulltext/ED540959.pdf

Katz, D. A., Greenberg, M. T., Jennings, P. A., & Klein, L. C. (2016). Associations between the awakening responses of salivary α-amylase and cortisol with self-report indicators of health and wellbeing among educators. *Teaching and Teacher Education, 54*, 98–106.

Kelchtermans, G. (2017). 'Should I stay or should I go?': Unpacking teacher attrition/retention as an educational issue. *Teachers and Teaching, 23*(8), 961–977.

Khalifa, M. (2019). *Culturally responsive school leadership*. Harvard Education Press.

King, E., & Butler, B. R. (2015). Who cares about diversity? A preliminary investigation of diversity exposure in teacher preparation programs. *Multicultural Perspectives, 17*(1), 46–52.

Kirkby, J., Walsh, L., & Keary, A. (2019). A case study of the generation and benefits of a community of practice and its impact on the professional identity of early childhood teachers. *Professional Development in Education, 45*(2), 264–275.

Klassen, R. M., & Chiu, M. M. (2010). Effects on teachers' self-efficacy and job satisfaction: Teacher gender, years of experience, and job stress. *Journal of Educational Psychology, 102*(3), 741.

Krathwohl, D. R. (2002). A revision of Bloom's taxonomy: An overview. *Theory into Practice, 41*(4), 212–218.

Kuhfeld, M. (2019). Rethinking summer slide: The more you gain, the more you lose. *KappanOnline*. Retrieved January 4, 2020, from https://kappanonline.org/rethinking-summer-slide-the-more-you-gain-the-more-you-lose/

Kumar, R., & Hamer, L. (2013). Preservice teachers' attitudes and beliefs toward student diversity and proposed instructional practices: A sequential design study. *Journal of Teacher Education, 64*(2), 162–177.

Ladd, H. F., & Sorensen, L. C. (2017). Returns to teacher experience: Student achievement and motivation in middle school. *Education Finance and Policy, 12*(2), 241–279.

Ladson-Billings, G. (1995). Toward a theory of culturally relevant pedagogy. *American Education Research Journal, 32*(3), 564–491.

Ladson-Billings, G., & Tate, W. F. (1995). Toward a critical race theory of education. *Teachers College Record, 97*(1), 47–68.

Lai, I., Wood, W. J., Imberman, S. A., Jones, N. D., & Strunk, K. O. (2020). Teacher quality gaps by disability and socioeconomic status: Evidence from Los Angeles. *Educational Researcher*. https://doi.org/0013189X20955170.

Lareau, A. (2011). *Unequal childhoods: Class, race, and family life*. University of California Press.

Lewis, O. (1959). *Five families: Mexican case studies in the culture of poverty.* Basic Books.

Lindsay, C. A., & Hart, C. M. (2017). Exposure to same-race teachers and student disciplinary outcomes for Black students in North Carolina. *Educational Evaluation and Policy Analysis, 39*(3), 485–510.

Malo-Juvera, V., Correll, P., & Cantrell, S. C. (2016). A mixed-methods investigation of teachers' self-efficacy for culturally responsive instruction. *AERA Online Paper Repository.*

Markowitz, A. J., Bassok, D., & Grissom, J. A. (2020). Teacher-child racial/ethnic match and parental engagement with Head Start. *American Educational Research Journal, 57*(5), 2132–2174.

Marschall, M. J., & Shah, P. R. (2020). Linking the process and outcomes of parent involvement policy to the parent involvement gap. *Urban Education, 55*(5), 699–729.

Martin, A. J., & Collie, R. J. (2019). Teacher–student relationships and students' engagement in high school: Does the number of negative and positive relationships with teachers matter? *Journal of Educational Psychology, 111*(5), 861–876. https://doi.org/10.1037/edu0000317

Maryland State Department of Education. (2020). *Excellence and equity: A guide to educational equity in Maryland.* Retrieved September 25, 2020, from http://marylandpublicschools.org/programs/Documents/EEE/MSDEEquityGuidebook.pdf

Maslow, A. H. (1943). A theory of human motivation. *Psychological Review, 50*(4), 370–96.

Maslow, A. H. (1954). *Motivation and personality.* Harper & Row.

McLaren, P. (1999). Research news and comment: A pedagogy of possibility: Reflecting upon Paulo Freire's politics of education: In memory of Paulo Freire. *Educational Researcher, 28*(2), 49–56.

Michie, H. (2019). *Same as it never was: Notes on a teacher's return to the classroom.* Teachers College Press.

Milner IV, H. R., Cunningham, H. B., Delale-O'Connor, L., & Kestenberg, E. G. (2018). *"These kids are out of control": Why we must reimagine classroom management for equity.* Corwin Press.

Mixon, C. S., Owens, J. S., Hustus, C., Serrano, V. J., & Holdaway, A. S. (2019). Evaluating the impact of online professional development on teachers' use of a targeted behavioral classroom intervention. *School Mental Health, 11*(1), 115–128.

Mo, Y., & Singh, K. (2008). Parents' relationships and involvement: Effects on students' school engagement and performance. *Research in Middle Level Education, 31*(10), 1–11.

Moll, L. C. (2019). Elaborating funds of knowledge: Community-oriented practices in international contexts. *Literacy Research: Theory, Method, and Practice, 68*(1), 130–138.

Moore, C. M. (2012). The role of school environment in teacher dissatisfaction among U.S. public school teachers. *Sage Open, 2*(1), 1–16. https://doi.org/10/1177/2158244012438888

Muhammad, G. (2020). *Cultivating genius: An equity framework for culturally and historically responsive literacy.* Scholastic Teaching Resources.

National Assessment of Educational Progress (NAEP). (2019a). *The nation's report card.* Retrieved December 20 2020, from https://www .nationsreportcard.gov/reading/nation/groups/?grade=4

National Assessment of Educational Progress (NAEP). (2019b). *The nation's report card.* Retrieved December 20, 2020, from https://www .nationsreportcard.gov/mathematics/nation/groups/?grade=4

National Center for Education Statistics (2018a). *Percentage of students receiving selected disciplinary actions in public elementary and secondary schools, by type of disciplinary action, disability status, sex, and race/ethnicity: 2013–14.* Retrieved December 1, 2020, from https://nces.ed.gov/ programs/digest/d17/tables/dt17_233.28.asp?referer=raceindicators

National Center for Education Statistics (2018b). *Percentage of public school students enrolled in gifted and talented programs, by sex, race/ ethnicity, and state: Selected years, 2004 through 2013–14.* Retrieved December 1, 2020, from https://nces.ed.gov/programs/digest/d17/ tables/dt17_204.90.asp

Newberry, M., & Allsop, Y. (2017). Teacher attrition in the USA: The relational elements in a Utah case study. *Teachers and Teaching.* https:// doi.org/10.1080/13540602.2017.1358705

Nieto, S. (2014). *Why we teach now.* Teachers College Press.

Okeke, N. A., Howard, L. C., Kurtz-Costes, B., & Rowley, S. J. (2009). Academic race stereotypes, academic self-concept, and racial centrality in African American youth. *Journal of Black Psychology, 35*(3), 366–387.

Ordoñez-Jasis, R., & Jasis, P. (2004). Rising with De Colores: Tapping into the resources of la comunidad to assist under-performing Chicano-Latino students. *Journal of Latinos and Education, 3*(1), 53–64. https://doi.org/10.1207/s1532771xjle0301_5

Osei-Twumasi, O., & Pinetta, B. J. (2019). Quality of classroom interactions and the demographic divide: Evidence from the measures of effective teaching study. *Urban Education.* https://doi.org/10.1177/0042085919893744

Ozmantar, Z. K. (2019). A phenomenological study of practicum experience: Preservice teachers' fears. *International Journal of Progressive Education*, *15*(1), 135–150.

Palmer, P. (2007). *The courage to teach: Exploring the inner landscape of a teacher's life* (2nd ed.). Jossey-Bass.

Paris, D. (2012). Culturally sustaining pedagogy: A needed change in stance, terminology, and practice. *Educational Researcher*, *41*(3), 93–97.

Park, Y. S., Chen, J., & Holtzman, S. L. (2015). Evaluating efforts to minimize rater bias in scoring classroom observations. In T. J. Kane, K. A. Kerr, & R. C. Pianta (Eds.), *Designing teacher evaluation systems: New guidance from the measures of effective teaching project* (pp. 381–414). Wiley.

Patrikakou, E. N., Weissberg, R. P., Redding, S., & Walberg, H. J. (Eds.). (2005). *School-family partnerships for children's success.* Teachers College Press.

Perrone, F., Player, D., & Youngs, P. (2019). Administrative climate, early career teacher burnout, and turnover. *Journal of School Leadership*, *29*(3), 191–209.

Pham, L. D., Nguyen, T. D., & Springer, M. G. (2020). Teacher merit pay: A meta-analysis. *American Educational Research Journal.* https://doi.org/10.3102/0002831220905580

Pianta, R. C., Hamre, B. K., & Allen, J. P. (2012). Teacher-student relationships and engagement: Conceptualizing, measuring, and improving the capacity of classroom interactions. In S.A. Christenson, A. L. Reschly, & C. Wylie (Eds.), *Handbook of research on student engagement* (pp. 365–386). Springer.

Podolsky, A., Kini, T., & Darling-Hammond, L. (2019). Does teaching experience increase teacher effectiveness? A review of US research. *Journal of Professional Capital and Community*, *4*(4), 286–308.

Poteat, V. P., & Scheer, J. R. (2016). GSA advisors' self-efficacy related to LGBT youth of color and transgender youth. *Journal of LGBT Youth*, *13*(4), 311–325.

Quintero, D. (2019). The benefits of Hispanic student-teacher matching for AP courses. *Brown Center on Education Policy*. Retrieved December 9, 2020, from https://www.brookings.edu/blog/brown-center -chalkboard/2019/10/11/the-benefits-of-hispanic-student-teacher -matching-for-ap-courses/

Rafa, A., Erwin, B., & Keily, T. (2020). 50 state comparison: Teacher employment contract policies. *Education Commission*. Retrieved January 10, 2021, from https://www.ecs.org/50-state-comparison-teacher -employment-contract-policies/

Rasheed, D. S., Brown, J. L., Doyle, S. L., & Jennings, P. A. (2020). The effect of teacher–child race/ethnicity matching and classroom diversity on children's socioemotional and academic skills. *Child Development*, *91*(3), e597–e618.

Redding, C. (2019). A teacher like me: A review of the effect of student–teacher racial/ethnic matching on teacher perceptions of students and student academic and behavioral outcomes. *Review of Educational Research*, *89*(4), 499–535.

Rychly, L., & Graves, E. (2012). Teacher characteristics for culturally responsive pedagogy. *Multicultural Perspectives*, *14*(1), 44–49.

Rizutto, K. C. (2017). Teachers' perceptions of ELL students: Do their attitudes shape their instruction? *Teacher Educator*, *52*(3), 182–202.

Rodriguez, J. A., Condom-Bosch, J. L., Ruiz, L., & Oliver, E. (2020). On the shoulders of giants: Benefits of participating in a dialogic professional development program for in-service teachers. *Frontiers in Psychology*, *11*. https://doi.org/10.3389/fpsyg.2020.00005

Rogers, L. K., & Doan, S. (2019). Late to class: Estimating the relationship between teacher assignment change and student sorting. *The Elementary School Journal*, *120*(2), 347–371.

Rojas, L., & Liou, D. D. (2017). Social justice teaching through the sympathetic touch of caring and high expectations for students of color. *Journal of Teacher Education*, *68*(1), 28–40.

Ronfeldt, M., & McQueen, K. (2017). Does new teacher induction really improve retention? *Journal of Teacher Education*, *68*(4), 394–410.

Roorda, D. L., Koomen, H. M., Spilt, J. L., & Oort, F. J. (2011). The influence of affective teacher–student relationships on students' school engagement and achievement: A meta-analytic approach. *Review of Educational Research, 81*(4), 493–529.

Russell, M. L., & Russell, J. A. (2014). Preservice science teachers and cultural diversity awareness. *The Electronic Journal for Research in Science & Mathematics Education, 18*(3).

Rychly, L., & Graves, E. (2012). Teacher characteristics for culturally responsive pedagogy. *Multicultural Perspectives, 14*(1), 44–49.

Sacco, T. L., Ciurzynski, S. M., Harvey, M. E., & Ingersoll, G. L. (2015). Compassion satisfaction and compassion fatigue among critical care nurses. *Critical Care Nurse, 35*(4), 32–42.

Santoro, D. A. (2021). *Demoralized: Why teachers leave the profession they love and how they can stay.* Harvard Education Press.

Shifrer, D., Turley, R. L., & Heard, H. (2017). Do teacher financial awards improve teacher retention and student achievement in an urban disadvantaged school district? *American Educational Research Journal, 54*(6), 1117–1153.

Shulman, L. S. (2005). Signature pedagogies in the professions. *Daedalus, 134*(3), 52–59.

Simon, N. S., & Johnson, S. M. (2015). Teacher turnover in high-poverty schools: What we know and can do. *Teachers College Record, 117*(3), 1–36.

Skaalvik, E. M., & Skaalvik, S. (2017). Dimensions of teacher burnout: Relations with potential stressors at school. *Social Psychology of Education, 20*(4), 775–790.

Skrla, L., McKenzie, K. B., & Scheurich, J. J. (Eds.). (2009). *Using equity audits to create equitable and excellent schools.* Corwin Press.

Smith, K., & Ulvik, M. (2017). Leaving teaching: Lack of resilience or sign of agency? *Teachers and Teaching.* https://doi.org/10.1080/13540602.2017.1358706

Sneyers, E., Vanhoof, J., & Mahieu, P. (2020). Bias in primary school teachers' expectations of students? A study of general and specific bias towards SES, ethnicity and gender. *Studia Paedagogica, 25*(2), 71–96.

Spittle, M., Kremer, P., & Sullivan, S. (2015). Burnout in secondary school physical education teaching. *Facta Universitatis, Series: Physical Education and Sport, 13*(1), 33–43.

Stacer, M. J., & Perrucci, R. (2013). Parental involvement with children at school, home, and community. *Journal of Family and Economic Issues, 34*(3), 340–354.

Steinberg, M. P., & Kraft, M. A. (2017). The sensitivity of teacher performance ratings to the design of teacher evaluation systems. *Educational Researcher, 46*(7), 378–396.

Stoll, L., & Louis, K. S. (2007). *Professional learning communities: Divergence, depth and dilemmas.* McGraw-Hill Education.

Sutcher, L., Darling-Hammond, L., & Carver-Thomas, D. (2016). *A coming crisis in teaching? Teacher supply, demand, and shortages in the U.S.* Retrieved December 24, 2020, from, https://learningpolicyinstitute.org/sites/default/files/product-files/A_Coming_Crisis_in_Teaching_REPORT.pdf

Sy, S. R., & Schulenberg, J. E. (2005). Parent beliefs and children's achievement trajectories during the transition to school in Asian American and European American families. *International Journal of Behavioral Development, 29*(6), 505–515. https://doi.org/10.1177/01650250500147329

Tajfel, H., & Turner, J. C. (1979). An integrative theory of intergroup conflict. In W. G. Austin & S. Worchel (Eds.), *The social psychology of intergroup relations* (pp. 33–47). Brooks/Cole.

Thieleman, K., & Cacciatore, J. (2014). Witness to suffering: Mindfulness and compassion fatigue among traumatic bereavement volunteers and professionals. *Social Work, 59*(1), 34–41

Toldson, I. A., & Lemmons, B. P. (2013). Social demographics, the school environment, and parenting practices associated with parents' participation in schools and academic success among Black, Hispanic, and White students. *Journal of Human Behavior in the Social Environment, 23*(2), 237–255. https://doi.org/10.1080/10911359.2013.747407

Towers, E., & Maguire, M. (2017). Leaving or staying in teaching: a "vignette" of an experienced urban teacher "leaver" of a London primary school. *Teachers and Teaching.* https://doi.org/10.1080/13540602.2017.1358703

Tuytens, M., & Devos, G. (2017). The role of feedback from the school leader during teacher evaluation for teacher and school improvement. *Teachers and Teaching, 23*(1), 6–24.

U.S. Department of Education. (2016). The state of racial diversity in the education workforce. *Office of Planning, Evaluation and Policy*

Development, Policy and Program Studies Service. Retrieved December 6, 2020, from https://www2.ed.gov/rschstat/eval/highered/racial -diversity/state-racial-diversity-workforce.pdf

U.S. Department of Education. (2017a). Number and percentage distribution of teachers in public elementary and secondary schools, by race/ethnicity and selected teacher and school characteristics: 2015-16 [Data set]. *National Center for Education Statistics.* Retrieved November 18, 2020, from https://nces.ed.gov/programs/digest/d17/tables/ dt17_209.23.asp

U.S. Department of Education. (2017b). Public elementary and secondary school enrollment, number of schools, and other selected characteristics, by locale: Fall 2012 through fall 2015. *National Center for Education Statistics.* Retrieved December 6, 2020, from https://nces.ed.gov/ programs/digest/d17/tables/dt17_214.40.asp

U.S. Department of Education. (2018). 40th annual report to congress on the implementation of the individuals with disabilities education act. *Office of Special Education and Rehabilitative Services.* Retrieved February 22, 2021, from https://www2.ed.gov/about/reports/annual/ osep/2018/parts-b-c/40th-arc-for-idea.pdf

U.S. Department of Education. (2019a). The condition of education, racial/ethnic enrollment in public schools. *National Center for Education Statistics.* Retrieved November 18, 2020, from https://nces.ed.gov/ programs/coe/indicator_cge.asp

U.S. Department of Education. (2019b). The condition of education, concentration of public school students eligible for free or reduced-price lunch. *National Center for Education Statistics.* Retrieved November 18, 2020, from https://nces.ed.gov/programs/coe/indicator_clb.asp

U.S. Department of Education. (2019c). Characteristics of public school teachers. *National Center for Education Statistics.* Retrieved December 20, 2020, from https://nces.ed.gov/programs/coe/indicator_clr.asp

U.S. Department of Education. (2019d). The condition of education, characteristics of public school teachers. *National Center for Education Statistics.* Retrieved November 13, 2020, from https://nces.ed.gov/ programs/coe/indicator_clr.asp

U.S. Department of Education. (2019e). Number and percentage distribution of teachers in public elementary and secondary schools, by instructional level and selected teacher and school characteristics: 1999-2000 and 2017-18. [Data set]. *National Center for Education Statistics.* https://nces.ed.gov/programs/digest/d19/tables/dt19_209.22.asp

Vagi, R. & Pivovarova, M. (2017). Theorizing teacher mobility: A critical review of literature. *Teachers and Teaching: Theory and Practice, 23*(7), 781–793.

Valtierra, K. (2016). *Teach & thrive: Wisdom from an urban teacher's career narrative.* IAP.

van Es, E. A., Hand, V., & Mercado, J. (2017). Making visible the relationship between teachers' noticing for equity and equitable teaching practice. In E. O. Schack, M. H. Fisher, & J. A. Wilhelm (Eds.), *Teacher noticing: Bridging and broadening perspectives, contexts, and frameworks* (pp. 251–270). Springer.

van Uden, J. M., Ritzen, H., & Pieters, J. M. (2014). Engaging students: The role of teacher beliefs and interpersonal teacher behavior in fostering student engagement in vocational education. *Teaching and Teacher Education, 37,* 21–32.

Vickery, A. E. (2016). "I know what you are about to enter": Lived experiences as the curricular foundation for teaching citizenship. *Gender and Education, 28*(6), 725–741.

Villegas, A. M., & Lucas, T. (2002). Preparing culturally responsive teachers: Rethinking the curriculum. *Journal of Teacher Education, 53*(1), 20–32.

Vincent, C., Rollock, N., Ball, S., & Gillborn, D. (2013). Raising middle-class Black children: Parenting priorities, actions and strategies. *Sociology, 47,* 427–442. https://doi.org/10.1177/0038038512454244

Vonk, J. H. C. (1995). Conceptualizing novice teachers' professional development: A base for supervisory interventions. *ERIC.* Retrieved December 21, 2020, from https://files.eric.ed.gov/fulltext/ED390838.pdf

Voss, T., & Kunter, M. (2020). "Reality shock" of beginning teachers? Changes in teacher candidates' emotional exhaustion and constructivist-oriented beliefs. *Journal of Teacher Education, 71*(3), 292–306.

Vygotsky, L. S. (1978). *Mind in society.* Harvard University Press.

Walker, J. M. T., Wilkins, A. S., Dallaire, J. R., Sandler, H. M., &

Hoover-Dempsey, K. V. (2005). Parental involvement: Model revision through scale development. *The Elementary School Journal, 106,* 85–104.

Ware, F. (2006). Warm demander pedagogy: Culturally responsive teaching that supports a culture of achievement for African American students. *Urban Education, 41*(4), 427–456.

Watkins, P. (2005). The principal's role in attracting, retaining, and developing new teachers: Three strategies for collaboration and support. *The Clearing House, 79*(2), 83– 87.

Watson, J. G., Kraemer, S .B., & Thorn, C. A. (2009). The other 69 percent: Fairly rewarding the performance of teachers in non-tested subjects and grades. *Center for Educator Compensation Reform*. Retrieved January 6, 2020, from http://www1.gcsnc.com/whatmatters/pdf/other69Percent.pdf

Wei, R. C., Darling-Hammond, L., & Adamson, F. (2010). *Professional development in the United States: Trends and challenges.* Retrieved December 27, 2020, from https://edpolicy.stanford.edu/sites/default/files/publications/professional-development-united-states-trends-and-challenges.pdf

Whitaker, M. C. (2018). Urban charter schools. In W. Pink (Ed.), *Oxford research encyclopedia of education.* Oxford University Press. https://doi.org/10.1093/acrefore/9780190264093.013.443

Whitaker, M. C., & Valtierra, K. M. (2019). *Schooling multicultural teachers: A guide for program assessment and professional development.* Emerald Publishing.

Whitaker, M. C. (n.d. [in progress]). *Mapping the evolution of teachers' ideologies.*

Whitman, G., & Kelleher, I. (2016). *Neuroteach: Brain science and the future of education.* Rowman & Littlefield.

Wilder, S. (2014). Effects of parental involvement on academic achievement: A meta-synthesis. *Educational Review, 66*(3), 377–397. https://doi.org/10.1080/00131911.2013.780009

Williams, T., & Sánchez, B. (2012). Parental involvement (and uninvolvement) at an inner-city high school. *Urban Education, 47,* 625–652.

Wong, H. K. (2004). Induction programs that keep new teachers teaching and improving. *NASSP Bulletin, 88*(638), 41–58.

Wong, S. W., & Hughes, J. N. (2006). Ethnicity and language contributions to dimensions of parent involvement. *School Psychology Review, 35*, 645–662.

Wright, A., Gottfried, M. A., & Le, V. N. (2017). A kindergarten teacher like me: The role of student-teacher race in social-emotional development. *American Educational Research Journal, 54*(1_suppl), 78S–101S.

Wynn, S. R., Carboni, L. W., & Patall, E. A. (2007). Beginning teachers' perceptions of mentoring, climate, and leadership: Promoting retention through a learning communities perspective. *Leadership and Policy in Schools, 6*(3), 209–229.

Zeng, G., Chen, X., Cheung, H. Y., & Peng, K. (2019). Teachers' growth mindset and work engagement in the Chinese educational context: Well-being and perseverance of effort as mediators. *Frontiers in Psychology, 10*, 839. https://doi.org/10.3389/fpsyg.2019.00839

Zeqeibi Ghannad, S., Alipoor Birgani, S., & Shehni Yailagh, M. (2018). Investigation of the causal relationship between academic motivation and academic engagement with the mediating role of achievement emotions and academic hardiness in students. *International Journal of Psychology (IPA), 11*(1), 79 97.

Index

Note: Italicized page locators refer to figures; tables are noted with *t*.

About the Author

Manya C. Whitaker, Ph.D., is a developmental educational psychologist whose work applies psychological theories to educational contexts. After completing her graduate training at Vanderbilt University, she joined Colorado College where she developed a cadre of courses on social and political issues in education. Her new courses, combined with her psychological training and community engagement with families, inspired her to write her first book, *Learning from the Inside-Out: Child Development and School Choice*, in 2016.

Since then, she's published numerous journal articles and book chapters examining the development and sustainment of teachers' diversity-related beliefs, particularly within the context of social justice-oriented teacher preparation. Those manuscripts facilitated her second book, *Schooling Multicultural Teachers: A Guide for Program Assessment and Professional Development* (2019), and contributed to the expansion of her consulting work with K–16 organizations. In addition to her teaching and research endeavors, she also serves as the Chair of the Education department and directs the Crown Faculty Development Center.

For Product Safety Concerns and Information please contact our
EU representative GPSR@taylorandfrancis.com Taylor & Francis
Verlag GmbH, Kaufingerstraße 24, 80331 München, Germany